# About th

**Gill Hines** has worked in education for over 40 years, starting out as an infant teacher before going on to work with children and young people with English as an additional language. In the 1980s she began training with a national charity for people living with HIV/Aids to lead workshops on living powerfully and creatively in the face of a terminal diagnosis, eventually leading workshops throughout Britain and in Paris. After a period of travel she began working in West London, bringing together her two passions, education and well-being. Originally working with pupils, students, staff and youth workers, she began extending her work to include parents and today runs dozens of parent workshops in schools and local venues on an ever-expanding range of subjects. She also has a growing list of clients for her parent and family consultation work. @GillHines

**Alison Baverstock** has had a life-long interest in encouraging people to read. She began her working life as a publisher, although she now researches and writes about the industry and teaches at Kingston University, where she jointly founded the Publishing MA programme. She likewise jointly founded *Well Worth Reading*, a national scheme to promote literature in libraries (now part of The Reading Agency), and set up *Reading Force*, a scheme to encourage shared reading within Service families. She is the author of around 20 books on publishing, writing, parenting and art. She and her husband have four children. @AlisonBav

Alison met Gill at a parenting workshop on how to help children manage the transition to secondary school and was immediately struck by her common (or rather *not* so common) sense attitude to raising children and, as a publisher, thought there was a book in it. They have now written three books on parenting together, all published by Piatkus.

# WHAT EVER!

## A DOWN-TO-EARTH GUIDE TO PARENTING TEENAGERS

Gill Hines and
Alison Baverstock

piatkus

PIATKUS

First published in Great Britain in 2005 by Piatkus

This revised edition first published in
Great Britain in 2016 by Piatkus

The extract on p. 289 is taken from *Where Did It All Go Right?*
by Andrew Collins, published by Ebury. Reprinted by
permission of The Random House Group Ltd.

1 3 5 7 9 10 8 6 4 2

A CIP catalogue record for this book
is available from the British Library.

ISBN 978-0-349-40952-8

Typeset in ITC Stone Serif by Palimpsest Book Production Ltd.,
Falkirk, Stirlingshire

Printed and bound in Great Britain by
CPI Group (UK) Ltd, Croydon, CR0 4YY

Papers used by Piatkus are from well-managed
forests and other responsible sources.

MIX
Paper from
responsible sources
FSC® C104740
www.fsc.org

Piatkus
An imprint of
Little, Brown Book Group
Carmelite House
50 Victoria Embankment
London EC4Y 0DZ

An Hachette UK Company

www.hachette.co.uk

www.improvementzone.co.uk

# Contents

# Foreword

## by Dame Jacqueline Wilson

I've written lots of books for young teenagers. I always write my stories in the first person, as if I was 13 or 14 or 15. People always ask me how I manage to do this, as I'm granny-age now, and have the silver hair to prove it (plus a big silver ring on every arthritic finger!). I'm not quite sure how I do it. It's a bit dangerous deliberating too much. It's like when you wonder how you breathe or how you walk – you immediately start wheezing and fall over!

I suppose the thing that helps me most is the fact that I have total recall of my teenage years. Ask me what I did last year (or even last month) and I will look blank and scratch my head. Ask me what my hair was like when I was 13, or the colour of my first pair of high heels, or the words of most 1960s pop songs and I know, straight off. Life has changed enormously since those long-ago times when I was a teenager, but feelings haven't. I can remember how awful it is to go out with a couple of friends and they get off with boyfriends, and you don't. I can remember my total life-is-no-longer-worth-living despair when I had a bad haircut. I can remember sudden urges of amazing happiness looking up at a starry sky, or jiving to rock music, or discovering poetry. I can remember the sweaty-palmed shyness on first dates and the astonishing joy of first love. I can remember feeling so angry with my parents, so bitter, so resentful – and yet when I left home at the age of 17 I suddenly felt horribly childlike and vulnerable and missed them miserably.

I feel I understand teenagers – but that doesn't always help me deal with them! I love my daughter passionately, and I also like and admire and respect her, but that doesn't mean to say her teenage years were totally plain-sailing. Because we'd been so close, up until she was 12 or so, I sometimes found it painful and worrying when she backed away from me and started to want to lead her own life in her own way.

I remember one time we were having an argument in the kitchen. It was a jokey argument, but we still got quite heated. I told her to get out of the kitchen. She said she wasn't budging. I started pushing her, and she started pushing back. We were still laughing but both of us were getting very red in the face. I pushed harder. So did she. I realised something alarming. My little girl was now stronger than me. Obviously brute force isn't the way to deal with teenagers!

We need to reason and rethink our reactions. This sensible, warm-hearted guide to all parents of teenagers is a tremendous help. It offers all sorts of strategies for taking the heat out of tense situations. It shows parents we're not alone. We all worry, we all fuss, we all feel we know best even when we don't. It's hard loving teenagers when they frequently find us irritating, embarrassing and impossible. But we do love them, and deep down they love us too.

Gill Hines and Alison Baverstock have a light touch, even when they're dealing with serious issues. Their suggestions are easy to read and simple to put into practice.

Happy parenting!
Jacqueline Wilson

# PREFACE

# Welcome to Whatever!

We met at a workshop on parenting in Kingston. Gill Hines is an educator with over 30 years' experience, who had been working with young people, and running workshops on parenting and relationships in local schools, for many years. Alison Baverstock is a publisher, writer and mother of four. She came along to a workshop on managing the transition between primary and secondary schools and got hooked on Gill's profound insight into the relationships between parents and children – and her straightforward, practical approach. Finding out there were no books on the market about parenting teenagers, she suggested they write one, and the result has won praise from teachers and specialists in education, parents and young people – as well as from the parenting press. First published in 2005, this is the second edition of our book – now fully updated to cover the latest trends.

## WHAT DO WE OFFER, IN A NUTSHELL?

Ours is a sound-bite culture. If everyone is famous for 15 minutes, they need to be able to say why they should be taken notice of equally quickly. During the writing – and rewriting – of this book, we were often asked to sum up what was our key contribution, the essence of our book. Three things consistently stood out:

1   The emphasis on encouragement. By encouraging your young person to have a positive attitude towards themselves, you help them deal effectively with so many of the difficulties associated with adolescence. And having worked on this principle, it quickly emerged that encouragement can enrich every other aspect of life – partners encouraging each other in the parenting of their young person; parents building the confidence of other parents – as well as in many other situations.

2   The reminder to remember how it was for you at the same age, because remembering how it feels to be a teenager enables you to parent your own young people more effectively.

> 'I was stunned by how fresh the memories of my own adolescence were, and how by thinking about how I had felt, and how I had handled issues myself (and could perhaps have done so better), was an excellent starting point for thinking about how to guide others.' **Alison**

3   Parenting teenagers takes time. And however pressed our lives become, it's something that should be prioritised – because it matters so much.

Ten years on from its original publication, we are proud to present a new edition of *Whatever!* and even more so that it has been hailed as a key text and found its way on to reading lists for those studying adolescence and preparing to work with young people.

We hope you will find the book useful, and that if you do so, you will in turn recommend the book to others who might benefit.

There are many people we would like to thank, but naming them would destroy the anonymity we promised. We will limit ourselves therefore to our publishers at Piatkus, notably Judy Piatkus, Penny Phillips, Gill Bailey, Anna Crago, Jo Brooks and Helen Stanton, Anne Lawrance, Meri Pentikäinen and Gemma Conley-Smith; Dame Jacqueline Wilson who wrote the Foreword; Olivia Sheldrake who wrote the powerful poem we feature in Chapter 3; and our partners, families and friends.

Gill Hines and Alison Baverstock

# CHAPTER 1

# What is a teenager?

The obvious answer is any young person whose age ends with 'teen', but when we talk about teenagers, read or write about teenagers or study teenagers it means a great deal more. It's not uncommon these days to hear parents describe even young children as 'like a teenager' as the term has come to mean a whole set of behaviours and attitudes. It would probably be more accurate to describe young people as adolescent, meaning the stage of becoming adult, and much of the literature these days does so, although parents and teachers generally still use the term 'teenager'.

The term 'teenage' was first used at around the end of the nineteenth century as an adjective to describe a young person but it wasn't until the 1940s that it started to be used as a noun, so a 'teenage boy' became a 'teenager'. The term probably started in America but by the 1950s it was widely used in the UK too, and the notion of a separate culture for teenagers began to grow. Like most cultural shifts this was most obvious in music, literature, film and clothing, as people in the creative industries began to realise there was a huge and growing market among adolescents. By the 1960s there were also television and radio programmes designed specifically for young people, which began to both reflect and direct teen behaviour and thought. As the teen market became more affluent from the 1970s, so there was an explosion of commercial development geared towards parting them (or their parents) from their cash, with fashion shops ranging from the designer to the cheap high street targeting teens, the traditional pub becoming a bar offering alcohol in new young-person-friendly ways (such as cocktails and shots), and the proliferation of fast-food outlets designed to appeal to the less health-conscious young.

Today we live in a world where young people have their own everything, from gadgets to bottled water, as every manufacturer considers what young people want as well as adults when designing their range of products. The millions of Western gap-year travellers have created a path around the world of shops and bars selling things teen travellers will spend money on, and the notion of a teenager has also spread.

But what characterises teenage behaviour? Most teens would answer that they want to have fun, they want to explore the world around them, they want to explore the strength, sexuality and energy of their 'new' bodies, and they want to be free to do all of the above!

Most parents would say that teenagers lack 'common sense' and often make foolish or even dangerous decisions, they are often rude or taciturn, and have periods of being full of energy they don't know what to do with or of being completely flat out for hours at a time. They eat too much or too little – and sometimes both – they are argumentative and can throw tantrums like a small child if they don't get their way, they take risks without realising it, experience life as an unending series of dramas, and dislike everything!

Of course those are just the negatives. They can also be funny, spontaneous, kind, passionate about injustice or unfairness in the world, fearless, loving, clever, willing to take on new challenges at the drop of a hat, vulnerable and thoughtful.

The trouble is they can show all of the above qualities – which, if nothing else, keeps you on your toes.

## REFLECTION EXERCISE

Take a moment to think about your teenager as they are at this time of their life – and perhaps as they have been in the last year or so.

Make a list of both the negative and positive attributes they display – try not to base your answers on how they were but on how they are now.

Perhaps two years ago:
- They were generous and kind but now they are quite selfish
- They were chatty and talkative but now they are uncommunicative or quiet
- They were happy to spend time at home but now they want to be out doing things all the time

| My teenager now: Positive qualities or behaviour | My teenager now: Negative qualities or behaviour |
| --- | --- |
| | |

If the list of negative qualities outweighs the positive then you are not alone. But now look again. Unfortunately many of the negative behaviours associated with adolescents can be so dramatic that we stop noticing the good ones, which, after all, have often been there for a very long time – and maybe are there still, just temporarily hidden from view.

Many adolescents are not having a wonderful time either as they can often feel that adults don't understand them or just try to be obstructive or controlling. Compared to their child self they feel very grown-up, but we with our wise hindsight know only too well that *being* grown-up is very different. Unfortunately for them they don't know this – but they will one day.

## WHAT MAKES A TEENAGER BEHAVE THE WAY THEY DO?

It is still the belief of most parents that these changes in behaviour are caused by hormones, and this was a widely held belief until fairly recently. We now know that hormones have some effect of course, but most of these are on the body and the sexual behaviour of an individual; the big changes come from a radical restructuring of the brain. So the bottom line is, your teenager really can't help it!

It has only been since the end of the twentieth century that scientists have been able to study live brains using MRI scanners, and they have discovered some amazing things about teenage brains that have changed the way we see them and their behaviour. These changes start around 11 or 12 years old (usually slightly earlier in girls than boys) with a massive explosion of new pathways in the brain, which makes the pre-teen years so important in terms of both education and parenting.

## THE TEENAGE BRAIN (IN VERY SIMPLE TERMS)

The brain has some recognisable areas which are very important for certain elements of our memory, character, personality or behaviour. It is how these interact with each other that makes us the unique individuals that we are.

Our genetic code, passed to us by our parents, plus anything that affects our development in the womb (such as nutrition, alcohol, hormones, drugs, stress, etc.) determine the physical structure and possibly the capabilities of our brain, and the rest gets laid down by our life experience, with different parts of the brain developing at different times. The main building blocks are billions of cells called neurons that make connections with other neurons as we experience our lives. These connections are called synapses and there are so many of them in everyone that they cannot be counted. They create 'pathways' in the brain so when we come across a situation we have experienced before we don't need a new pathway, we can use the old one. As a baby we learn everything this way, from language to how to get our parent's attention – what worked once will be used again. In this way, one tiny pathway at a time, we develop into the people we are.

The bit of the brain associated with logic and thinking things through is the prefrontal cortex, basically the large part that sits at the front and top of our brains. This grows synapses throughout our lives to help us make use of all the information stashed away elsewhere in the brain. Our emotions come from a part of the brain at the back, near where the spine and all its nerves join the brain.

In teenagers the whole brain is being 'pruned' – getting rid of many of the pathways that are no longer necessary as they have been superseded with more appropriate ones – and this pruning starts essentially at the back of the brain, creating some disturbance in the emotion centres as the old pathways no longer work as they did, and progresses forward to the front brain. The prefrontal cortex is the last part of the brain to be restructured in this way, and is not completely 'streamlined' and fully operational until the person is in their early to mid-20s.

'I remember the moment I realised I had grown up. It was when I was working in my first teaching job and struggling with everything I needed to do. I was at home writing my lesson plans for the morning when a friend phoned and invited me to join a group of friends in the pub. My first reaction was relief at getting out of the flat and talking to non-teachers for an evening but my second thought was that if I go to work without being adequately prepared I will have a very bad day. I chose to stay home and do my work.' **Teacher**

MRI scanning also suggests that as parts of the prefrontal cortex are effectively closed for business, other areas of the brain take on a lot of the workload. One of the most noticeable effects of this is in communication. In adults our communication is filtered through our logic centre (most of the time anyway), but in young people the part of the brain that lights up when they communicate is the emotion centre of the brain. This is why if you've ever travelled on a school bus with young people you can feel as if war is about to break out although they feel they are communicating normally with each other. It also helps to explain why young people experience emotions so powerfully as they haven't got the buffering capability of logic to make sense of how they're feeling.

The prefrontal cortex also operates as a central control system, sending signals to the part of the brain that is best equipped to deal with them. When this isn't working properly signals can indeed end up going astray, so that the reaction of a young person to something might be hard to understand and hard for them to verbalise. A typical adult reaction is to ask why they did something. This is often met by an emotional outburst or by blaming you when what they really mean is 'it's not to do with any part of myself that I recognise'.

There are some other changes in the brain which are worth knowing about too as they contribute to the typical teenage behaviour pattern. Some structures in other parts of the brain are streamlined early on in the process, such as the area of the brain that deals with pleasure and reward. However, this part of the brain, called the *nucleus accumbens*, tends to show an exaggerated response to medium and large rewards and almost no response to small ones. So in days gone by a smile or a thank you would have given your child pleasure; now it needs to be money or a new iPad! Your pleasure (or displeasure) at their behaviour will also barely register for most young people.

Other tasks of the prefrontal cortex are letting us know when we are safe and helping us spot errors in our own judgement. In young people their changing brains impair these, leading to the predictable outcomes of increased risk-taking and poor choices. If you incorporate the heightened desire for medium to high reward and poor processing and error judgement, you get much of the behaviour that characterises a teenager. Some will be blindly taking risks; others may be overwhelmed by anxiety as they feel everything is a huge risk.

Also during this period of development the brain starts to encase synapses with a substance called myelin, making them, to all intents and purposes, permanent. This means that many of the experiences and behaviours begun in adolescence from the age of 11 to 12 until the early 20s can become 'set in stone'. Many people remember the music, friends and clothing of their teenage years far more clearly than any other period of their life due in part to this process. As we age we tend to lose synapses, but the longer they have been there in a protected state, the longer they tend to remain.

Research has also shown that adolescents temporarily take a backward step with some of the skills of late childhood, such as the ability to empathise and the ability to read other people's emotional clues – including body language, facial expression and tone of voice. What we see as rudeness, selfishness or not caring about others may often be simply a reflection of these changes. It isn't that young people don't care, it's that they don't see or understand the impact their communication and behaviour has on others. Their prefrontal cortex isn't letting them know how others will be affected by their behaviour, nor is it letting them see what the impact is of their highly emotional response to criticism or curtailment.

Unfortunately what is going on inside the brain cannot be seen, and it's also hard to understand for both us and them – young people can often feel as if they are going crazy, because they are experiencing so many conflicting emotions at once. When trying to use their prefrontal cortex to work things out, evidence suggests they tend to over-use it, to over-think, which may leave them unable to make choices or to see conspiracies everywhere!

## PHYSICAL CHANGES

The physical changes of adolescence are well known to everyone and include the development of the sexual body parts and sexual hormones. They also include an increase in sweating – often accompanied by a particular adolescent body odour – a rapid increase in body hair (and developing facial hair in boys), and some odd side-effects like uncontrollable blushing or itching in intimate places.

'When my son was about 13 he would sometimes have several of his friends over to play computer games and I used to let them use the back room downstairs. After they had left it used to smell strongly – like hamsters! They were all lovely boys but they all let off a very strong "animal" smell. I used to have to open all the windows

– and keep the door shut – for a couple of hours to air
the room out once they'd left.' **Mother**

The development of sexual body parts and functions can be
embarrassing or difficult for young people and it is not
uncommon for them to feel particular discomfort around the
parent of the other sex, so boys with their mothers and daughters
with their fathers. Boys who are experimenting with masturbation and possibly porn may find it hard to meet their mum's
eye (we sometimes have a long-seated belief from childhood
that mums can read our minds through our eyes); girls may
feel shy or embarrassed during their early periods being around
their dad, particularly if they know he is aware of what is
happening for them.

It is normal for children approaching puberty to become
more secretive about their bodies, which can mean parents are
shut out of many discussions or sharing of anxieties that go
on. Making sure your child has access to good information,
good friendships and knows where to go for advice is probably
as much as you can do once puberty has begun, but a wise
parent will make sure they talk with their child about body
changes and the changes of adolescence long before the
hormones kick in.

## OTHER GENERAL CHANGES

Just like in babies, the brain changes of an adolescent happen
while they are asleep – thankfully. So it is both understandable
and necessary for young people to need a great deal of sleep
so all that restructuring can happen. They may be full of energy
one minute and out like a light the next, or perhaps go to bed
and not emerge for 24 hours after a busy day or reduced sleep
the night before. Their body clocks are geared towards the
needs of their brains and not the clocks the rest of us use. One
of the problems with modern life for adolescents is that they

don't usually even start to feel sleepy until about 11 p.m., when a key substance for sleep called melatonin starts to be produced in their brains. Most of them, lacking the ability to consider possible outcomes and consequences properly, will resist sleep for as long as they can – especially as much of the more desirable TV is on later at night. If they are getting up for school or college at 7.30 or so this is obviously going to be difficult, and more than one parent has resorted to throwing a glass of water over their dozy child to get them up.

The double trouble of a rewiring brain and escalating sex hormones can make some young people become acutely self-conscious when out in public and they may even act quite out of character if they feel other people are watching them, particularly younger men and women. They can act extremely shy or embarrassingly loud and showy; they can play it cool to the point of looking slightly ridiculous, or be so excited and boisterous they create silence around them everywhere they go in public. As far as they are concerned, adolescents are at the very centre of the universe; they lack the ability to see themselves as others see them – to understand that to others they may come across as completely self-absorbed. For them, for a while at least, they are living their lives in the spotlight, all eyes are on them at every moment. Some will even 'play to the cameras' when they are alone.

Your temporarily self-centred teen might find it incredible that you haven't spent all day working to make their life happier or more comfortable, that you haven't remembered every detail of the complex story they told you a fortnight ago, or that you haven't washed and ironed the outfit they want to wear in two hours' time because *you know* they are going out and *you know* that is their best outfit!

Living with a teen can be frustrating and very hard work, and living with two or three at different stages of the process can seem like an uphill struggle. But the good news is it will pass. All the time and talk you put in will not be wasted.

Helping them make sense of the world and their own minds and bodies will help them move through this sometimes difficult and sometimes dangerous transition to adulthood with relative ease – and have plenty of stories to share at a later date.

# CHAPTER 2

# Parenting a teenager

'After years of being the one in charge of the children I suddenly find my authority and judgement questioned all the time by my teenagers. This has come as quite a shock.' **Mother**

When a baby is born, we learn how to feed it, change its nappy and get it to sleep. We are firmly in charge. Then, as the child grows, we are there to be supportive and encouraging, and to put things right when they go wrong.

Parenting teenagers is different. Strangely, the realisation that the goalposts have moved often takes parents by surprise. All of a sudden we find that our children are young people with their own strong opinions, who often don't accept our judgement, and the practices and tricks we relied on when we were parenting small children don't seem to work any more.

Doing everything for your children can be a hard habit to break. Yet raising confident teenagers means renegotiating boundaries and encouraging them to take the initiative. Encouraging your teenagers to do things for themselves can mean that everything takes much longer, and makes a lot more mess (and probably noise), and this can be very irritating. But such encouragement is in everyone's interests. There's no point in driving teenagers everywhere if it means they don't, or can't, recognise danger signals when they first meet them in the street, or in making their breakfasts and doing their ironing if it means they can't do anything for themselves once they leave home.

We also need to consider gender balance within the family. There is evidence suggesting that mothers go on doing things for boys longer than for girls. Girls are given more responsibility (despite generally being allowed far fewer freedoms and less money) and are expected to take care of themselves far sooner. And so they do!

As well as recognising that all teenagers need to do things for themselves, you need to renegotiate your role as a parent. Whereas parents of younger children are assumed to be right, parenting teenagers calls for a much more consensual approach – and admitting you are not always right is a really strong start. You are beginning a dialogue that encourages your teenagers to make their own moral and ethical choices, helping to foster their sense of self.

While at one level letting go is many parents' dream, letting go too soon is most parents' nightmare. To a parent, teenagers so often (in the right light!) still seem like vulnerable, downy-cheeked children, and our knowledge of the world means we're aware just how easily a wrong choice could damage and hurt them.

The great challenge of parenting teenagers is to let them become who they are going to be, even if you had your heart set on their being something else – like a world leader or an Olympic champion. You have to let go step by step, while dealing with your own fears, insecurities, unmet dreams and hopes – and life after they have moved away.

## HOW TO SPOT A SUCCESSFUL YOUNG PERSON

The purpose of this book is to help you raise independent, self-assured and confident teenagers. So it helps if we start by thinking about how to spot a successful young person.

A successful young person:

- Is considerate of the feelings of others
- Accepts and understands cause and effect, and knows that their actions have consequences for others
- Is able to empathise
- Is in contact with their own sense experiences (knows how they feel)
- Knows how to communicate and express their own sense experiences and feelings
- Feels accepted and valued
- Has a sense of their own rights
- Is developing a sense of morality
- Understands that different behaviour is appropriate in different contexts
- Has good self-esteem
- Maintains friendships with both sexes
- Is able to discuss problems with friends of both sexes
- Communicates effectively with a sexual partner/potential partner
- When in a sexual relationship, thinks about, plans and implements safer sex strategies and negotiates the use of contraception
- Is self-motivated and can use their time well, including study and free time
- Is able to make choices by considering options and consequences
- Recognises when help is needed and knows how to access it

It's interesting to think about how many of the attributes listed above also relate to you, the parent. Confidence, values and fairness run in families, but I doubt they're genetic!

In the course of hundreds of hours' work with parents, some basic principles for raising confident teenagers have developed.

I'll be referring to these again and again in this book, and they underpin all my recommendations.

## My parents' teen toolkit

1 **Talk, don't tell.** Everyone responds better when they're talked to rather than told what to do. Telling easily becomes nagging, which simply doesn't work. Talking is particularly important after disagreements. If we don't establish why something happened, then hurtful words and threatening behaviour can become a pattern that gets repeated next time a similar situation arises. I've always found a good way to start is with an apology – for ignoring them, being cranky, not listening, being obstinate or whatever I've done to inflame things. But it has to be sincere!

2 **Don't expect them to get your viewpoint!** Empathy is learnt behaviour, and it develops over a lifetime. Parents often dismiss teenagers as selfish and self-centred, concerned only with their own priorities and unable to identify with others. But to help your young person to understand both your feelings and their own, and to encourage them to be sympathetic to others, you have to show them how to do it. Discussing soap operas or news stories and then asking questions like 'How do you think she felt about . . . ?' is a great way to start.

3 **Learn to recognise and express your own feelings** – not just anger. Teenagers often typecast their parents as angry about most things. Anger is often a mixture of many emotions – fear, sadness, frustration, jealousy, loneliness, hurt, feeling left out – but if all you show is anger, that's all they'll get. So when you feel angry, try to take a step back; walk away until you are calmer. Then ask yourself what this situation is really about. Is it just about your frustrated desire to be

in control or are there other feelings or worries to be aired? Being able to identify your own real feelings, however conflicting or confusing, will help them to be clearer about theirs.

4  **Wait before you speak.** There are many circumstances that require a conversation about a particular issue – such as what time your teenager is to come home by or what they wear to go out. But the time to have this conversation is not when the situation arises – then there will be too much emotion in the air. Instead, wait until you can talk on an equal basis and in a rational frame of mind; don't start just as they're departing through the front door for a night out – or at 3 o'clock in the morning when they promised to be back by midnight. And talking before an incident is always better than after.

5  **Negotiate.** Think how you feel if a decision is imposed on *you* from above . . . decisions arrived at through negotiation are much easier to stick to. Give and take on both sides makes freedoms and privileges more highly valued, and increases the young person's sense of responsibility. What about a clothing allowance in return for additional help at home; permission to stay out late in return for a serious discussion of personal safety issues? By making a problem or issue partly ours we can also make it clear that it's up to everyone to get things sorted – it's not just their mistake or their behaviour that needs to change. Practise using non-blaming language: instead of saying 'You hurt me' you could try 'That hurt'.

6  **Try to forget that you know best.** We all learn through experience, but usually our own experience (or that of our peers) rather than our parents'. So it doesn't matter how many times you tell your teenagers that a particular action may have difficult consequences; nothing will stick in their memory (and guide them in the future) like finding

the same thing out at first hand. And if things do go wrong, nothing is more annoying than a judgemental 'I told you so'.

7 **Your young person has a point of view.** It will probably be shaped by the way they as individuals respond to the beliefs and attitudes they have grown up with at home, as well as to peer pressure and external role models. What's more, about many things, they know more than you do. Accept this and respect it. Even if you don't agree with their viewpoint, they have a right to it. You can't control someone else's actions or thoughts. The art of living harmoniously with teenagers is about just that: living with them rather than trying to manage them.

8 **Family life is no picnic.** But learning to negotiate with others, to read signals and to respond to needs is hugely valuable. Take the rough with the smooth – and remember to celebrate every good moment.

9 **Show them that you love them.** And take pride in their demonstrations of affection, wherever they occur, however infrequently. If you spot the highs as well as getting through the lows, life with teenagers becomes much more enjoyable.

10 **Be flexible.** There are times when teenagers want you to treat them with distant respect and others when they're happy with hands-on contact; their requirements may move back and forth between the two as circumstances demand. A young person with a broken heart may need some very hands-on nurturing, whereas one in the first stages of an exciting new relationship will probably want to be taken very seriously – but tell you little. Flexibility is the key: allow them to be nurtured like a child, but not necessarily seen as a child, as the situation demands.

11 **Take a moment to see it from their point of view.** I know only too often it feels that they're the ones not seeing it from ours, but let's face it – how can they? We've been

where they are; they have never been in our shoes. Sometimes, when you find yourself locked in yet another example of their gross lack of consideration for others or determination to break the rules, try to let go of your adult, intellectually based decisions and put yourself in their emotionally based process. Try the following exercise as an example.

## FLASHBACK

Here's a flashback exercise for you to try, to encourage you to try to think back in time. Try to remember being 14 or 15. Now try to consider:

- Whose opinion mattered most in all the world to you?
- Was it a friend, some cool older peer, or even a sibling?
- Maybe there was someone you fancied who hardly seemed to know you existed – whose praise you would have liked to have had more than anything else?

Now take this reflection a stage further and try to see yourself at the same age, but now in in a shoe shop with your mum.

- What are her criteria for choosing a new pair of shoes to buy for you?
- Does she think cost, durability or school-worthiness matter most? Or is she juggling a combination of these things?
- Meanwhile, what are your criteria for choosing a pair of shoes?

Looking back, you can probably see your mother's point of view. But did you do so at the time? Now the positions are reversed and it's you in the parental role, and you are probably adopting the same criteria as your mother. The bottom line is that the person paying is not using the same criteria as the young person who will be wearing them. Armed with this understanding perhaps there's some compromise that can be made? Perhaps she can top up the cost from her allowance? Perhaps she'll go without something else that she was going to have? Perhaps you can get her two cheaper pairs and have one for out-of-school wear?

Parenting teenagers isn't rocket science – though at times it may require the patience of a saint. You simply need to recognise, and perhaps hone, all the interpersonal skills you've acquired yourself throughout a lifetime of adventures and knocks. You can't give them that wisdom directly, but you can teach it to them through example.

## WHAT MAKES A GOOD PARENT?

Through discussions with hundreds of parents and dozens of workshops I have produced the following list – in no particular order – of attributes for a good parent from the point of view of the teenager:

- Listening without judgement
- Setting clear boundaries and enforcing them
- Making sure there is enough to eat
- Making sure the home is warm and safe
- Loving you
- Helping you to sort out your problems
- Making sure you eat well
- Offering advice and support
- Letting you be yourself
- Being friendly

- Managing the day-to-day routine for lots of people
- Ensuring nothing gets forgotten
- Keeping an eye out for you without being intrusive
- Managing the family finances
- Driving you about
- Being willing to bend the rules sometimes
- Showing affection
- Being an arbiter in family disputes
- Providing guidance in situations where a moral choice has to be made

Which of these do you think are the most important? If your child is willing, get him or her to think about it too, and then each write down the numbers in your own order of priority. How do your lists compare? Are your priorities the same?

I asked a 14-year-old to draw an ideal mother. Her drawing is shown below. Before you look at it in detail, can you draw an ideal teenager? Drawing is an excellent way to prompt thinking – because you are using a different part of your brain. Sometimes, when asked to explain how they feel in words young people, and in particular young men, can't think what to say. By using a more creative approach (perhaps a list, a series of lines or a drawing) they can choose a method of non-verbal communication that gets across what matters to them.

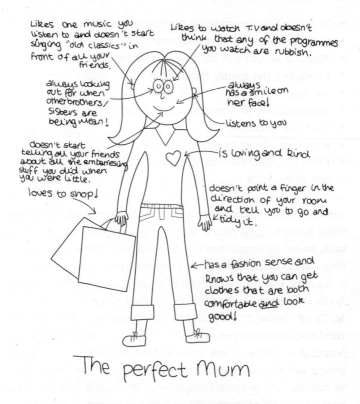

Likes one music you listen to and doesn't start singing "old classics" in front of all your friends.

Likes to watch T.V and doesn't think that any of the programmes you watch are rubbish.

always looking out for when other brothers/sisters are being mean!

always has a smile on her face!

listens to you

doesn't start telling all your friends about all the embarrasing stuff you did when you were little.

is loving and kind

loves to shop!

doesn't point a finger in the direction of your room and tell you to go and tidy it.

←has a fashion sense and knows that you can get clothes that are both comfortable and look good!

The perfect Mum

## THE KEY TASKS OF A PARENT

Most people (both teenagers and their parents) see that parenting falls into three main areas. These are:

- Managing (ensuring there is enough food, enough money)
- Nurturing and caring (loving and showing affection)
- Guiding (setting clear boundaries, listening without judgement, making moral choices)

When asked, teenagers usually say they regard the roles of nurturer and guide as the most important – and so do their parents. But parents often feel that their daily lives are so taken up with management tasks (ensuring the fridge is full, getting the teenager to the right place at the right time), that they don't have enough time for the nurturing and guiding. If this sounds like you, perhaps you need to allocate more time to the priorities at the top of your list above.

The importance both you and your young person attach to the setting of boundaries is worth a look. Parents often find them much easier to set up than to stick to; teenagers are likely to complain about them whatever they are. But feedback from teenagers consistently shows that they think the very act of setting boundaries shows that you love them and care about what they get up to. So while they may complain about having to be home by a certain time, or about their stingy allowance, they would rather you set rules than didn't. And they're not going to get any fun – or kudos – out of bending the rules if the rules are made of rubber in the first place.

It's important to remind yourself that, as I said earlier, you can't control someone else's actions or thoughts. However much you may sometimes wish things were different, parenting a teenager is about working with them in all things. You are not in control. You may be in charge of the family finances, and your children are financially dependent on you, but they still have minds of their own. For example:

## Who is parenting your teenager?

We've got used to the concept of 'time famine', and there never being enough time to go round. But just because you're out all day, and your teenagers no longer legally require a child-minder, doesn't mean that the need to parent them goes away. Try asking yourself: are your teenagers being brought up by you, or by the Internet or the television, or by the other kids they meet on the train or the estate where you live?

## REFLECTION EXERCISE

Spend a moment thinking about who is influencing them and shaping their values. Suggestions might include:

- You, their parents. Are you having conversations with them on a regular basis? Do you know (or even have any idea) what they really think?
- Grandparents. Even if not geographically close, relationships with grandparents can be active via Skype or mobile phones. The often greater availability of grandparents can make them a particularly useful support to your young person.
- The extended family (e.g. aunts, uncles, cousins) who can be significant role models for your young person.
- Their peer group, now not just available to talk to when they meet, but available to them constantly through social media and messaging technology.
- Teachers and administrators at school or college; in addition to teaching staff many schools now offer supporting staff such as counsellors and advisors.
- Celebrities and those in popular culture can have a big influence on young people who follow their every word, often whether relevant to them or not, and derive their own meaning from what they say.
- Popular culture portrayed by the media – about money, jobs, the value of being famous – can all impact on how young people feel about themselves and others.

Below is a simple diagram with levels of impact marked in the form of rings. I suggest you fill in the diagram for your young person by entering all the people or agencies that influence them in terms of their thinking, behaviour or self-belief. Try to think not only about which ring you place them in, but also where within each ring.

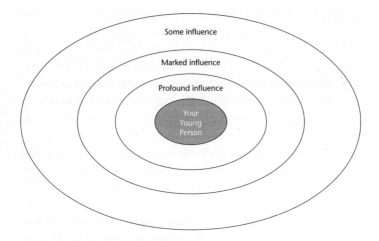

You many find, as adults often do when considering young people, that you have placed these influences according to how you would like them to be or how they were for you.

Now ask your young person to look at what you have put on the diagram, and ask them to change it or adjust it to reflect their reality.

By far the most profound influence on the way young people behave and the choices they make are their peer group. It has always been the case that during adolescence young people begin to identify more strongly with peers than adults. Adults' views can become the marker for all that is out of date or irrelevant – which is why young people rarely wear what a parent suggests or want to spend time on leisure activities identified by adults.

While peer influence was important to us in our development it has changed dramatically in the last few years in that young people are now almost constantly in touch with their peers through social media and gadgets. They are relaying every decision to friends, commenting on every action and thought of others and inhabiting a virtual space with their peers at all times. In turn this peer group is constantly influenced by the actions and thoughts of key individuals that they have decided to follow through popular culture and mass communication. More than any generation in history your young person is being parented by the people they like and admire in a remarkably intimate way. Whether it is a footballer, a musician, an actor or a non-specific 'celeb', their choices, words and actions are as close and immediate to your teen as you are – and sometimes closer!

All the above were available to us in some form. What has, however, changed for our young people is the ongoing extent to which they can be accessed today – mostly online. The young person generally has access to online information on anything they choose, and given the power of screens to absorb attention to the exclusion of everything else, information available online can be highly influential. But being able to access information in this way does not mean that what is being accessed is either unbiased or broad-ranging.

## WHY GOOD PARENTING MATTERS

How we have been parented ourselves is the foundation of what we, in turn, are able to offer as parents. It's not a good idea to assume that others in a leadership role, such as teachers and school administrators, are also parenting your young people: they may be meeting their material needs but almost certainly lack sufficient time to really develop them as people. Most professionals will not present moral or value-led opinions through their work, and teachers and youth workers are trained to be inclusive of a range of views and thoughts. This is a strength of their practice, but while parents will want to promote both acceptance and inclusion as principles they also need to provide a framework for their children on what is and what is not acceptable. Professionals may be setting and reinforcing clear boundaries, but their reasons may be more professional or institutional than emotional. Love doesn't come into it.

Even if it can sometimes feel restrictive, nothing compares to being loved.

Among young people there's a strong correlation between those who have been brought up in care and those who become parents themselves at a very early age – perhaps looking for love from a child of their own when they have received little themselves.

Given the general selfishness apparent in society, many parents may question whether it's worth teaching values at all. Surely it's more useful to teach them Mr Boffin's (*Our Mutual Friend* by Charles Dickens) philosophy of 'scrunch or be scrunched'?

In fact, it's because there is so much selfishness in society that we need to teach our young people to behave with consideration and kindness for others. If more people take responsibility for their own actions the world will be a better place.

It's a good idea to teach young people respect for the law too; to encourage a positive attitude towards those who have positions of authority over them (the police, teachers, probation officers) that is supportive rather than running them down. Parents often feel that they have little impact upon teenagers, but principles they have heard around them all their lives do tend to be absorbed, and they will be sure to pick up attitudes they hear expressed around them if such attitudes suit their purposes.

Empathy for the experiences of others is something that is learnt rather than something we're born with. With this in mind, think whether the impression you create at home is one of mutual respect. The tone of voice you use when requesting help can be particularly significant. Do you thank them when they do something for you or treat it as your right? Do you return the compliment and hold doors for those who have held them for you? Do you shake hands with young people when you first meet them?

I recently heard someone say, 'As a parent, you get them through childhood, the diseases and the risk of being knocked down by a car, and then you get to a certain stage – maybe 14 or 15 – and think, well I'm irrelevant now, I've done my best, and now it's up to you, mate.' I don't agree. I think the job of parenting is no less relevant as your children get older, but gets more demanding, because you have to observe and guide without taking over, and help them make the right decisions – in the hope that the experience will last them a lifetime. For both the future of our individual families and the future of our society as a whole, nothing could matter more.

## WHO ELSE CAN HELP WITH PARENTING YOUR TEENAGER?

1  **Other adults you trust.** Involving other adults widens your teenager's horizons. This is particularly important if yours is a single-parent family and your child has little or no contact with the other parent; involve members of both sexes in their upbringing.

2  **Family members.** Allowing your teenager to go and stay with a grandparent or uncle or aunt can be a very positive experience, and particularly useful if things at home are getting fraught. Reports back ('so helpful', 'so willing', etc.) often suggest that a different teenager has been to stay! Rather than feeling let down that you do not see this side of them very often, take strength from this clear evidence that they really do know how to behave.

3  **Their friends' parents.** Seeing how a different family organises themselves can be really mind-broadening – and you might pick up some useful ideas.

4  **Neighbours and friends.** If you can't be there when your

teenager comes home from school, is there someone else who can pop in for a cup of tea occasionally? Elderly people are sometimes glad of the company.

5 **Carefully chosen mentors.** It's quite common to read in autobiographies of famous people about schoolteachers who had a profound effect on them, encouraging them when no one else seemed to. Often, best-selling writers highlight one particular English teacher who spotted their talent and nurtured it.

6 **Books make good parenting assistants.** They are often full of (disguised) morals and usually carefully checked before they are published (unlike much of the information on the Internet).

7 **Role models in the media.** Sports biographies and interviews in the press open young people's minds to possibilities in their own lives.

8 **Information.** It's a good idea to put together a fact file containing some of the information that a young person might need access to: phone numbers for the doctor's surgery, taxis, the cinema; bus times; pamphlets on contraception, AIDS and other sexually transmitted infections. Keep it in a place where everyone knows where to find it.

You already have everything you need to be an effective parent to your teenager, and of course you don't have to go it alone. If you choose, you can:

- Ask advice from professionals (teachers, developmental experts, counsellors).
- Go to workshops and read books on parenting skills.
- Talk to friends – parents of other young people can be a tremendous support, as can knowing that you're not the only one facing these difficulties.

- Talk to your teenager's friends. If your teenager does not seem to want to talk to you alone, you may find you get more out of them if their friends are there too.
- Access information: from libraries, online.

# CHAPTER 3

# A teenager's world

It's a long time since I studied Physics at school, but I do remember one experiment with particular clarity. It was the one when you had to determine the balancing point for a long wooden rod over a fulcrum. The balance achieved was always very precarious and the rod would sway dramatically one way and the other before achieving stability. Add an additional weight to one end of the rod, and the same process of trial and error had to be gone through until a new balancing point was found.

Teenagers often find themselves in a similar position, trying to achieve stability in a situation that is so easily upset, and which constantly throws new challenges at them. They veer between responsibility and neediness. They are inconsistent – they may protest their desire to be left alone and get on with life, but if it does all go wrong they may want to be allowed to revert to being a child, who is cared for and everything 'made all right'. And then, once the crisis has passed, they will want you to forget about it, and the key part you played, and allow them to be independent again.

For parents this can be tough. You know about the world, more about how things work, systems and chances, as well as threats. You may see a landscape bulging with opportunities that your young person is ignoring. You may also want to protect your young person against the setbacks, knocks and mistakes you made yourself. You can also feel a strong sense of urgency; there is so much information you want to pass on, and so little time in which to do it, that it can seem better just to issue instructions about what to do than to take time to explain your point of view to your young person, to allow time for them to absorb the message at their own pace.

But while parents may know more about the world they see, they do not know more about the young person's world. There are issues they are dealing with that were not part of our growing up:

> 'I've been on Facebook since I was 11. At first I used to check it just a couple of times a day but since I got an iPhone at 13 – the age most of my friends got one – my social-media use has increased dramatically to the point where it forms the backdrop to my whole day. As a teen-ager today, having a social media presence is mandatory. No one calls or texts anymore because you have to pay to do that so most communication takes place on apps or online.' **Izzy Mackay**, 15, interview in 'Technically Addicted,' *Sunday Telegraph* magazine, 16 November 2014

And their lives are driven by the emotions they feel. It's important to understand that young people feel a wide variety of different emotions, and may relate to their world in terms of how things 'feel' rather than what they think. Young people often experience lots of different (and frequently conflicting) feelings at the same time, such as:

- Irrational anger
- Stress
- Sudden awareness of new sides to their personality, for example they may experience – and be frightened by – suicidal thoughts or intense feelings of self-hatred; a sudden desire for secrecy and to suppress rather than share their feelings

- An increased need for love, reassurance and affection and yet great embarrassment if their parents show it
- A mouthful of harsh words that rush out without thinking ('I wish you were dead')
- A new urgency to say absolutely nothing, having been a chatty person up to now
- A desire to blame: you for making their life unhappy; themselves for being useless at everything
- A real desire to hurt, sometimes just those close to them, sometimes everyone
- Extreme anxiety, even panic attacks that seem to come from nowhere and may be around areas of their life they managed easily in the past

The likelihood is that these feelings will be expressed not through negotiation or explanation but through an extension of the 'stress-communication' mechanisms they have always used – just this time in greater measure. So if they have cried or shouted to get their own way in the past, expect more of the same, but for longer periods and louder. If they are sulkers and seethers, expect some door-slamming and long-drawn-out silences.

When expressed to close family, many of these feelings can be very hurtful, but really this is the safest and best place for this to happen; it's important to allow them to explore their emotions without long-term loss of love. Parents need to understand that while the intensity of the feelings they experience will not last, they are still very real at the time.

By understanding that young people need to explore the explosive range of their feelings, you can even learn to find some pleasure in the fact that when they explode and tell you they wish you were dead, they are doing their job of growing up and learning to relate to others – and you are doing yours by creating a safe and secure relationship for them.

## FLASHBACK

Think back to your first serious crush on someone –
perhaps when you were 13 or 14. Take a few moments
now to picture the person and recall how it felt when
they looked at you – or ignored you. Can you remember
what they looked like, and what their smile was like?
What does thinking about the person now, after all these
years, do to your insides?

Most of us can remember our first crush, and it can be
a surprise, if you have not thought about the object of
your affection for many years, to realise how much you
still remember – both about them and how you felt at
the time. Though now you might use the word 'crush',
there might have been a very different word or phrase
then.

When I have tried this experiment in workshops for parents,
many have reported feeling that 'the bottom suddenly dropped
out of my stomach', or they felt a quick attack of 'butterflies'.
Teenagers experience this intensity of feeling on an hourly
basis. A smile can make the sun come out, while being ignored,
or having the loved one smile at someone else, can be a tragedy
to put *Romeo and Juliet* in the shade.

## COMMON TEENAGE THEMES

Of course not all teenagers are the same. Some are kind and
loving, others funny and sharp. Some cringe at the idea of
wearing high fashion, others would rather be struck down with
bubonic plague than be seen in supermarket trainers. However,
when teenagers talk about what they do and don't like about
their parents, some common themes appear:

• They resent being talked down to. They do not feel like

children any more and do not want to be treated as such, even when they behave like them.

- They see you as in the way: of their happiness and their freedom. You basically stop them having all they want, though you may see yourself as the provider of all.
- They see your experience as irrelevant and the idea of you being in love, or having sex, as ranging from distasteful to disgusting. After all, it was such a *long* time ago in their eyes and the world has changed.
- They will kick at whatever boundaries you set, because the process of distancing themselves from their parents is something that is essential to them. Whatever boundaries you create, however reasonable, are likely to be resisted – simply because they are there. It does not follow that no boundaries are the way to an easy life, because they do understand in some way that boundaries equal love – and anyway, they need to kick at something.
- They want past boundaries regularly checked out and some previous arrangements to be forgotten about. For example, if they have always liked to talk to you while they have a bath, the bathroom door will suddenly be locked and they will want you to forget you ever had the intimacy you shared before. They will want you to knock before entering their bedrooms and do not want their siblings marching in without permission, especially when they are not there. However generous they may have been in the past with their things, they may suddenly no longer want to share.
- They feel excited and threatened, at the same time. At one moment they are thrilled by opportunities, at the next terrified by the idea of missing them or the responsibilities that go with them.
- They look for immediate gratification and are not good at planning long-term outcomes. They may even be unable

to imagine how consequences will affect them. For example, a 13-year-old may well say 'Don't worry, if anyone tries to grab me I'll kick them and run.'

- Bodily changes, hormones and a brain that is rapidly both growing and pruning itself mean they are experiencing considerable confusion as well as strong and sometimes conflicting emotions, which they feel unable to discuss with their parents. And it is important for parents to understand how quickly these changes happen.
- There is an immense drive to 'belong', to be seen as one of the group, but at the same time to be seen as an individual.

## How this feels, first person

Here is a slam poem written by Olivia Sheldrake, a sixth-form student, reflecting on her time in secondary school:

### HIERARCHY – THE DEVIL'S PLAYTHING

The second we enter high school we are automatically
    divided, automatically judged on the version of
    ourselves that we happen to be that day.
You walk through those gates in your neatly pressed
    uniform and it doesn't matter that everybody else is
    wearing the same as you, it is about how you wear it,
    how you walk in it, what shoes you wear with it.
It is what bag you have, how you wear your hair, where
    you hang around before class.
It is the sound of your voice, how much you scratch your
    nose or bite your nails with nerve because you know
    that anyone who thinks that they are better than you
    will judge you if you step out of line for a single
    second.

I was in high school, and when I arrived aged 11 to the
shock of many I did not know how to be whatever
they had decided was the definition of 'cool' that day.

I had my skirt at my knee because that was a rule that I
had apparently not got the memo about being okay
not to follow.

My blazer was almost the same length as my skirt
because my mother wanted me to grow into it so she
wouldn't have to buy another next year.

And worst of all, my backpack was black. I did not
particularly like that colour at age 11 but I had asked
my mother especially to buy that one, and you know
why? It was because I knew that it was a neutral
colour so therefore I would be judged the least for it.

That is surely not what an 11 year old should have to
think.

The bag in which I kept my school supplies was suddenly
an important part of my education and although I had
no idea why I went with it.

I had merely experienced half a day of introduction to the
school and to my classmates before I had this idea
fixated into my head that if I could not conform to the
rules of the prettiest and the cleverest of my year
about skirt lengths and backpack colour schemes that I
must instead keep my head down and become as
unnoticed as humanly possible.

Because of a small collection of other 11 year olds I
suddenly felt compelled to do as they say or stay out
their way, and although doing the latter made me
feel more unimportant than I have ever felt I found
myself conforming to their system for three years of
my life.

Isn't that insane?!

I had become belittled by my own peers simply because I
happened to be a person who surprisingly enough was

not interested in being a part of their gang with the
ringleader's name on the door.

I was a nothing, a reject.

And why?

Because I had passion burning inside of me for the things
that they chose to find uninteresting?

Because I didn't take the same generic selfie that they
took?

Because I didn't actually enjoy conforming to their made
up rules about how school hierarchy is meant to be
sorted?

You see this is what happens in high school. Every tiny
thing that you do is stamped on your forehead.

You read a book? Nerd.

You put your hand up in class? Keen.

You struggle with a subject? Lazy freak.

DO YOU NOT UNDERSTAND?

We have a legal obligation that we are trying to make the
most of and yet all we hear is the tapping of your
heels as you walk down the hallways, the 'it's okay'
sympathy from favouring teachers, the constant
reminders that no matter how good our grade card
looks at the end of the term we will never look as
good as you at prom.

PLEASE, tell me why we can't be ourselves.

With the benefit of hindsight, most of the teenage themes above
are fairly easy to understand – but that doesn't mean they are
easy to deal with when they happen. A teenager who up to now
has been a reasoned and reasoning young person, who suddenly
reacts to perfectly logical ground rules with ferocity, can be a
shocking experience. Being told that you are hated, 'in my way'
or 'ruining my life' can be similarly devastating. But the process
of pulling away and separating from parents is essential if they
are to achieve the status of independent individuals. The more

they become fully independent and self-sufficient, the more likely it is that you can establish a long-term and meaningful relationship with them in the future.

## THE TROUBLE WITH TEENAGERS – AND PARENTS

Parenting teenagers can be a rocky ride. It may feel at times that no one else has ever had to go through what you have to go through – or that no one else's children have turned into such self-obsessed monsters. It's sometimes helpful to look at what both parents and teenagers find most difficult – so that you can tell yourself that you're not the only one when things are bad, and congratulate yourself that things are not as difficult as they might be on the good days!

### What gets parents down:

- Your own experience of the world is rejected; they take more notice of their friends than you – even when you absolutely know you're right
- You can see them making the same mistakes you made and they will not listen to your advice. They will swear that the outcomes will not be same for them, even when you know they will
- They are rude and uncooperative, even when there is no reason to be
- They have lost their individuality, and behave as part of a crowd
- They look unattractive, with greasy skin and spots; they smell – and show no inclination to do anything about it
- They need to stay constantly in touch with their peers by way of a gadget even when you are having some precious time together

- They veer between wildly enthusiastic (something that involves friends) to negative and sneering (anything that involves you!)

## What gets teenagers down:

- Their friends and relationships, which shift and realign constantly, and the pressure to be 'in the loop' all the time
- Attraction-based relationships, dates, sexual bargaining and how far to get involved
- Exams and pressure at school, often mirrored by pressure at home – e.g. the frequently stated advice that 'good grades mean good prospects for you, so you must do your homework'
- Self-image: clothes, skin, weight, hair and spots
- Their bodily development, how fast in comparison with their friends and the terrible uncertainty of not knowing how they'll end up
- The future
- The past, and you bringing it up in front of others

It's interesting to note that the things that get parents down are mostly to do with how they relate to their teenagers, and how things have changed, whereas the issues the young people concentrate on tend to be to do with the much wider world. They are looking onwards and outwards, and the changes and uncertainties can be hard to live with, while their parents are harking back to 'how things used to be'.

There are occasional truces – such as when a teenager is ill, needs your help and is willing to accept your love, and is grateful for what you do for them – but the day-to-day reality of living with teenagers can be an existence of ongoing conflict and stress. However, it will pass, and with love, support and endless patience (all yours, alas) the dust will one day settle.

## COMMUNICATION

Much of the time within families, communication tends to be pretty factual and actual. Parents frequently complain that their children stop talking to them as they enter the teen years. More and more communication ends up as a string of questions fired at the young person, followed by, and interspersed with, periods of nagging – or as the young people might put it, 'pointing out the f****** obvious'.

Parents frequently justify this 'question and complain cycle' by saying that their children no longer either talk or listen to them. I can't help feeling that there are mismatched approaches here. Firing questions at someone is never a good way to make them communicate freely, and nagging has never worked. In fact most people, particularly males, have really good 'nag filters' to block out anything that comes close to a repeated complaint or criticism by the time they are ten. Sooner or later most of us have had one of those 'I sound like my mum/dad and I swore I never would' moments.

### FLASHBACK

Think of your relationship with your own parents. Now try to put yourself back in the position of yourself as a teen-ager. What phrases and actions annoyed you then? Do these phrases still have the power to make your blood boil?

### Parents' deadly phrases

- 'It just is'
- 'You are so self-centred'
- 'Just do as you are told'
- 'Because I said so'
- 'You treat this place like a hotel'

- 'Just you wait until your father gets home'
- 'If I say black's white, it's white'
- 'I know what I'm talking about'
- 'In my day . . . '
- 'I would not have dreamed of talking to my parents like that'
- 'It's just your attitude'
- 'You always have to have the last word, don't you?'

(The above list was compiled during workshops with parents.)

## And now the good news – what teenagers do want

- Your unconditional love and support. To know that there is nothing they could say or do that would make you stop loving them
- Your attention (but when they want it, not when you feel able to give it)
- The knowledge that you are proud of them
- To know that you will always forgive
- Negotiation
- To know that you are not trying to tell them what they should do
- To know you are on their side even when they mess up

## Parenting pitfalls

This is very definitely what teenagers don't want:

- Nagging
- Telling them how it was for you again and again (particularly stories you are very fond of telling)
- Using phrases that are clichés and get used without thinking ('You'll be sorry when I'm gone'; 'Because I say so')

- Being angry and shouting ('Get to your room'), even if they have provoked your anger in the first place
- Constant restating of what they did wrong
- Emphasis on things they think are trivial (e.g. not picking up their school bags), especially when you interrupt their tales to tell them
- Constant emphasis on things that they could have done better
- Pointing out the other person's point of view when they are telling you about an event they are outraged or angry about
- Having the last word again. One of the hardest challenges for any parent is to say nothing; to allow our previously stated point of view to stand and not to come back with a final retort. Being able to say nothing is such an effective way of communicating with teenagers, because it shows we are really listening to them

Parents want the world to be safe for their teenager, they want to restrict, cosset and protect: 'Take care on the way home'; 'Let me know when you get there'. But these phrases can have the effect of restating the dynamics of the relationship. What is masked as social politeness is in reality a restating of 'I'm in charge', a paternalistic view of risks they choose to take, and their charting of the world.

## RELATING

Having stated the problems from both sides of the fence, the key theme of this book is the tremendous opportunity on offer: the chance to really get to know your young people, and encourage the development of a relationship that will last for the rest of your lives.

I will be looking primarily at how we can do this through better communication; exploring how we can really hear each other and, in the process, both encourage and extend our understanding – of our young people, of the situations they face, and of ourselves.

# CHAPTER 4

# The feel-good factor: promoting self-esteem and self-confidence

This is one of the most important chapters of the book. As we saw in the list of qualities that go to make up a successful young person in Chapter 2, good self-esteem is a key part of the recipe. High self-esteem is a key part of resilience, the secret ingredient that helps get many young people through adolescence relatively unscathed, while those with poor self-esteem risk falling into one of the many traps along the way.

It would not be true to say that all young people with good self-esteem behave better than their less confident peers, or that they are less likely to get themselves into troublesome situations or make bad choices. What is true is that young people with high self-esteem are less likely to be pushed into situations where they feel vulnerable or give in to negative peer pressure. They are more able to distinguish between actions and events that are their own responsibility and those that they found themselves caught up in or affected by but for which others made the real choices. Overall they are more likely to take responsibility for themselves, be better able to negotiate safer boundaries, to make and maintain positive friendships and relationships – and be better able to plan safe outcomes.

Not all young people with low self-esteem will have diffi-culties or come to any harm, but the majority of those who do encounter serious problems will have self-esteem issues. While not everyone has the same notions of harm, anyone who believes in their own worth is less likely to take part in any action or behaviour they can see is harmful or dangerous to their well-being.

## WHAT SELF-ESTEEM IS AND IS NOT

Self-esteem is all about how you feel about yourself; it is not about how others feel about you. How you feel about yourself acts like a filter. We tend to notice and agree with anything that comes our way that reinforces our existing sense of ourselves. For example, someone who believes they can't add up will notice every time they get it wrong, but may miss the many times they get it right, or dismiss those occasions as worthlessly easy. Unfortunately it does not help to be contradicted by those who think they know you best; when talking to your teen contradiction can serve to further isolate a young person as it may seem to them that you don't know them at all.

Simply refuting their self-view just makes them wrong again – it doesn't make them feel better. So although it is tempting to contradict negative opinions about themselves that you hear from your young person, far better than arguing the point is to encourage them to reflect on their own feelings; to help them notice the feelings of satisfaction or pride in achievement or effort that they experience. So if, for example, your teenager says 'I'm useless at Maths', it's best to encourage them to reflect with a question such as 'What do you mean by useless?', rather than with an automatic response of 'Oh no you're not'. Even if your perception is valid, it's their perception of the situation that matters to them. So if you want to talk about the way you see things, do it as your own personal point of view rather than deny their point of view, or make your opinion into 'fact'. For example, 'I think you're very good at general Maths, but what are the things that you feel you're not good at?'

## UNDERSTANDING SELF-ESTEEM IN TEENAGERS

For a teenager, self-esteem is about how a young person sees – and therefore values – themselves. It is often described as confidence. Confidence is how they express their inner feelings to the world – the way they operate and behave in relation to their inner belief. However, a young person displaying outward self-confidence does not necessarily hold themselves in high esteem, as people can learn to override inner feelings as a coping strategy. It's also accepted by many that we have more than one sense of ourselves, so it's perfectly possible for individuals to be able to operate well in some aspects of self while disliking themselves or feeling inadequate in other aspects. For example, your teenager may speak well in public, get their point of view across very effectively in a discussion or be the life and soul of the party, but still not, deep down, like themselves very much.

Some young people operate brilliantly in the learning environment but feel totally inadequate socially; some may feel confident and capable in a sporting environment but be unable to make small talk. For young people with a generally good sense of self-esteem these 'low' areas can present them with challenges to be overcome. For those with low self-esteem they may become 'no go' areas to be avoided at all costs. Some young people may even put all their emotional eggs in one basket and concentrate solely on one area of their lives and personalities – because that's where they feel most successful.

The simplest way to understand self-esteem is to see it as the comparison between two different internal viewpoints – our 'perfect self' and our 'self-image'.

All young people carry around inside them a blueprint of how they would like to be – or even should be – and how they should behave. This 'perfect self' varies from person to person, will vary in different situations, and has a lot to do with how they are parented – how many 'shoulds' or perhaps 'should-nots' they had pointed out to them in their formative years. (One of the many reasons why nagging doesn't work and can be harmful is that it puts another 'should' into the perfect self.)

Most of us can easily identify what's in our perfect self because it is full of 'shoulds'. Every time we say the word to ourselves we are referring to that blueprint for perfection we have never – and will never – live up to. Some of mine include:

- I should get up at the first ring of the alarm clock
- I should always be kind and thoughtful to the neighbours
- I should never lose my temper with the kids
- I should get to the gym three times a week
- I shouldn't have that piece of cake

The list is endless. For most people the 'shoulds' contain impossible ideals they wouldn't dream of imposing on others, such as always giving and never taking, always being supportive but never showing or expressing need, allowing others to express their feelings but always putting on a 'brave' face themselves. In really extreme cases the 'shoulds' may contain damaging or harmful things, like weighing 30 kilograms or giving in to damage or abuse. For many young people these 'shoulds' may even be opposed to each other, such as 'I should keep my room clean and tidy' and 'I should be my own person and make my own decisions – not do what Mum tells me'.

While many of our early 'shoulds' and 'should nots' come from parents, as a child begins to move towards adolescence the power of the parent voice wanes and is increasingly replaced by the peer voice. This voice also has some very powerful messages about what a perfect young person does or does not do, and while for most people the two sets of ideals eventually merge, and reasoning skills discard foolish or damaging ideals, for a while at least the peer voice is running the show.

There are some telltale signs to spot if your young person has high self-esteem or not – although there can be daily fluctuations.

## HOW TO SPOT A YOUNG PERSON WITH GOOD SELF-ESTEEM

A young person with high self-esteem will tend to:

- Take on new experiences willingly
- Have a go at things they have not tried before, and have another go if the first experiment does not go well
- Persevere
- Be open to making new friends. When they meet new people they will be curious and interested rather than just showing off
- Be willing to admit their mistakes (albeit not necessarily at the time they occur)
- Be able to separate 'this is my fault' from 'this is someone else's fault'
- Be willing to take responsibility for themselves and their actions
- Be willing to be criticised (if constructive)
- Be self-accepting and willing to let others make mistakes without pointing the finger
- Be willing to believe they are likeable and loveable
- Be able to believe that people care about them and want to be with them
- Be able to understand that others believe in them and want to support them

- Be able to treat all with consideration and respect – including themselves
- Understand that everything takes different people different amounts of time and support to learn, and so it's acceptable to take time
- Be able to understand that not everyone has the same skills so it's OK not to be the best at things

## HOW TO SPOT A YOUNG PERSON WITH LOW SELF-ESTEEM

A young person with low self-esteem will tend to:

- Shy away from new experiences
- Only try new things if pushed and give up straight away if they make a mistake or if anyone teases their efforts
- Declare the task or event 'stupid' or make some other derogatory statement
- Be very judgemental of others they hardly know and very protective of existing friends – and try to put friends off making new friendships too
- Lie and deny as long as possible. Blame everybody and everything for their mistakes – ultimately it's your fault for having me
- Let others take the decisions and therefore the blame if things go wrong
- Get very angry, aggressive or overly self-deprecating when criticised. 'I'm going to run away.' 'I'm going to kill myself.'
- Find great delight in the faults of others
- Feel insecure and be in constant need of reassurance
- Feel they constantly have to do things to make the other person like them – giving gifts, doing favours, lending items or clowning
- Consider all offers of help to be a criticism of how badly they were doing or how inadequate they are

- Put some people on unshakable pedestals while others are harshly judged
- Take little real care of themselves
- May abuse alcohol, drugs, sexual contacts or self-harm
- Constantly compare themselves to others and decide they are 'thick'
- Stop trying and opt out of learning by truanting or behaving badly
- Be overly competitive at those areas they do well in
- May be boastful or brag or use put downs
- May be obsessive about their one area of skill, e.g. sport, singing, etc.

## SELF-IMAGE

As well as how they think they should be, young people also have the other part of their self-esteem, their self-image. Their self-image reveals how they think they are.

This self-image may bear very little relation to how anyone else sees them or to the feedback they get from others as they go about their lives. It is the picture they see in their mind's mirror regardless of anyone else's view of them and they filter out what does not fit their own self-view.

For example, a teenager's self-image may include a sense of herself as a foolish person who is always getting things wrong. Every time she makes a mistake or does something silly her poor self-image is reinforced, but she fails to notice either that she also gets plenty of things right or that she is popular and others see her as friendly and successful. She also fails to notice that everyone else also makes mistakes fairly frequently as they are all learning and developing or that they are also sometimes wrong-footed and foolish. Our self-image bears no relation to how others see us, it is simply how we see ourselves.

For teens self-image has a strong link to appearance and how attractive they deem themselves to be. Whilst all adults know that teens, regardless of skin break-outs or wonky eyebrows, are beautiful – their energy and passions are compelling – teens often feel ugly or even deformed. This may be increased by aspects of the media presentation of beauty (both male and female) as the ultimate in human value. Research has shown that easy access to porn has also had a profound effect on how young people view the human body with its emphasis on surgical enhancement and hairlessness. The unnatural portrayal of (particularly) female bodies from a young child's Barbie to the airbrushed perfection of media images of celebrities can lead a lot of young women and, increasingly, young men to have unrealistic views of how a person should look. If this is compounded by a household where weight is constantly an issue and where food intake is monitored by calories and fat content rather than health properties or taste, it is common for young people to have problems around food and eating. They may either deny themselves food (or types of food) or binge eat to fill the 'emptiness' of feeling inadequate.

Youthful obsession with selfies and social networking taps into an important stage in becoming an adult: the recognition of oneself as an individual within society and social groupings, which is displayed and marked by appearance. Such markers as clothing, hairstyle, jewellery, skin colour or tone, body-fat and body-art all contribute to how we categorise others and recognise people we feel allied to. Of course, such instant judgements are often wrong, but research continues to show that we assign traits to others based on appearance. People deemed attractive are often assigned positive traits whilst those viewed as unattractive are considered less able or less pleasant – even when this has proved incorrect time after time.

Young people looking in a mirror frequently judge themselves the same way, using the same incorrect set of assumptions. If they think they look good in relation to the desired grouping they aspire to belong to, they believe themselves to be capable, pleasant and successful within that group's criteria, whereas if they see themselves as bad in relation to those criteria they will feel like an outsider. The hard thing for young people is that their view of themselves can change rapidly and even swing dramatically from one extreme to another within a very small timeframe. A simple criticism from someone whose opinion they value can send them into uncertainty and misery – but this won't apply to most parents! Whilst a parent's criticism of their teen as a person may cut deep, teenagers do usually accept that parents know them well, so a parent's negative assessment of their appearance seldom causes any upset – though a positive one might.

All children and young people need to learn that what they see in the media, whether in an advert, a film or in porn, is not necessarily 'real'. They should understand that the images they see are frequently air-brushed, that bodies are surgically enhanced and that people behave and look the way they do to encourage others to purchase products. Playing around with their bedside lamp and a mirror can teach a young person a great deal about how lighting can make a huge difference, and most schools will use film clips or photo-editing software to show young people how images are manipulated.

Essentially self-esteem is the difference between the perfect self and the self-image, or, in other words, our self-esteem is how well we think we shape up in relation to our own view of perfection!

When we think about ourselves in relation to others all of us, including children and young people, have a very strong sense of hierarchy; we compare ourselves with those within the societies we are part of and decide who is higher on the scale and who lower. For most adults this may mean people at work or within the social groups they belong to, and though many people still operate competitively in these arenas, mostly adults accept that everyone has equal value (though exceptions may persist for some people). However, for young people the position of an individual in any given hierarchy may be confused with the value of this person. So someone at the top level of popularity might be viewed as a 'better' person, a more worthwhile person, than someone at the lower edges of popularity, whereas the truth is that some people adopt behaviour that makes them more popular but everyone has equal value.

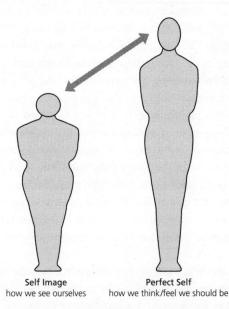

Self Image
how we see ourselves

Perfect Self
how we think/feel we should be

What constitutes 'top dog' in any grouping may vary or change according to the make-up of the group. Interestingly, when asked what they like about their friends, most young people will list humour, loyalty, kindness, fun and fairness as important characteristics. But when asked to identify what a 'perfect' example of a young person would be, they almost always refer to physical characteristics and achievements.

For groups of young men, haircuts and football (the right moves or the right team) are very important; for groups of young women, hair (again) and body weight are seen as markers of value. Designer labels, fashion, game-playing skills, language, attitude, money and independence are also common markers of 'value' to young people.

Having this strong sense of hierarchy has many functions. It helps groups of young people to bond, creates society and to some degree keeps things ticking along nicely. However, it can be limiting and even damaging if it is the only way a young person relates themselves to the world around them. If a young person believes they are worth more or less than others in their peer group, or believes that other people are quantifiable in this way, they may make choices about their behaviour in relation to this information. At an extreme level we see this manifest as 'isms'. Racism supposes that race determines a person's worth and that some people are of more value than others from birth. Likewise sexism determines that the qualities and behaviours associated with one sex are of less value or worth in the world than those of the other. Hierarchical thinking is also strongly ingrained in those young people who are likely to bully or use power tactics over others as it allows whatever qualities are deemed desirable by the group to be more important than broader concepts of fairness or value.

A more healthy view of the self in relation to others is to see it as a recipe that contains the same 'ingredients' as everybody else but in differing quantities and mixtures. We are all unique but all made up of the same bits and pieces. Some of us have skills in some areas, some of us don't. Some of us have one kind of motivation in life, some of us have many and we change motivations as we develop – perhaps a love of music is supplanted by a love of amateur dramatics after coming across an enthusiastic local group. We are all different but we share a broad cloak of humanity and common experience. We are therefore able to empathise with people we have never met and whose lives are very different from our own.

I've often heard it said that everyone is good at something.

I'm not sure I completely agree. I think many people are average at most things and they are still unique, worthy and valuable. It's not being good at something that matters: it's being some-body. And it is entirely by encouraging your young person to understand and share this view that parents can influence their child's life-long self-esteem.

Our role as parents is to help young people see themselves in a positive light. We need to help them form a manageably broad perfect self and a healthily robust self-image.

## GETTING THE 'PERFECT SELF' IN PERSPECTIVE

So if everybody carries around a little blueprint in their head that they use either to beat themselves up ('I shouldn't have said that') or pat themselves on the back ('Good try'), it's a sound strategy for parents to help their young person develop a healthily supportive inner map.

This can best be done by getting rid of the 'shoulds'. As we have seen, every 'should' given goes straight into a teenager's 'perfect self' picture to prove just how wrong, bad and useless they are – even when we're not around to remind them. The quick antidote to the 'should' phrase is the 'everyone . . . but' phrase. For example, instead of: 'You clumsy thing – look what you've done, you should have been more careful', you could try saying: 'Everyone drops things sometimes – we all have accidents, but I find concentrating a little harder usually helps to avoid them.'

The first option is blaming and shaming, while the second offers understanding and some advice (based on personal experience) in an assertive way. Getting rid of the blaming 'shoulds' not only helps self-esteem but probably allows them an easier apology when one is indicated – while allowing you to stay calmer too. Adapting your vocabulary or tone of voice can make a huge difference to how easy you are to listen to – and how readily your young person will respond!

### FLASHBACK

What were some of the 'shoulds' your parents used? Can you remember five common ones? How are you with these five things today?

## SOME COMMON 'SHOULDS' AND THEIR ANTIDOTE PHRASES

You should have been out of the house by now.

*It is past your usual time to leave.*

If I tell you to do something then you should do it without arguing all the time.

*I find it frustrating when you argue with me so much. I have asked you to do something and I would like it done please.*

You shouldn't talk to your brother like that.

*If you are trying to get someone to respond, I find it works better if you say it in a kind and friendly tone of voice.*

At your age you should be able to keep your room tidy.

*It's difficult to find things calmly in a muddle. Your bedroom needs a good sort out.*

You really should listen.

*This is important information so please can I have your attention now; these are things I need you to know.*

You should be doing your homework.

*If you want to have your homework ready for tomorrow it might be a good idea to programme in some time for when you will be able to do it this evening. Bearing in mind your other commitments, what time is best?*

## GROUP 'SELF' ESTEEM AND
## THE ROLE OF SOCIAL MEDIA

For young people growing up with technology, self-esteem has new ways of both manifesting itself and being reinforced or damaged. In past generations young people would, as now, find a social group that accepted them – usually a friendship group. These groups are important to all of us in our lives, and never more so than during adolescence when the family group is becoming less important as the provider of mores, rules and reinforcement. Being shunned by their social group, or finding themselves the centre of negative reports and feelings, can be terrible for young people and they may find themselves facing the prospect of having to leave an established grouping and finding another to 'adopt' them – a situation akin to the old fear of rejection by their family that younger children sometimes feel when they have broken family rules.

The differences between what it was like for us and what it is like for young people now are many and the most obvious one is the size and extent of their social groups. While we may have been in social groups of a handful of people, and linked by that small group into several other handful-sized groups, today, thanks to social media, a young person can feel them-selves to be in a virtual group of hundreds. While in the past we would confide in our few closest friends and trust them to honour our confidences, today many young people share all their 'secrets' with dozens of people, who in turn pass on anything of even mild interest to their own networks of dozens more. The more interesting the news, the wider and quicker it spreads and the more likely the sharer is to get the much sought after 'likes' to their comments, pictures or shares.

These virtual 'likes', along with the number of virtual friends an individual has in their network, have become the means that many young people use to measure their social value. Rather than embodying the virtues of friendship – being a good friend – many of today's socially successful young people operate in ways that we would have considered being very bad friends indeed, by sharing secrets, listing their friends' failings and humiliations and commenting on others' behaviour and feelings. This is done without reproach because they are 'only saying', a term which often means anyone taking offence is considered by the group to be overly sensitive.

I meet many young people who are desperately lonely and frightened by the power of social networking, though none of them is necessarily experiencing the online bullying so frequently commented upon in the media. They fear the rejection which might ensue if they are seen to be 'overreacting' or supporting values not generally shared or exhibited by the group. Their loneliness is often caused because they have no one to truly trust as their painful dramas are pulled apart and commented on by all, and their social network may well include those who are the cause of the upset in the first place. Many young people share networks with the majority of their school year, for example, so everyone knows who is hooking up with who and whose boy or girlfriend has cheated. While this is probably not behaviour that is unique to this generation, the scale and speed of the passing on of information is very new, as is the use of photos and the posting of opinions on everyone's behaviour for all to see:

'After supper I watch TV with my phone, and Facebook and Tweet and chat to friends on Snapchat. Then I take my phone to bed. It's normal for me to be on my phone from 10pm to 11.30pm – all my friends are.

'I've got 560 followers on Instagram, which I'm pleased with. I may post pictures of me or me with my friends, then often people will comment.' Interview with **Izzy Mackay**, 15, in 'Technically Addicted', *Sunday Telegraph* magazine, 16 November 2014

## WHAT'S THE BEST WAY FOR PARENTS TO SUPPORT THEIR TEENAGERS?

Many young people feel parents have no idea about their associated problems or issues – because their parents did not experience the pressure of social media in anything like its present form. They may also be unwilling to allow parents to know what is going on because they don't want their private lives made known to them or for them to offer their opinions on the actions of their friends. Similarly, parents may feel at a loss to deal with upsets in the virtual realm as they have only experienced such things from a sensible adult perspective.

- All parents need to make sure they help their young person develop strong personal values and beliefs before they venture into social networking. When they are young and first exploring networking sites, only give them permission to join if they 'friend' you too so you are aware of the exchanges and can talk about issues as they arise.
- Encourage dialogue about the use and importance of social media and virtual friendships – the good, the bad and the mean! Help your young person think through the importance of the choices they are making on their sense of themselves.
- Social networking can be addictive and exhausting as young people feel enormous pressure to keep up to date with everyone and everything. Help them keep some perspective by having some healthy rules about not using phones or tablets during mealtimes or when spending time with family members.
- Limit screen time and set download limits to encourage some personal boundaries and choice.
- If you see anything on your young person's network sites or in their emails or texts that you feel is bullying

behaviour, speak to them about it – and don't be afraid to report it to their school or even the police if it merits that level of action. Young people need adults to make decisions about safety and well-being for them when they are unable or unwilling to do this for themselves, but always talk it through with your young person first: they may be able to offer another solution.

## 13 top tips for helping teenagers' self-esteem

1 **Avoid making comparisons.** Comparisons are seldom helpful. It's not a good idea to make statements like 'Joanne is such a polite, helpful girl – why can't you be like her?' That just gives the perfect self a face and name! Within families it might also lead to a level of sibling rivalry bordering on warfare. Constantly question all stereotypical notions of beauty, body image and value, especially in the media. A little healthy cynicism in relation to supermodel thinness or 'bad boy' behaviour from footballers will help them develop a more realistic and healthy perfect self to live up to.

2 **Question, but don't argue with, any self-deprecating comments.** Your young person may make such comments for a variety of reasons, perhaps because they genuinely do feel negative about themselves, or perhaps to provoke discussion or denial. While it can be hard to distinguish which is which, the accompanying body language can be revealing. For example, if your young person says 'I'm so ugly', ask them 'What do you mean by ugly?' or 'Why are you saying that?' The object is to let them know you're not going to play the 'Oh no you're not', 'Oh yes I am' pantomime game, but that you are prepared to have a serious discussion should they want one. The chances are they are seeking reassurance and comfort – in which case ask them if that's what they

want before offering it. The difference between a friend and a parent is that a friend strokes the ego and a parent educates.

3 **Let go of that horribly British modesty!** Let them talk about things they feel proud of and encourage them to notice those feelings. There's a world of difference between boasting and feeling good about yourself. Boasting is when we use something good about us to put someone else down – and I'd call it a form of bullying. Feeling good about ourselves is when we recognise an achievement, and that we are the source of it. It doesn't mean we can't see the flaws or that we become big headed, just that we know we are capable of things.

4 **Encourage a sense of achievement.** Look through photo albums together sometimes and ask them to remember how it was to find so many things difficult that they now find easy. Keep an album with a few photos for each year of their lives, one album per child, and add captions together for the selected pictures to reflect the successes and growth areas of the year. Christmas and birthdays are ideal times for these rituals. Achievements don't have to be big things, just things that provide satisfaction. For example, finally completing a piece of homework they had been putting off, or tidying up their bedroom, are both worthy of positive feedback.

5 **When they do something praiseworthy** – however slight, let them know it pleases you and that you are proud of them. On its own, your pride won't change anything, but over time, knowing that you believe in them will. Especially as so many young people feel their parents hate them and can find nothing right.

6 **Give praise and approval in adult ways.** Specific praise is much more motivating than a general well done. Specific praise means someone has really taken the time to look and observe how you made a difference to a project, and is very

motivating. So instead of 'That was lovely of you' try: 'Thanks, I appreciated the help with the shopping. Without you it would have taken twice as long.' Be sure to recognise effort and intention and not just the end result.

7  **Quit nagging.** It does not work and it makes anyone on the receiving end miserable. It does not feel good for the person doing the nagging either!

8  **Criticise, if you need to,** in a constructive way, and always in the context of trying to be positive. For example: 'I know you have tried, and I was really pleased to see you making such an effort, but I am still not happy with where we are on this.' Try to criticise the actions rather than the person. For example, rather than saying 'Don't talk about your grandmother like that, you're so rude and selfish!' try instead: 'That sounds like a rather selfish thing to say. I know your grandmother cares about you very much.'

9  **Encourage young people to be kinder to themselves.** Not to beat themselves up over failures to be perfect, but rather to take comfort in what they have achieved, such as 'Well I know it must be disappointing not to have done better but you did organise your study well and worked on some of the hardest areas. That will begin to pay off in time.'

10 **Try to parent rather than mould.** Try to guide rather than take over the decision-making and planning; to help them come to terms with disappointments but not see them as the end of the road. If you help them spot options, you begin to help them learn to analyse a situation when you are not there to show them how to do it. This skill will in time increase their confidence in dealing with let-downs constructively, rather than choosing not to take risks that might hurt if they don't pay off.

11 **Remember that your young people's first influence is their parents.** Are there self-esteem issues that you need to work on yourselves? Self-esteem tends to run in families.

12 **Teach them to be critical** of things they see and hear in the media, including advertising, and to look at why things are portrayed as they are. Is someone profiting from this? Is someone using their take on this issue to manipulate people and if so, to what end? Many interesting discussions can be held around the table or on the sofa.

13 **Keep any insecurity about your own body weight or appearance to yourself.** Everyone has some from time to time and not everyone finds self-acceptance easy, but don't teach your young person that disliking your physical self is an OK choice. Avoid constant remarks about appearance (even positive ones) but give compliments that are about the person. Rather than 'You look pretty', try 'You look confident and happy'.

## QUESTIONS & ANSWERS

**Q:** My daughter is completely stuck in her ways and is refusing to try anything new. She won't go to new places, new holiday destinations, try any new hobby or listen to anything new. Nor will she consider changing her clothing or hairstyle. How can I help her adjust to life?

**A:** That's quite a list of things she won't try. Does she know you want these things to change? With such a long list of her shortcomings I expect she feels she's not good enough for you already and is unwilling to risk your disapproval or criticism even more by trying and getting things 'wrong'.

It could be that she's just internalised change as dangerous or difficult, or it may be that she feels scrutinised and criticised every time she does anything, either by you or by herself, and just wants you to back off. Look first at your own behaviour in relation to her and new experiences. Who decides them, you or her? Do you question her in detail about them? Do you offer 'advice' to her? The best way of getting someone to change the way they behave is to change how we behave towards them!

Encourage your daughter to trust her own judgement and move outside the totally predicted by recognising that her fears are real. Change unsettles many of us, and whereas the fears she experiences may not equate with losing a job or a major health scare, within her limited experience of life they are just as challenging.

You could also ask yourself 'Where did she learn to be afraid?' Young people pick up the attitudes and beliefs we put over, and if your daughter has watched you agonising over choices and then regretting that you made the wrong one, she may be equally reticent about moving beyond what she knows.

You could encourage her to do something new with a group of friends, so that she has someone to try out new experiences with. If she is frightened to go into town on a bus by herself, could you arrange for someone else to go with her? Or does her fear grow out of not knowing what to expect? Could you break down the process into a series of stages so that she knows exactly what is likely to happen?

And when she does manage to do something new, give her lots of praise and ask her how she feels about herself in face of the challenge!

**Q:** My daughter hates being alone. She will not go out at all on her own and regards being seen doing anything on her own as the sign of a loser. How can I help her have more confidence?

**A:** Young people can be very status conscious, and aware that being seen with the right or wrong group of people will affect how they are viewed in future. Similarly, they are often aware that being seen alone may mark them out as losers.

If she is unhappy about being alone can you help by suggesting she organises a group activity based from your home? If she suggests a theme to a couple of other acquaintances, it may seem less of a commitment than an open-ended day with no specific plan. For example, could you make a pretext of needing to go to a nearby town and offer your daughter and a couple of friends a lift there if they get the bus back? Could you suggest she sets up a cinema trip for herself and two others who like the look of a new film?

Whatever you do, don't dismiss her feelings of rejection at being alone and tell her how much you value five minutes' peace yourself!

**Q:** My daughter really seems to dislike her appearance. She is always making comments about how fat her face is or how ugly she looks. How can I improve her self-confidence?

**A:** There are two possible scenarios here. Is your daughter saying these things only to have you disagree with them or does she really mean it and is very dissatisfied by her appearance?

If your daughter is using these statements as an attention-seeking device – in other words, saying these things only to have you disagree with her – then you are best advised 'not to play'. While it's pleasant to be told occasionally that we look good, continually fishing for compliments by saying negative things about ourselves is not healthy and is very irritating too. So if she keeps on asking, you could try telling her how it feels to be used as a recorded message that is not listened to: 'How often do I have to tell you that you look good? Please don't use me like this.'

Someone who is really upset by their appearance may find it more difficult to tell you they are ugly; it may be their behaviour that leads you to think that they feel very unhappy. In this case, you may need to take the lead in showing them they are attractive and loved. You could:

- Go through a photograph album with her and show her pictures of her looking happy and attractive. Point out things that appeal: 'Don't you look lovely in that photograph.'
- Tell her how much you enjoyed experiences you have shared together and the part her presence played in making it much more special
- Take every possible opportunity to say something positive to her
- Reassure her that having negative thoughts about both yourself and other people is part of growing up
- Analyse together what makes a person appear attractive. Sometimes it may be physical perfection, but in most cases it's posture, expression, energy and attitude that make the difference

If you feel your daughter's preoccupation with how she looks and with being fat is more serious, or if she is constantly agonising about food, you might consider talking to a doctor or checking out some of the information given on the Young Minds website (see Appendix 2). Most people think that a young person is fine as long as they are not getting too thin, but body weight is not the real indicator of a problem. Young people with Compulsive Eating Disorder may indeed be too fat. In fact by the time there are visible health problems it means the disorder is established and will be harder to treat. Look out for the warning signs and get help early if you think there's a problem. Such telltale signs that a young person may have, or be developing, an eating disorder might include any or all of the following:

- Obsessing about food – maybe watching cookery programmes, reading cook books or diet books, calorie charts, etc., especially if eating little
- Eating alone or out of sight, such as always taking their meals up to their room

- Frequently saying they have already eaten when offered food and turning down treats
- Binge eating – occasional 'blow outs' possibly followed by shame or self-loathing
- Finding hidden food in their cupboard or bag, including stashes of food wrappers
- Disappearing after eating to the bathroom or loo for a long period of time. Possibly returning smelling of toothpaste or mouthwash – or with a reddened face
- Cessation of periods in a girl
- Excessive and frequent exercising
- Frequently complaining of feeling 'bloated' after eating small amounts of food, or feeling sick after eating
- Using food to 'fix' or keep down feelings

**Q:** I find it impossible to compliment my son. He rejects any positive thing I say.

**A:** Instead of saying 'You are kind' try 'I think you are kind'. This is impossible to argue with as it is your opinion not his. You could support your argument by reference to your wider understanding: 'You are not the only young person I know, and I think you are very kind.' You could also quote a third party: 'Mrs Cobbold told me she overheard you sticking up for a younger child on the way home from school the other day. She commented on how kind you were. I felt really proud to hear that – how do you feel?'

Encourage your son to spot his own successes, to feel good about little incidents that say something wider about him and his value to other people. For example, if he is phoned regularly by a friend you could comment, 'It's really nice that Rory wants to talk to you so often.'

If you get positive feedback, pass it on (paraphrasing if necessary to miss out embarrassing words such as 'young man' or 'pleasant'!); help him see himself as others see him and notice the effect they have on the world: 'My hairdresser asked how you were the other day. She remembered your name having only cut your hair once – she often has trouble remembering mine!'; 'Mrs Stanhope commented on how she likes having you round at her house'.

# CHAPTER 5

# 'Did you hear me?'
## Language, swearing, lying and learning to communicate

Parents of teenagers habitually complain about their language: the incomprehensible way in which they talk to each
other; the swearing; or just the lack of real words. Many young
people seem to cease talking to their parents and rely on grunts
when they reach adolescence.

I think it is important to take a wider view than just grumble
about how teenagers talk and to look at the way in which the
rest of the world communicates with them – their parents
included. This can seem just as alienating to them as grunts
do to us.

One of the interesting things about how modern teenagers
communicate is that they do it through so many other methods
than just their mouths. As well as the almost constant stream
of electronic chat, teenagers can communicate through the
way they leave their clothes on the floor, through the angle
of their shoulders, the way they eat or drink, the way they
look up at you without moving their heads. What is more,
their chosen methods of communication are often radically
different from those preferred by parents. For example:

- Parents tend to like quiet as the backdrop for conversation.

- *Teenagers generally prefer noise.*
- Parents may think a sit-down talk with lots of eye contact is the best method of communication.
- *Teenagers may prefer it if there is no eye contact at all (say when driving).*
- Parents tend to like real conversation, face to face or on the phone.
- *Teenagers often prefer to send a text message, an email or to chat online.*

Language allows us to communicate. To use an obvious analogy, while body language and tone of voice can impart some inform-ation, two people who do not speak the same language may be able to understand some of what is being shared but cannot communicate effectively. Although most parents speak the same language as their children, teens do not necessarily use the same parts of their brains to communicate as their parents. Adults tend to use the areas of their brains more associated with logic; young people during adolescence use primarily the emotion centres. This can mean that the way each interprets the shared language, or chooses which words to use, can vary enormously – and misunderstandings can be frequent and painful.

Teens also may lose much of their previously acquired skill in 'reading faces' – they may genuinely be unable to tell the difference between your humorous face and your critical one – and so even gentle teasing can cause a blow up.

When we put together the over-use of the emotion centres of the brain, the different styles of modern communication, the changes in language and syntax between generations and the general inability to understand body language, it is not surprising that there are frequently communication breakdowns. We are barely using the same language as far as our brains are concerned.

One of the skills developed in effective communication is

matching the style of language to the person we are trying to ensure understands. For example, when talking to babies we repeat the same terms again and again and use a limited vocabulary; when academics write for each other in professional journals they use a complicated syntax and as many long words as possible. When communicating with teens we may need to help them understand by giving a little more information than we might with adults, for example how we are feeling or the wider picture and its impact on others. It might seem strange but teens almost need a verbal version of the written 'lol'[1] to know when things are being said in a jokey way, and may need 'I am angry' spelled out for them when appropriate.

Parents also need to be aware that their young person has few grey areas in their thinking and so may see contradiction and hypocrisy in things adults understand easily. Parents may say they require total honesty from their young people, but teenagers learn that total honesty is not always in their best interests – or even required by society at large. I remember being quite shocked when I had a small accident while learning to drive. It was obviously my fault – I had rolled backwards into a car after failing to apply the handbrake – but the first thing my father said to me before getting out of the car was 'Don't admit anything.'

Young people are learning this selective application of vocabulary and tone of voice to particular situations, and are often confused by the mixed messages they receive. Furthermore, all young people are naturally bilingual. They speak one language with their friends, another to their parents. They may have yet another for other adults such as their teachers and their friends' parents.

Finally, while considering language, it's important to grasp that it changes all the time; words fall in and out of currency – they are the ultimate fashion accessory. Young people feed

---

[1] Text speak for 'laugh out loud' – not 'lots of love' as parents often assume.

off this with an immediacy that we adults cannot hope to keep up with; by the time their parents hear a piece of slang, and understand the context in which it is used, it will almost certainly be out of common use. For this reason, parents are best advised to steer clear of trying to talk like their young people; you risk looking out of touch.

## PARENTS AS COMMUNICATORS

Parents tend to see themselves as the ones who get it right and their teens as the ones who have room for improvement. While this may often be true, it is important to remember that effective communication is a two-way process – we too need to be upholding our side of the dialogue effectively. We all know that there are some people that we find easy to talk to about anything and others that we find almost impossible to chat with, but with whom we can still share important information when necessary. When considering how we communicate with our teens we need to ask ourselves:

- Are they able to communicate the things that matter?
- Do they communicate to make me feel part of their world?

It may be that they do one without the other, both or neither! For any parent the priority should be the first of the two, because keeping your young person safe is always the priority. Interestingly, for some teens, too much intimacy may make talking about the things that matter more difficult. Although as their young person approaches adulthood a friendlier and more equal relationship may begin to develop (although this is by no means automatic), parents are not their friends. Young people who are on very friendly terms with parents may find it difficult to talk about difficulties or personal issues as they feel that the parent will want to deal with things at a more intimate level than they are comfortable with – they would rather have a more distant parental reaction when difficulties arise. For example, I have worked with a couple of young women who were on very friendly terms with their mothers but who had never told them they had started their periods – because they didn't want to hear about their mum's experiences of such a personal issue.

Maintaining some distance will help your teen tell you the things that matter. Similarly, sharing your life with them, within respectful boundaries, will also, in time, help them share more – not less – with you.

When running workshop with young people around communication, their views on parents include the following. Parents are:

- Always in a rush
- Always angry
- Not really listening and easily distracted
- Inclined to get hung up on small details rather than hearing what the speaker is trying to say
- Not understanding what is being communicated – missing the point
- Often rude or sarcastic
- Nagging

These show a striking similarity to the comments often made by parents about their young people, with the possible exception of nagging – which is a uniquely adult pastime according to teens.

## HOW TO MAKE TIME FOR YOUR TEENAGER

Before we get on to the issue of how to talk to a teenager, let's tackle the issue of how to make time for them – or how to signal that we are prioritising, and hence value, their company.

Parents often talk about the need for quality time with their children, but by the time they are teenagers their desire to be out with their friends all the time (or perhaps just as worryingly, their preference to be on their own in their bedrooms) can mean that we get out of the habit of seeking time together. To make matters worse, accessing that time can be really difficult when both parents are working all week, and weekends have to be filled with a combination of childcare for younger children and domestic tasks. Juggling too many things can mean conversation is overlooked. Here are some top tips for finding quality time with your teenager:

1   Learn to spot the quality experiences – and accept that quality time can assume many different forms. It doesn't have to be perfection – however you define that. So spending ten minutes in a real discussion with your teenager about something that is important to them can represent quality, even though you would never have prioritised that subject as particularly meaningful yourself.

2   Get rid of that 'to do' list – which is in any case almost invariably overstretched. Just because you had set yourself a list of things to achieve during the day doesn't mean you have to work through them all before you allocate time to your family. Powering on through them may mean you may miss the moment they *are* ready to talk – and by the time you have reached the end of your list, the opportunity for conversation has moved on without you.

3   Switch off your mobile phone when you get home – and do this publicly, so they can see you are focused on being with your family rather than still technically back in your place of work. Resist the opportunity to communicate with colleagues or via social media. If you are offering a running commentary on your life it will probably make them less likely to communicate.

**4**   If they do seem inclined to talk, stand in the same room while you are talking to them – don't move out of the room while continuing the conversation. Even if you can still hear them, and you were in the middle of doing something else, it conveys an impression that your routine matters more than their company.

**5**   Watch what they are watching on the television (but don't keep interrupting the programme for a detailed explanation of what's going on). In the process you may discover that programmes you may have been inclined to dismiss as worthless displays of consumerism are in fact being watched in a spirit of irony rather than adulation. Which can be quite comforting if you had thought that all they were up to was absorbing lifestyles they could neither emulate nor you afford to fund.

**6**   Take advantage of needing to deliver them somewhere. While not recommending that you offer a permanent taxi service, and replacing their use of public transport, the occasional opportunity for communication without eye contact can be a real bonus. Get them to think about the route.

**7**   Don't assume it has to be the whole family spending time together or nothing. Individual communication, one-to-one, can really boost relationships.

**8**   Prize the odd – and hence the likely-to-be-memorable. Families that have shared experiences feel bonded – they have memories they can share. Memories can be built on very simple things; they don't have to be expensive. You could suggest picnics in the winter (get them to make the sandwiches or heat up soup for eating in the car); stopping to look at something that looks interesting when you are walking along; really allowing them to choose something rather than making the choice yourself because it is quicker.

**9** Show them how to do something. Precisely what, matters not. You could chart them around anything they might need to know how to do in future, and over which you have some life experience that could be useful: how to change a fuse or a light bulb or clear the filter on a washing machine – or how the process of applying for a mortgage works.

**10** Take the time they are willing to offer rather than using every offer as a starting point for negotiation. So coffee together at a local snack-bar, willingly given, is better than insisting on their company for a whole afternoon – when they make it clear they would rather be somewhere else.

## TALKING TO TEENAGERS

Teenagers often complain that those who talk to them target the message wrongly; they phrase things in a style that is too young for their age and they therefore feel patronised or 'talked down to'. A common parental retort of 'If you behaved more like an adult, I would talk to you more like one' only makes matters worse.

On the other hand, should you have to make concessions to the way teenagers speak? Should you have to adapt your way of speaking to ensure you are understood by your young people? Or is learning to use the grown-up vocabulary that is part of everyday life just part of what teenagers need to learn in order to communicate with the rest of the world?

There are certain language requirements that parents do well to stick to when communicating with teenagers:

**1** **You must be clear.** The teenage brain is juggling lots of different stimuli at the same time and can find sequencing and pulling out the most important pieces of information difficult. If you are imparting really key details, write them down (or send a text message), repeat the information several times using different words – and then get them to tell you what you have just told them in their own words. A couple of 'What if?' type questions will help you check on whether or not they have understood, and will also help them have ready-made strategies to use should something unexpected occur. For example:

- 'I want you to be back here by midnight.'
- 'So what will you do if the last bus does not turn up?'
- 'What if the friend who is giving you a lift back from the party has had too much to drink?'

2   **You must be precise.** Teenagers are expert at spotting gaps in your argument; they are all barristers in the making. They may not point out the loophole you have left wide open, but afterwards, in discussions about what took place, they will refer back to what you said. For example:

- 'You said you were happy for me to ask Granny for money for my birthday instead of a present. You did not say anything about not suggesting how much she gave me or not spending it all straight away.'
- 'I *was* back by midnight. I was back in Watford, just not back home.'

3   **You must talk in an appropriate manner.** Not matey or cool, avoiding their jargon and any nicknames associated with infancy; this is particularly vital in front of their friends.

4   **Don't fire questions at them.** This feels more like an inter-rogation than a conversation and may actually confuse them as they can find processing ideas hard going. Open-ended questions (ones for which a basic yes or no cannot be given) work best, for example:

- 'How do you think Maria feels about being left out of the hockey squad?'

If they answer 'dunno', tell them it feels such a putdown to be answered that way and give them more time to answer. Then really try to take in what they are saying before asking anything else. If they still can't answer, try:

- 'Well, see if you can work it out and get back to me.'

## SOME COMMON COMMUNICATION BREAKDOWNS

### Swearing

Swear words tend to be common in the vocabulary of young people; they use them all the time and in the process their shock value can be completely diminished. Words that may disgust elderly members of your family can seem little more than adjectives to your young people. If your young people are swearing all the time when talking to each other, it's very easy for swearwords to slip out at home, so before you get enraged about them swearing at you, consider whether it was an act of defiance or simply an act of forgetfulness. They might also be looking to push back the boundaries and see how far they can go!

Matching the vocabulary to the situation is an important skill for young people to grasp. Words they use when talking to each other should not be used when talking to you, or to their siblings, or in front of younger children, or out of an informal context. If they continue to swear in front of you:

- Try asking them if they really understand the words they are using in such a casual manner. Providing a precise definition (frequently biological) for the term they just used can make them understand why its casual use causes such offence.
- Are they using swear words to attract your attention? Is

it clear to them that you really are listening to them? If
you are doing something else while talking to them maybe
you should stop and give them your full attention.

- How important is what they are talking about? If the
subject is one of high emotion, then picking them up
on their swearing means you are listening to their words
rather than what they are saying. Pointing it out now
will not improve their mood!

- If they swear in a situation without high drama, walk out
of the room and make it clear that you will not resume
the conversation until they talk in a more reasonable
manner. If including swearwords in their conversation
means they cease to communicate effectively, they may
reconsider their vocabulary. But try to point this out in
a non-judgemental way rather than through anger: 'I
know you swear at college, but when you swear to me
it gets in the way of me hearing you. It offends me and
I would much rather you did not swear when you are
talking to me.'

- Try not to swear yourself! Never swear at the children. If
you do, apologise to them afterwards.

## Starting a swear-box

A family swear-box, into which the offender puts money every
time they swear, highlights the misuse of language in the home.
But once established it must be stuck to – by parents as well
as young people. A general cry of 'swear-box' can draw attention to words that otherwise get ignored.

Having a swear-box is also an effective way of thinking
about language and how its use can be an act of aggression,
even when no swearing takes place. For example, there may
be terms that offend certain groups of people and so should
be avoided, even though they are not officially swearwords.
You can differentiate between language that is unusable in any

context (e.g. racist or sexist terms) and terms that are best avoided (general abuse and body parts).

There should be family discussion about what to do with the money, perhaps giving the proceeds to charity rather than using to save up for a treat – otherwise there is an incentive to contribute! Alternatively, repeat offenders can be allocated an increase in family chores.

## Lying

Parents of teenagers often complain about the extent to which they lie, usually about the key battlegrounds of adolescence: where they have been and with whom; what time they were back home. What parents tend to forget is that they are often less than completely truthful themselves. Most adults lie habitually: sometimes to protect themselves, sometimes to protect others. So if we understand the reasons why we lie, we are better equipped to explain the value of truthfulness to our young people.

Before thinking about how teenagers lie to us it's worth spending some time thinking about the big lies put over on them. We encourage them to be fair in a world that is patently not so, and to be honest when many business fortunes are based on exactly the opposite principle.

Adults tell 'white lies' to preserve the social order and avoid hurting other people's feelings. We express warm thanks for gifts we hate; make excuses for turning down an invitation we had already said yes to if a better offer turns up; simplify situations so that the truth is lost ('I was only on the zig-zag line outside school for five minutes, it's completely unfair that I got a parking ticket'). And our children watch us do this.

So before thinking about imposing moral standards on young people, and insisting that they tell us the truth, it's worth thinking about how our own values shape up.

## FLASHBACK

Can you isolate five little white lies you have told in the last month? Whom did you tell them to and why?

### Why teenagers lie

All behaviour has a payback, otherwise it is simply not worth the effort. So the key question to ask about teenagers not telling the truth is, why are they doing it? What is their payback? Are they lying because they suspect you would not approve if they told you the truth, to stop you worrying, or are they deliberately not telling you the truth because they want to preserve the situation whereby they know something that you don't?

By changing our reactions we can help teenagers tell the truth. So if instead of reacting with anger we modify our response, we can help analyse the problem. 'Can I think about it and get back to you later?' is a really good reply as it gives you time to think before making a decision.

### Why we need teenagers to tell the truth

If we encourage them to tell the truth we encourage them to take responsibility, to plan effectively and to improve their negotiating skills. We encourage them not only to plan for what they want, but to take responsibility for the wanting and getting of it. We also encourage them towards a simpler life, and less complicated relationships with others:

'If you tell the truth, you don't have to remember.'
**Mark Twain**

## *The habitual or persistent liar*

A persistent liar is someone who constantly lies in order to get their own way or to avoid the consequences of their actions. For the habitual liar, the payback is an exercise in power. A habitual liar tells so many lies that a lie becomes the default mechanism. The object is not securing something that is desired, but a feeling of power. Only the liar knows the real truth. By withholding this at will the young person can to some extent manipulate those around them.

Habitual liars do not become so overnight, but the longer you put off dealing with the situation, the harder it will be to influence their behaviour. You should look out for the following, which may signify a growing problem in telling the truth:

- Arguing the toss about everything.
- When cornered, putting the blame on to someone else rather than admit a fault themselves.
- Picking on points of grammar or language in the accuser to detract attention away from the accusations being made.
- Being very specific in their analysis of your question – to take away attention from the fact that they are lying.
- Scoring points to detract attention from the key issue.

The level at which such behaviour becomes an illness or personality disorder is debatable, but in the long term a habitual liar may need emotional or even psychiatric help.

A good way of dealing with a persistent liar is to reduce the freedoms that are given out. For example, you could:

- Insist that they phone home when out to confirm their return time (embarrassing).
- Agree that you will ring them at a particular time to confirm the same thing (ditto).

- Drive them to an event they want to attend rather than allowing them to take the bus with their friends.
- Allow them to take small decisions and then praise the responsible way in which they handle them (if appropriate).
- At all times use non-judgemental language – 'Can we just clarify that?'; 'Are you sure?', rather than 'You are a liar.'
- Explain the consequences of not being thought reliable. 'The boy who cried wolf' was never trusted again and his safety was compromised; the consequences of being uncovered as a liar and losing other people's respect do not feel good.
- Only allow the old freedoms back slowly as their honesty or trustworthiness develops. Take it all away again at the first whiff of an untruth or fake alibi.

## ENCOURAGING YOUR TEENAGER TO TALK TO YOU

'I can still remember the anguish that I experienced when hearing my mother/father/parents speak in public. I would cringe with embarrassment. At particular stages of adolescence I did not want to have anything to do with either of my parents and I would fantasise that I had been adopted at birth and would one day be claimed by my real parents.'

This was an almost universal response from all the parents I have spoken to on the issue!

Respect your teenager's urge not to communicate, particularly about their 'private' life – and for a teen this might mean every aspect of their life that does not contain or refer to you, such as school, friends, parents of friends and what they do when away from home!  They have a right not to talk to you if they don't want to – after all, you can't force someone to communicate – but you have an equal right to talk about how you feel about this. Most teenagers do not stop talking overnight; they gradually withdraw, so the sooner you notice this pattern the better you will be able to keep communication going.

Make use of an occasion conducive to chatting. Ask your young person if they want a cup of tea and sit down at the kitchen table to drink it together. Rather than offering them a piece of cake, put the cake on the table, cut it and hand it to them to eat with you. When out shopping, suggest having a drink in a café together. Don't make these occasions too formal. Sound casual when you suggest it – if you imply you are really looking forward to it, this may put them off the idea. Make use of opportunities that crop up and try to build time for communication around them: car journeys are great for conversation as the lack of eye contact builds intimacy.

'My son had to have braces fitted last year and this required trips back to the orthodontist every two months. This began as a bore, but we discovered that two doors down from the surgery was a coffee shop, and made a point of always going in for a drink afterwards before returning him to school. Sometimes we would read the tabloids together, sometimes we would talk. Always we would people-watch and talk about what we had seen on the way home. We both grew to value this time alone together, and it was strange that it came out of something that was outwardly so unappealing – for who really wants to have braces?' **Mother**

## DEMONSTRATING HOW TO CHAT

Some young people have yet to learn the art of easy conversation, so show them how to do it – chat about things you have done that day. You can ask their opinion, or check occasionally that they are listening (either through their body language or ask 'Am I boring you?'), but if they don't give more than a monosyllabic answer and don't fall asleep, chat on a bit more.

If your young person loves to chat or text it might be a good idea to engage with them on their gadget of choice occasionally. A simple 'out shopping – anything special you want me to get?' message or a reminder of an appointment after school are easily done by text and may get more attention and response than verbal communication.

Young people learn so much by example, so why not allow them to see the pleasure that social intimacy brings you? If they have a friend round to visit, why not ask the parent to come too and have the opportunity for a chat yourself at the same time? Most young people get really irritated if – when out with you – they have to wait in the street while you talk to a friend, but try explaining that just as they like to have friends, you do too.

A good rule of thumb is to talk about the past rather than the present; share the hilarious (as long as it is not anything they are embarrassed by). It's much less intrusive to talk about things you have shared in the past than to debrief them on what they have done, action by action, during the whole day.

If you are doing something, describe it! For example, if they find you cooking, or changing a fuse, ask them if they know how to do what you are doing – the explanation that they are going to have to learn in order to do it for themselves is a flattering reference to their emergence as independent adults. But be aware that if you keep up a monologue they may not feel there's much to say. So once in a while simply try being quiet together; this can give a wonderful feeling of intimacy.

## WHAT NOT TO DO AFTER YOUR TEEN HAS TALKED TO YOU

Post-conversation, however, there are two big no-go areas as far as most young people are concerned: blaming and fixing. So if your young person tells you they have had a huge row at school with a classmate that has resulted in everyone taking sides, listen like a friend not like a parent. Say how mean it all sounds, make a shocked face, ask questions to help the story flow such as 'what did she do then?' or 'what did you say?' So often adults respond in full-on parent mode, with comments such as 'well you could have been kinder to her, you know she is having a hard time at the moment' or 'you should go and talk to the teacher to see if they can calm things down a bit'.

Like all of us, teens need time to process events and to sort out for themselves who is right, who is wrong and what can be done to help things move forward. Telling them your take on their lives will almost certainly result in being locked out in the future. Of course you want to help them process their difficulties and find good solutions, but listening sympathetically in the first instance, and later asking them questions to encourage their reflection, can be far more helpful than passing judgement or giving unwelcome (and adult-style) advice.

---

10 top tips for communicating with your young person

1   **Really listen!** That means sit down, make eye contact when appropriate and make sympathetic noises to show you are listening, such as 'Did you really?' or 'I bet he didn't like that!'

2   **Resist the temptation to slip into parent mode.** Try to

contribute to the conversation without taking over, affirming rather than dominating. So avoid telling them they were wrong, criticising their past behaviour, belittling or making fun of them, giving advice (if not asked) and pointing out their mistakes. Rather, by giving time and space, encourage them to open up and think about their own ideas; exploring a problem through conversation often makes it seem less of a problem, or allows the solution to emerge. Even if they don't see the obvious conclusion that strikes you, leave them be and the ideas may sink in – you can always ask them about it again later. If you find separating your parenting role from your support role difficult, try saying 'I'm wearing my parent hat right now' or allowing them to see that your body language is different.

3 **Improve the opportunities for conversation by turning off the television now and again.** Play games, have visitors round that you all enjoy, listen to music (theirs as well as yours!).

4 **Make family rituals.** For example, Sunday breakfasts with chats about the papers or everyone sitting around the table for a meal once a day. Stick to them. Teachers say that the children who regularly eat with their family stand out a mile!

5 **Have a family meeting on a regular basis.** In family meetings everyone has an equal voice and behaves with equal respect for everyone else (see Appendix 1). Gripes can be aired (and not answered), decisions made, feelings owned (though not fixed) and relationships allowed to mature.

6 **Tell them things they would not know unless you told them.** For example tell them how you felt on being let down by a friend; a row you had in the supermarket. Encourage them to listen sympathetically without trying to solve the problem and sometimes ask for their advice, for example: 'How do you think I should tell her?' Let them know the next instalment.

7 **Use text or email to remind them of details such as appointments or things to bring home** – that way they can look things up if they forget.

8 **Never talk to another adult on behalf of your young person with them present.** If an adult engages your young person in conversation and the situation allows it without being rude, walk away and leave them to get on with it. And don't announce what you are doing (doubly embarrassing!). Along similar lines, talk to them in advance about how they want things to be for parent consultations at school: who will do the talking and what you will say in front of their friends and their teachers.

9 **Be honest with yourself** – and with them – about your feelings. Anger is just the short version of many more complicated emotions. If you get cross, go and calm down – that way you will know how you really feel and be able to communicate better.

10 **Never try to be cool!**

## QUESTIONS & ANSWERS

Q: My son's language is appalling. How can I encourage him to be more civil?

A: There is a huge difference between the language young people use at school, in order to be part of the crowd, and that which they use at home. They need to distinguish between the two and understand the same words are not appropriate in both contexts. When they were small and made the same mistakes we used to think they were cute. Now they are so much taller, it's hard to hang on to the cute response, but do hang on to the fact that the behaviour provoking the reaction has not changed. Although your teenager now probably sounds more offensive or aggressive, he's still trying to learn to get the tone of voice right.

Think though about why he is using bad language. Is he feeling it is the only way to get your attention? Are you really showing him that you are listening, and thinking of the question he really wants you to ask? Or is he just unwilling to drop the habit of swearing that he uses with his friends. If so, leave the room for five minutes every time he swears at you. If swearing is ceasing to attract your attention, he may learn to stop doing it.

**Q:** I really dislike the cynical way in which teenagers talk. How can I encourage them to be more positive?

**A:** Negative talk can be a cloak to wrap oneself in to feel part of the crowd, but it does not necessarily reveal true feelings – in the same way that baggy clothes do not mean the young person underneath is enormous.

Teenagers are often deeply cynical in the way they express themselves – perhaps in part because they are full of a desire to do new and exciting things, but don't know how to start. With a raging desire to be burning energy, and almost no pleasure response from everyday activities, teenage brain changes can make life feel desperately dull.

My advice would be to let them talk how they like. Resist the urge to mention it at all. If at any time they show any enthusiasm for anything, reward the behaviour with attention and some positive affirmation such as 'How lovely your laugh sounds'. Resist all urges to add 'I'd almost forgotten what it's like'.

**Q:** From being a chatty 12-year-old, my 14-year-old son is now completely monosyllabic. How can I get him to communicate with me?

**A:** This is a very common complaint from parents. But let's face it, he's got things going on in his body and mind that he cannot talk to anyone about and the last people he thinks will understand (and he could be right) are his mother or father. The outside world is known, the inner one is new, powerful, terrifying and exhilarating, but also has huge shadows of guilt, shame and forbidden pleasures embedded in it. How do you share that when you are 14?

Perhaps the first thing to consider is whether your son is like this with everyone, or just with you. If withdrawal of communication is solely from you, it may just be part of the separation that a teenager must make from his parents in order to function effectively as an independent adult. Withdrawal from society as a whole is more serious if it goes on for any length of time and may require specialist help (see Appendix 2 for details).

'My parents were endlessly critical of my teenage self. If I tried to talk to them about the things we argued about my mother would leave all the talking to my father. He would talk in constructed paragraphs with subsections that led logically on, making it difficult for me to butt in and say anything. "I have three things to say to you" meant I had to wait until point three was over, and by then I had forgotten what my objections to points one and two were. If I did butt in he would pause his monologue, and then, the moment I finished talking, pick up directly where he had left off. This made me feel he was not listening to what I said at all.' **Mother**

Q: Why do teenagers shout such a lot and how can I stop them shouting at me?

A: When it comes to general shouting, in part they do not know they are doing it. They are used to lots of surrounding noise, and whereas adults tend to turn down the other distractions in order to be heard, teenagers just tend to talk louder.

As for shouting at you, remember that most behaviours work on a cause-and-effect basis: a particular piece of behaviour is produced in order to secure a particular response. So if they shout to get your attention, and you do not reply, they soon learn that they must come and find you!

Occasional shouting is a great way of dealing with anger, does not hurt anyone and can be an appropriate way of getting the emotion out. The problem is that this behaviour can become a pattern, which needs to be avoided as it may be hard for others to take.

To deal with repetitive shouters: don't shout back (however tempting); touch the shouter (reaching out your hand, touching them, at the same time saying 'I am listening' often breaks the pattern); and giving lots of eye contact (are they shouting because they think you are not really listening?).

'We have a house rule. Anyone returning home can shout out to find out who else is there, but if they want to talk they must go and find the person before continuing the conversation. And everyone has to stick to this, parents as well as young people. The only exceptions are emergencies, and we are quite loose in our definitions of these – needing a roll of loo paper or a bathroom towel both count.' **Mother**

Q: My son forged my signature on his school report. What should I do?

A: In a small context forgery can look like initiative; in a larger one, a crime.

Did he do this to get something, or to get out of something – a positive or negative reason? He needs to realise you can't change the outcome by forging. His action means he is not taking responsibility for something already done; he is trying to change the past.

**Q:** My husband told our son what he thought of his music, and it was not very complimentary. Now he won't speak to us.

**A:** Was this really an act of honesty or an act of spite? Are you concerned that rather than offering objective criticism, your husband was taking pleasure in demolishing your son's music taste? Be honest. There is a world of difference between honesty and brutality. This is a classic example of the 'young bull/old bull' struggle, and I suspect the issue was about winning rather than a serious debate about music.

**Q:** My sister's daughter appears to have no opinions about anything. She agrees with whatever I say to her. How can I encourage her to open up a bit?

**A:** Young people who develop too much of a social filter can be particularly difficult to communicate with. They may never express an opinion for fear of getting it wrong, and risk not developing close relationships with friends because they worry about letting their guard down.

Try to show her how to chat (see the tips above on pp. 86–8). Make time for her and above all ensure she knows you will not breach her trust – and will not relay information back to her parents, and that you stick to this. It's really valuable for a young person to have an adult whom they trust, and who is not one of their parents, to talk to. Bear in mind, though, that she may have chosen someone else to talk to, and not you.

**Q:** I was just about to go out to work when my daughter told me I looked a mess. I felt crushed. How do I make her realise how unkind she was being?

**A:** Tell her. Let her see the consequences of her actions. If she replies that she was only joking, say that when being attacked you feel threatened and it's very hard to read a tone of voice. She should know how much she has hurt you, but then move on – don't hold it against her.

**Q:** My son refuses to tell me where he is going when he goes out. How can I persuade him that I need to know?

**A:** Let's start with the basics. Do you really need to know or just want to know where he is going? This is a hard question to answer honestly, so perhaps a few supplementary questions will help. What will change through your knowing where he is? Will it make him safer or will it just mean you will be notified sooner if an accident occurs? Will knowing where he is mean you worry less? Or will knowing mean that you don't feel so left out, not so superfluous to his new grown-up life?

How much information parents need before a young person departs for an evening out is debatable. If they are staying locally, you need to know roughly the direction, and whom they are with, but perhaps not much more.

If you ask them for a detailed breakdown of their precise movements you remove all sense of it being their adventure, and of course provide endless scope for you to ask them questions about it the next morning (which they will resist above all things). So, put your efforts instead into making a plan that will ensure that he is safe while he is out. By concentrating on the mechanics of their trip you emphasise safety to them and stand back from being part of the adventure, which is what they so want to avoid. For example:

- Has he got something on him carrying his name and address?
- Does his phone work (is it charged and in credit)?
- Does he know how to make a reverse charge call?
- Have you got an agreed strategy on boundaries (how late

he can ring; who he will and will not travel home with)? Is safety prioritised?

- Have you agreed what constitutes an emergency? If he rang from the mainline station having missed the last train, would you turn out to pick him up or (as he is in a public place) make him wait 3 hours for the first outgoing train of the morning?
- Would you lock the front door after a certain time; does he know this? Would you really do it if he is still not home? (You may find that rather than ensuring he is back by the agreed hour you have given him the excuse to stay out all night.)

After all this, have you trained yourself to go to bed and not to worry? Your worrying will not make any difference to the outcome, and learning to separate yourself from your children is very healthy for both you and them.

**Q:** My 13-year-old daughter has an extremely manipulative friend. She will suddenly start to refuse to speak to my daughter, coming up with a mysterious pretext ('You know what you have done') and spreading stories about her. Lots of tears and side-taking follow, then a dramatic 'making-up' when she swears undying friendship and is more intense (and demanding) than ever before. While the reconciliations are always a relief, this behaviour upsets my daughter, who is starting to see a pattern, and to feel manipulated. She has asked me for advice.

**A:** Your daughter's friend is hooked on attention, which she is seeing as a substitute for love. This craving for attention means she is setting up situations in which she is likely to get a lot of it, attract loyalty and receive sympathy. In the process she is testing her friends and getting them to prove their adoration. She gains intimacy in both the duration and the making-up after a fight, and finds emotional satisfaction in the consequent anguish – which is much greater than in their more usual day-to-day relationships.

It's a good idea to discuss the pattern of this relationship with your daughter. Encourage her to describe what is going on and ask her questions to enable her to see how she is being manipulated. Maintaining a cool friendship in future is probably the best response – so that she still has a relationship in public, but is not the person chosen for an artificial fight the next time her friend needs an emotional fix.

**Q:** My daughter just has to have the last word. It drives me mad. What should I do?

**A:** It sounds to me as if she might say the same of you! Wanting to have the last word in an argument is a very human characteristic. And if your daughter wants it too, perhaps you should sympathise rather than get angry – the last word does not have to belong to the parent. In fact, letting your daughter say something without you having to say something back is a really powerful way of allowing her to see that she is valued as an individual. Wanting the last word is so predictable – your silence will show you have really listened to her. Try making your last contribution: 'I hear you' and saying nothing more.

# CHAPTER 6

# The role of the family

What makes a family? Given the huge amount of social change that has taken place, it's sensible to adopt a more flexible definition of what a family means. A family is a group of people that you have not chosen but from whom you cannot walk away; you are both emotionally and physically connected. Belonging to a family means belonging to the hurly-burly that trying to connect several lives from the same living space involves; a real family will survive the hustle and bustle and remain connected. Your family is a group of people whom you care about and who care about you, and with whom you stay in touch. Your family is a strong and on-going influence.

Throughout this book I have used the word 'parent'. A parent is a person who has assumed the role and responsibility of raising a child or young person to adulthood, but they may not be biologically related to that child. Consequently a child may have more than two parents as new members to the family take on that responsibility. There are also times when a bio-logical parent chooses to relinquish their role, and this can be heartbreaking for a child who had always seen 'forever' as a given within the relationship. Many people still maintain their parent role even when the core family has broken down, however, providing a greater stability to the child and another adult for support and affection.

For the teenager, a strong family is an important asset. A strong family provides a safe harbour, a place where they feel protected, valued and from which they emerge with a sense of their own identity: the perfect resources with which to grow up. If the family bond is strong it also means that a young person has a place they feel secure to 'act up' in – knowing that they'll be loved no matter what. It is not the measure of closeness in a family that determines how well behaved the children are – when talking about teenagers the opposite may well be true.

The family in which a young person grows up usually influences both heredity and environment. Young people inherit one set of characteristics, but are hugely influenced by what they observe and experience around them. A family is where children try out different behaviours and observe the response they get, for example:

- When to sulk
- What happens if you throw a tantrum
- How to get attention
- What happens when you argue with your siblings/parents/ friends
- How to relate to other people

Young people will observe what happens when adults use these behaviours and also try these things out themselves. They will note, subconsciously or consciously, whether these behaviours get reinforced (i.e. if they are an effective strategy for getting your own way or attention) or squashed.

It's commonplace for teenagers to be parented the way their parents were treated: the values that were reinforced to you as a child are likely to be the ones you pass on to your young person, whether consciously or subconsciously. The values you had passed on to you as a child tend to be the ones you take for granted; the phrases that come instantly to mind when situations are stressful or distressing are those that were used to you, and the chances are that you will find the same things that annoyed your parents are irritating to you. Even if you are making a conscious effort to be different from the way your parents parented you, their behaviour is still the dominant influence on the way you bring up your young person.

## FLASHBACK

Think about the values that you inherited and grew up with. Can you name five things that were held sacrosanct in your family when you were a teenager? For example, I grew up with the firm impression that eating anywhere but in the kitchen or dining room was sloppy, and that the *Observer* newspaper was always right.

Consider your five remembered values and think how many of these you are passing on to your own young people. Are there some values on the list that you are deliberately reacting against and determinedly not passing on? What priorities do you want to pass on to your own young people?

## FAMILY VALUES

Certain family values will have been reinforced and hence influenced the way you behaved. For example, parents who value humour will comment on a child's amusing sayings and reinforce this as an attractive thing for their child to do. A family that values boisterousness will tend to comment positively on their children's physical stamina and activities. Most parents do this quite unconsciously.

The same goes for negative feedback. If your own family regarded personal vanity in a negative light, and you were never complimented on how you looked, it can be difficult to make positive comments to your young people. Alternatively, you may react against the way you were raised and comment on your teenagers' appearance all the time.

Your values might fall into a range of categories, such as domestic (e.g. how things are organised at home), political (e.g. what political values/parties are supported), social (e.g. do you have friends visit often?) and economic (e.g. what is the attitude to money at home; how much is available?).

'All they ever do is tell me to shut up.' **13-year-old girl**

'If I do tell them anything they never listen.' **14-year-old boy**

'All she ever does is shout.' **13-year-old boy on his mother**

'They're always busy.' **15-year-old girl**

## A FAMILY IS WHERE WE LEARN TO BE WHO WE ARE

No two children have the same experience of being in the same family. Most parents try to be fair (or say they do), but personality and circumstances mean that their children have a variety of different experiences. For example, a young person's experience of family life will be influenced by:

- **Placement.** The order they were born in; eldest children sometimes have stricter parenting than younger siblings and have fewer people to learn from when it comes to social behaviour or manipulating adults. Younger siblings always have an older child to watch as they win or fail at getting their own way. Children learn more about social interaction from watching how older children do things and interacting with them than they ever do from adults.

  Eldest children also have that period of time when they are the only (and therefore most adored and fussed over) child in the family, so resentment at younger siblings can be strong. Younger/est children are frequently made a lot of fuss of by everybody and so may learn to love the limelight.

Middle children miss out on the level of attention either their eldest or youngest sibling receives, with the possible outcome that they become attention-seeking, without necessarily differentiating between positive or negative attention – any attention is better than none.

- **Sex.** A girl born after three boys might find life rather different from an eldest girl who then had three more sisters.

- **Arrival.** Some couples go through a great deal of physical and mental anguish and pain as well as a great deal of money and personal sacrifice to conceive or become a parent to a child. This may result in a child being treated by family members as 'extra special' or even a miracle child.

- **Whether they were the youngest child.** Older children can resent the subsequent relaxation of rules that were firmly implemented when they were younger – often due to parental relaxation – or tiredness. The youngest sibling is often perceived as being the favourite, although from their point of view they may feel they are never truly accepted as having grown up.

Parents usually say that they love all their children the same; deep-down most have favourites, perhaps those you find it easiest to get on with or those who share your interests. This may never be materially evident, let alone discussed, but it is still experienced by your children.

Learning to understand yourself can be a life-long journey. Who we feel we are is a combination of the character we are born with, the personality we develop within our family and how we interact with the world around us; the experiences we have (e.g. moving house at a key stage or the birth of a sibling); and the values that are reinforced within the family that surrounds us.

## CONFLICT WITHIN A FAMILY

Just because you were born into the same family does not mean you are going to get on with each other. Many parents report that their children are in a constant state of war with each other. If this is your experience, look for underlying causes of conflict. Do your children feel there is favouritism or discrimination? Most sibling battles come from jealousy or boundary issues. Work on these and many disputes can be solved. It's also a good idea to try to develop a family identity ('We are the Lewises'), which emphasises the children's links with each other, rather than the tensions.

When conflict does arise, as a parent you should avoid taking sides. So if you have two children who are fighting, and given age disparities you are worried that physical injury will result, talk to your elder one about why hitting their younger sibling is not appropriate, but also talk to the younger child about what it was about their behaviour that irritated and caused the lashing out. Be aware, however, that children of all ages need to learn to take responsibility for their own behaviour and choices, and jumping in with judgements can increase resentment. When intervention is required stay as neutral as possible. A lot of sibling issues are caused by parents sticking up for a child who may be operating quite differently out of sight of their parents.

Once everyone has cooled down (including you), talk through the situation with them. What happened, in what order and what was the result – and try to help them find a mutually acceptable way to resolve their differences. Young people should understand that a civilised atmosphere is possible even if they would not choose each other as friends. When they are independent adults, living away from home, or in the workplace, they will not be able to thump those they disagree with.

## SIBLING RIVALRY

Sibling rivalry is an issue in most families where there is more than one child. It may be particularly apparent in families where there are step-siblings. When step-siblings are at war it is often because one or more of them are afraid that their 'own' parent prefers the newcomer to them; that they are being supplanted in their affections. If this is the case it is important to ensure there is still one-on-one time with the parent and their child, and that love and affection are clearly given unconditionally, even when there are upsets. A child who has had a parent 'replaced' may have underlying feelings of rejection and hurt. They may well take these out on a new parent and siblings. They need to know that everyone is going to stay this time so the issues are around 'how do we make this work?' rather than 'let's find what it takes for this one to leave'!

Most sibling rivalry comes from feelings of inequality, and so the issue is really the way they are parented rather than the way they relate to each other. A good response to arguments therefore is not to take sides, but rather to explore the position as mediator: to look at the choices each young person made and examine how what they said or did affected the other party. Moving on, you could talk about how they might have reacted and how the outcome would have been affected had they made different choices. Avoid blaming language and instead explore their options and their feelings:

- How that made me feel
- How I could handle that differently next time
- How that would make the other party feel

If siblings truly do not get on, do not force the issue; they did not ask to be put together in the same family, and while they should be civilised with each other, they cannot be forced to be friends. (Read on for a four-stage guide to resolving conflict.)

Within a family, it is very important that each young person feels they have an independent and valuable relationship with their parents, both singly and as a couple, so don't always feel you must do everything together.

If it is possible, you and your partner could make time to do things with each sibling individually and to do things relevant to each as an individual (e.g. picking up on their particular interests or hobbies), as well as allowing each one some time with both of you on their own. When this happens they tend to emerge from the more usual role of combatant to communicate with you directly.

If you have the space to allow it, separate bedrooms allow each sibling to express their own personality and to have withdrawing space in which they feel safe. If you don't have the space and they have to share a room, there are strategies that can be used to give each young person their own space:

- Put a curtain down the middle of the room
- Make a partition or screen to separate the room into two halves
- Allow them to decorate the two halves differently (who said a room had to be painted the same way throughout?)
- Using sticky-backed plastic, put a dotted line down the middle of the carpet to indicate whose territory stops where
- Ensure each child has enough storage space (shelves, cupboards, pin boards) to allow them to store their things safely

The problem of sharing space can get more acute if the siblings have different attitudes to tidiness: a tidy child forced to share a room with an untidy sibling can be a particular cause of tension. One solution that has worked well in several families I know of is for the untidy child to pay the tidy one to keep the room in a good condition.

## FOUR STEPS TO CONFLICT RESOLUTION

### 1. Listening

Use 'active' listening techniques to find out what the person/ people are feeling. Take turns to listen to everyone and keep repeating that you will hear everyone in turn. Active listening means showing that you are listening: for example, sitting down at eye level with those you are talking to, keeping eye contact and adding 'go on'/'mm'/'ah' occasionally.

### 2. Acceptance and understanding

Restate the key issue to clarify what is being said. Recognise the feelings expressed. Keep restating what you hear: 'So you are saying . . . Is that right?'

After each key point or event has been established from one point of view, establish it from the other/s. As you do this, be absolutely impartial.

Often the act of explaining or clarifying how someone views the situation can make a line of argument look weak. But this is not the time to start adding your opinion, however tempting, or to allow others a second 'speak' before everyone has been heard for the first time. Try to get consensus on events.

### 3. Get those involved to state their position

Encourage them to use 'I' statements to explain their feelings, and do the same for your position in the dispute if you have one. This is not about passing judgement. If you have no personal position and are simply attempting to facilitate a process, give feedback on what you observe. Do not accuse or use blaming language ('You should have done X' is both undermining and completely pointless – because the situation is in the past and therefore cannot be changed).

Check that everyone agrees or recognises each other's viewpoint – keep listening and going over things until they do.

## 4. Negotiate a solution

For the argument to be resolved, each party may have to compromise and allow the other party to retain dignity. In order to negotiate such a 'no-lose' solution, both (or all) parties will need to accept that it is not about being right or wrong, winning or losing.

To negotiate, start by asking all parties to state what they want. If possible come up with several possibilities as a list, or brainstorm some ideas. After the list of possibilities has been completed, consider each in turn, discussing the pros and cons. Get all parties to agree to the solution that has the best 'fit'.

## DEFUSING A DIFFICULT ATMOSPHERE

Start the ball rolling by looking at yourself. Take five minutes to think about how you could have done things differently to get a different outcome. And do this even if you think you haven't done anything wrong!

For example, if two of your children were having a big fight and you separated them, but now they are sulking and snarling at each other. Go back into the fray and discuss your observations about your actions, and get them to join in (they will!). You could say: 'You guys were fighting so I shut you up for some peace and to make sure no one got hurt, but now I find the atmosphere in the house is like cold treacle and I am wondering if I did the wrong thing. What do you think? What could I have done differently? Should I have left you to carry on fighting and see what happened, with the risk that someone would get really hurt?'

By shifting the focus to the least-involved party you can get everyone to begin to work together again.

## HOW TO SAY 'NO' AND STICK TO IT

1  Take your time to say 'No'. One way might be the 'three strikes' rule: 'Once I have said no three times you had better believe it.' This leaves some leeway for discussion and changing minds but ultimately says: 'No is no and I am not moving'.

2  Once a definite 'No' is given, ignore all attitude, pleading, shouting, temper or threats. Really ignore. Pretend you can't hear it at all. Be warned, this is only a reasonable approach if you've done step 1.

3  Sometimes the results in the short term of sticking to your 'No' can be very painful. Dealing with a major tantrum or a string of abuse in public, for instance, can be ghastly. However, give in once and they will have a brilliant new weapon in their armoury, which they will use more and more frequently to get their own way. Don't give in and they will be left feeling rather foolish and will learn not to go there again.

4  'Don't sweat the small stuff.' Be prepared to negotiate as often as you can, but when you have given your inch just say 'No' and mean it.

# 13 top tips for creating strong family ties

1 **Grow your own family traditions.** Traditions create a sense of belonging to a particular organisation or institution and families work in just the same way. Having a takeaway meal on a Friday night, watching a film together on a Sunday afternoon, having an ice-cream after school one day a week, reading the papers together over Sunday brunch, the way you celebrate birthdays and Christmas are all traditions worth building upon.

2 **Mealtimes are an excellent opportunity for communication** and strong families use these as ideal times to talk together. Prioritising family meals – even if only once a week – creates a sense of community. It also helps to develop resilience and is a great way for the modern gadget-crazy teen to practise the skills of face-to-face conversation. Learning to pick up on simple clues in facial expressions to help judge when to speak and when to stop are hard to explain and can only be learnt by spending time face to face in groups, so meal-times are ideal. Your young people's table manners will undoubtedly improve too, even if they do not display them in front of you, and understanding how a formal meal works can be beneficial when they are visiting their friends' houses or taken out to eat. Make sure all phones or tablets are left on silent, and expect people to stay at the table until everyone has finished.

3 **Have a family meeting** (see Appendix 1) to discuss issues that affect you all in an equal and 'no-blame' way that is all about finding solutions, as well as to formalise the exchange of important information.

4 **Play board games.** Computer games tend to be intense and solitary. A board game needs communication and empathy – to encourage younger players to take part. Card

games and word games work well too, or try charades, quizzes with 'teams' or consequences.

5 **Do something together** – go to the cinema or theatre. This may not be as expensive as you think as lots of cinemas and theatres offer very good value family tickets. Museums, galleries and exhibitions become more appealing if you offer to visit the café or shop before you come home.

6 **Make something together.** There are pottery shops where everyone can paint their own mug, which you could then make a point of using for family meals. Get everyone involved in digging the garden, sweeping up leaves, making a formal meal or painting a room; tolerate the additional mess in the interests of a shared experience.

7 **Enjoy treats together.** These do not have to be expensive, so as well as saving up for a trip to a theme park, you could all go swimming together, cycle a local park trail or tow path together or take a pile of 2p pieces to the kind of slot machine that nudges coins over the edge. Allow every member of the family to choose a treat in turn and insist that everyone goes on each excursion with a willing spirit, and not just to those that appeal to them.

8 **Talk about shared memories.** Talking about things you have shared – and valued – boosts a sense of community and the young people's sense of grounding in an institution they value. Most young people love to hear about when they were born; it's their personal history and knowing that someone else values it can be a tremendous boost to self-esteem.

9 **Listen to things together:** humour that appeals to everyone; music (theirs too). Story or music CDs or tapes played in the car can be an ideal shared experience, particularly on long journeys.

10 **Watch TV together.** *Neighbours* may not be the best show in the world but watching it with teenage children can

prompt all kinds of good conversations and creates a situation that you share. Keep a blanket or spare duvet in the room that houses the television so that those who are sitting on the sofa can watch in comfort – and cuddle up to each other.

11 **Compile scrapbooks and encourage your teenagers to do the same.** Encourage them to print a few favourite photographs, put in things from special outings (bus tickets, leaflets and programmes). Look back through family photograph collections and talk about what you were doing and how you felt. Show them scrapbooks and photograph albums from your own youth.

12 **Design a family Christmas card together.** Each person can have their own area to manage such as creating the design (and deciding which option is most popular with the other family members), getting the design on to the computer, printing and adding finishing touches such as a ribbon or glitter. Get them to sign their names in those you send out. When there are family birthdays and other special occasions, encourage everyone to sign the card and help suggest an appropriate present.

13 **Put up a notice board** in a prominent place in the house and encourage everyone to have a special section. Here they can pin up items that matter to them – so if they have had a 'good note home' from school this could go up, as could a ticket from a concert they have been to. This will attract interest from callers to the house and provide them with the opportunity to talk about their achievement or experience.

## QUESTIONS & ANSWERS

**Q:** I can't bear my son's table manners and so end up commenting on them all the time. My husband says I am drawing attention to them and should leave him alone. Who is right?

A: You both are. Firstly, bear in mind that attention is the most significant reinforcement of behaviour, so the more you comment on what he is doing, the more he feels he is centre-stage. Depending on his personality, and status within the family, this could be a very attractive position to be in.

Particularly when other people are present, parents often tend to draw attention to something they disapprove of through humour or mock outrage. But by doing this, you may be giving him more of the attention he really seeks. So rather than saying: 'It's like sitting next to a washing machine when you are chewing, I can see the entire contents of your mouth', it might be more effective to say: 'Please close your mouth when you are chewing'.

You may also be drawing attention to your son's failings and not noticing those of other young people sitting around the table. It's common for parents to concentrate on what they don't like in a young person's behaviour rather than what they do like. A valuable strategy here is to comment positively on what they do when they are behaving well. So if you have a younger child at the table with good manners, reinforce the desired behaviour: 'It's a pleasure to eat with you, you have such beautiful manners.' By the time they reach the teenage years they want you to leave them alone, so then is the time to reverse your role: good behaviour buys them time on their own without your presence.

Q: My husband and I seem to disagree completely about the best way to raise children. What should we do?

A: We are all brought up in different ways, so whereas a certain overlap is likely in order for your own relationship to have got going in the first place, it's also probable that both of you will bring some new (and different) values to the parenting of your own children.

You will also have had different experiences of growing up that are due to gender rather than culture. Most parents treat boys and girls differently, and you will find that gender affects how you treat your own young people. For example, many fathers find the emerging sexuality of their daughters difficult; mothers often find it hard to stop doing chores for their sons.

Because they are individuals, situations that will reduce one parent to distraction may leave another emotionally unscathed. It's a very good idea for parents to compensate for each other's strengths and weaknesses. For example, if one of you is more likely to lose your temper, perhaps the other parent can spot the warning signs, and offer a break until calm is restored. But for this to work effectively, some honesty about each other's weaknesses is required.

The best practice is to discuss between you what is best, to encourage both of you to take part in parenting rather than excluding one party, not to take any big decisions without involving both parties, and to accept that there is not just one way to parent.

Avoid making deals with a young person that exclude the other parent. 'I'll let you do this but don't tell Mum' is divisive, excludes the other parent and puts the young person in a position they can manipulate. If you have to make a tricky decision in your partner's absence, have a family meeting once you all get home to bring the issue out into the open: 'We decided to do the following, but let's just talk it through with Mum now she is back.'

**Q:** My wife has two children by her former husband. We now have a son of our own. Her former husband lives close by and I find that if I try to insist on issues with my two stepsons, they say that their father allows whatever behaviour I have just commented on.

A: Whoever's home you are in has the right to set the rules, so if you are commenting on behaviour that offends you, and you are at home, the boys should do as you say. Having said that, there should be complete consistency between you and your wife on what is (and is not) worth enforcing.

Lack of consistency between different places and situations is not a problem for most young people; they deal with it all the time (e.g. different words for the same things at school and at home, different language with their friends compared with their parents). The important thing is that their parents and carers should be consistent in what they ask of them.

If you feel particularly strongly about certain issues, and the behaviour you consider acceptable is completely different from what is being advocated in their other household, then you should discuss this with the former partner and your wife.

Many young people will play the 'you're not my Dad/Mum' card here and if it works will continue to do so. They should be firmly reminded that while this is true biologically, you are their parent because you have taken on the role and its responsibilities until they reach adulthood.

Q: My wife postpones disciplining our teenage son until I get home from work. This means that the first contact I have with him each evening is negative, and I am responding to a situation I did not witness, reliant on her account only. Is this OK?

A: Postponed discipline never works. Disciplinary issues should be dealt with there and then – when the issue arises and should be tied in with a long-term strategy. Issues of acceptability (e.g. times in and out, allowances and what they are to be used for) should be agreed beforehand so all parties know what is acceptable.

It's very difficult to deal with a situation you did not witness, so why not start by getting both sides together and talking through what happened? Both sides can then put their point of view.

In the long term, your son's behaviour during the day is a problem that you all need to sort out. If your wife does not deal with it and then passes it to you to handle, you are distancing your son from his responsibilities. The behaviour is primarily your son's problem and he must be involved in the solution, together with you.

**Q:** My mother comments that although I threaten my teenagers with sanctions, I never carry them out. Surely most people do this?

**A:** It's common practice, but a slippery slope. If you threaten a sanction, you must stick to it – otherwise your young people will soon learn not to take you seriously. Remember too that if you keep imposing threats, they have to get bigger and bigger in order to be effective.

There is no point in having sanctions if you do not see them through; without carrying them through they become meaningless. It follows that you should be careful about imposing sanctions you do not want to carry out. And if you do end up enforcing a sanction that you do not feel is fair, the learning point may be yours rather than theirs! If you genuinely feel you have been over-harsh, you could try offering your teenager a compromise, but don't dispense with the sanction all together: 'If you work at it between now and next Tuesday perhaps we could agree a compromise, of you going until 10 p.m. instead of overnight.'

A good sanction should be of appropriate severity, immediately applicable, and not given in the heat of the moment, but calmly thought through.

'One half term, on a shopping trip set up by my mother, I spent all my allowance on clothes. My parents refused to allow me to go out that evening on a prearranged theatre trip with a friend for which the ticket had already been bought. There was no advance warning about not spending all my money, it was mine to spend, and my father only imposed this last-minute disciplinary measure because my mother worked him up into a frenzy (he always got angry very quickly). Their argument was that I should have planned ahead and would need money for the remainder of half term. The worst thing was they rang my friend's parents and told them I could not come out "due to a disciplinary incident". I was mortified, and writing about it 30 years later can still feel the resentment incurred.' **Mother**

Injustice hangs around for ever. If you want a mature relationship with your young people, based on mutual respect, then impose sanctions wisely.

**Q:** When angry, my partner told my daughter she could not go to a party I know she had been looking forward to for weeks. I feel this was over-hasty but I do not wish to undermine his authority.

**A:** Your decision not to undermine him is a very good starting point. It's good practice not to argue in front of your daughter, but to discuss this rationally with both parties, without actually taking sides. You could encourage your daughter to put her point of view to your partner, making connections between his anger at something else – presumably not connected with the outing – and cancelling something she had been looking forward to. You could have the same discussion with him. Feeling calmer now, does he still feel that the punishment (for that is how she will see it) is appropriate? If not, then encourage him to discuss the situation with your daughter and consider reformatting the sanction. But any decision to change what was set up must be his rather than yours.

If you are able to reach a compromise, a follow-up discussion between all of you about why the sanction was prompted in the first place can be very helpful: what was the behaviour that led to anger, which in turn produced a sanction? By talking about it in this way you imply there were mistakes and lessons to be learnt by all parties, not just your daughter, and long-term outcomes are hopefully improved.

**Q:** My son always leaves the bathroom window closed after his shower. Each morning starts with me reminding him, yet again, to open it before he leaves the room. How can I encourage him to see how selfish he is being?

**A:** Other parents raise similar issues about shoes in the hall, rucksacks on the stairs and hanging jackets up.

This is an ideal issue for a family meeting (see Appendix 1). Explaining why you continually raise an issue that to them probably sounds very boring, may mean that you are listened to for the first time – rather than sounding like a recorded message. You could start by asking whether anyone can guess why you want a particular action carried out. Explain that opening the window after a shower allows steam to escape and prevents the walls going mouldy.

**Q:** My parents-in-law tell my children off in front of me and disagree with me quite publicly. I feel undermined and marginalised. What should I do?

**A:** The role grandparents play in their grandchildren's lives can be a source of support and happiness – but also frustration.

Whoever's house you are in has the right to set the boundaries within it. So if your children are acting in a way that displeases their grandparents, and they are in their grandparents' house, they have a right to comment and ask that the behaviour is discontinued. In your house, however, they have no right to set the moral climate (unless they are left in charge in your place).

The problem is made worse in many families because rather than talk about difficulties – for example whether it is a good idea for grandparents to comment on what they dislike in teenage behaviour, or whether ideas have changed since their adolescence – individuals brood silently and build up resentment.

If something your parents-in-law do really annoys you, and it is a situation that is both worthy and capable of resolution, try to deal with it yourself and do so quickly. Leaving the situation for discussion with your partner (their blood relation) means that the situation escalates further than it would if you dealt with it quickly yourself. If you feel unable to tackle this yourself, and it is something worth fighting for, say so, using non-blaming language. Alternatively, ask yourself if this is an issue really worth fighting about. A trainer who runs courses in assertiveness told me recently that the key to being truly assertive is to pick issues you genuinely care about, rather than becoming a routine fighter.

Q: My sister-in-law and her husband lived in Africa for years and many of their views are frankly racist. I have silently resented this for years, but the possibility of their restating of these views in front of my teenagers fills me with horror. What can I do?

A: There is an initial problem in that you have silently tolerated the situation for so long. By remaining silent they may have long concluded that you agree with them.

Talk to your partner about this. Perhaps your partner (or you together) could talk to them about the wider issue, which is that children today grow up in a multicultural world and that quoting offensive attitudes that they hear at home will cause damage to both the society they find themselves in and the relationships they are able to form. It's a backhanded compliment for relations to be told that their attitudes really do influence the next generation!

If your relations do make a racist remark in front of you and/or the young people, you should make a comment, even if it is simply to say that you do not agree with the views expressed. If your children see you just accepting such views they will assume you share them and may repeat them to others.

A desire to avoid confrontation may be your reason for not challenging beliefs you do not agree with. But your teenagers will not necessarily be scarred by seeing that adults do not agree: they see this all the time, in the media, at school and at home.

**Q:** My parents give my young people money. They do this without me seeing. We give them an allowance and I do not want them to receive additional funds.

**A:** Is this really about the funding of your young people or about your relationship with your parents? As adults we receive income (and demands) from all quarters, expected and unexpected. A lottery win may supplement the family coffers, a parking ticket deplete them.

If your parents enjoy giving to your children, and the amounts are not so large (or small) as to subvert their value structure, why not let them? Don't you remember the sheer pleasure of an additional £5 and the equally great joy of spending it?

Encourage the relationship with grandparents in ways other than money – which may just be the one they find it easiest to fulfil. Time with a grandparent, or other member of the extended family, can be a wonderful way of boosting a relationship between two people who do not see each other very often.

**Q:** My parents-in-law do not seem at all interested in my children. It really bothers me that they don't come and take them out in the holidays. How can I make them take an interest?

**A:** Again, is this about your relationship with them or theirs with your children? I wonder if your children even notice – unless you have pointed it out to them and encouraged them to dwell on it. Children's expectations tend to be based on experience, so if they have no memory of their grandparents' attention, they are unlikely to resent the lack of contact.

In terms of making them take an interest, the short answer is that you can't. But I do wonder if they realise that you would like them to be involved – what do they say about the relationship and the lack of contact?

Perhaps you should suggest that they come and visit, or make a plan to leave the children with them for a weekend and go off with your partner for a short break? Offering to help may not have occurred to them – simply because they admire the way you parent your children. In other words, their lack of volunteering may be a compliment to you. They may be waiting to be asked.

**Q:** It is really clear that my parents favour one of their grandchildren – the third child of my sister's family. This is so unfair – what can I do?

**A:** It may be unfair but who ever said life was fair? Most parents, if they are really honest, find one of their children easier to deal with than the other(s). Young people accept this – they are used to this in relationships with their friends and family; they may even find one parent more empathetic than the other!

If there is no difference in the love, care, kindness or generosity offered to the various grandchildren – just a difference in the empathy you witness – then you might decide to do nothing more, and just accept that we all get on better with some people than others. If the treatment is biased, you should discuss this with the grandparents, without the young people being present.

**Q:** My daughter writes a diary every day. Should I read it?

**A:** The short answer is no. If she is choosing to confide in a diary rather than in you, or other people, you should respect that decision, the important thing being that she is communicating her feelings. On occasion, however, young people have been known to leave their diaries lying around in a prominent place – in order to be found. Parents have found in this a tacit mechanism for telling them what is going on, without the need for a formal conversation. This is the kind of situation that has to be judged on its merits.

'My daughter has written in a diary for years. Although I have found her writing it, I have never known where she kept it and I have certainly never read it. Last summer however she was going through a difficult time with a boyfriend and I suddenly found the diary was on top of her bed, day after day. I decided she wanted me to read it and then was able to understand the problems she was facing. We talked about the issues in general terms without ever discussing the people involved. I hope this helped. The diary has now disappeared again.' **Mother**

**Q:** I hear people talk about quality time with their children. Most of mine seems to be spent running them from engagement to engagement.

**A:** It's true that 'quality time' is more important than quantity of time. You can have more communication during an hour of being together and talking than during five hours of simply co-existing in the same space. But don't confuse delivering your young person to the schedule you (or she) have set up outside the house with parenting. Running them from French classes to modern dance and then on to their Saturday afternoon coaching session is not parenting – particularly if you have the radio on in the car so you cannot talk to each other!

Parenting does not have to take place in formal one-to-one sessions; indeed if you always make a point of having a heavy conversation during a car trip they may come to dread this and bring a 'prop' (a mobile phone, Game-boy or friend) to avoid the need to talk to you. Effective conversation can take place over any activity. So if you are changing a light bulb or cooking pasta why not show them how you do it and talk to them at the same time? You'd be amazed how much satisfaction there is in carrying out a simple task when you are not used to doing it. And describing how you do something gives the teller a great sense of purpose – hence morale boost all round!

> 'There is a woman that I regularly see on the bus in the evenings. She has evidently just picked up her son from his after-school care and I see him sitting beside her, good as gold, as she talks into her mobile phone about work arrangements. She makes one call after another. Yet this is the time for such easy communication – he has not seen her all day, and they have the chance to chat. It makes me sad that she makes so little use of it.' **Gill**

**Q:** My husband works long hours and leaves the parenting to me. He is often away and tired when he is at home. I get on with it, but resent it. What should I do?

A: Parenting works best when two people are involved, and in the long run this question raises a choice that you both have to make about your priorities.

Your frustration at single-parenting will be evident to your young people, and their self-esteem – at being worth so little time from one of their parents, and being the full-time (and resented) burden to the parent who is around – will be affected. Whatever the material consequences of the decisions you make, is the long-term relationship between you and your young people really worth all the time at work?

If you do have to tolerate a partner's heavy work schedule (say as a short-term measure), then look to your own support mechanisms. Do you have friends to talk to, an exercise routine to keep you healthy, and help at home? And when your partner does get time off, it's important that he is able to feel welcome there. So it's good practice not to save up all the disciplinary and organisational issues for the moment he arrives back, but to allow him to reconnect in an inviting way, say through a meal or some family time.

When it comes to looking back over their lives, most people's regrets are to do with lack of communication with families and friends, rather than work commitments not met.

Q: My son refuses to eat with the family. I call him when his meal is ready but he usually appears after half an hour or so, takes the plate and heads back upstairs to his computer and games console. I used to put his food in the oven but I don't now; I leave it out to get cold but it makes no difference. One day last week he came down for it after an hour and then heated it up again in the microwave!

A: Have a relaxed one-to-one chat with him about his mealtime choices, perhaps when you are both in the car going for a longish journey or sitting on his bed if he stays put in his room all the time.

Be clear about your expectations and don't let him sway you. Perhaps you want him to join you and the family every evening, or perhaps a couple of nights a week he can make his own choice? If so negotiate which days he is to be at the family table and which he can make choices for. It is probably wise to give him a reasonable warning before dinner is ready if he is gaming as it can be extremely frustrating to leave a game halfway through, but it is his responsibility not to start a game 20 minutes before mealtimes.

I suggest that if his timekeeping continues to be unacceptable you don't just leave his dinner to get cold but you put it in the bin. He won't starve as there are undoubtedly plenty of things he can eat in the fridge or cupboard, but knowing that he cannot have a nice cooked meal without upholding his side of the deal matters.

## CHAPTER 7

# 'All my friends are allowed to': peer influences and friendships

Who are your young person's peers? Parents tend to lump a young person's peers into very broad categories, and so may see all teenagers as peers. From the teenager's point of view, their peers are usually a much less defined group: a shifting alliance; a group that is defined by mood, timing, tastes in fashion and music, use of language and many passing fads. Peers can be highly exclusive or very inclusive, depending on the time at which the grouping is made, and the grouping may not last very long. Here are some examples:

- A family of four children of differing ages may behave as peers when they want to exert pressure on their parents to do something, but form very different peer groups on a day-to-day basis when allowances and freedoms are being discussed.
- A girl may not feel that the boys in her class are her peers until united behind an issue that involves them all, such as a discussion with a teacher over deadlines for coursework.
- A 13-year-old boy attending a gig for the first time will quickly adopt the behaviour of the rest of the audience who, even though they may be much older, become his peer group for the evening.

The peer group consists of those the young person relates to as having an overlapping background, tastes and interests, even for a short while. But not all peers will become friends or are even people they have met. Young people form friendships of a variety of different stages of intimacy, just as their parents do. They will have relationships with people in a variety of different degrees of closeness. For example, there may be those whom they:

- Nod to in the street
- Have a long, intimate and detailed conversation with once but never meet again
- Gossip with
- Have things in common with
- Do things together with from time to time
- Phone or text but rarely meet
- Share everything with
- Think about all the time but have little contact with
- Have an online relationship with but have never met

Significantly, you may not be able to distinguish one relationship from another, and may make the wrong conclusions about who has most influence on your young people. Your daughter may be hanging out with one person most of the time, but her real influencer is someone she has very little day-to-day contact with.

Essentially a peer is anyone a young person perceives as being like themselves either in age or behaviour, circumstance or setting. For example, at a family gathering a 14-year-old may consider a 10-year-old a peer (albeit a rather young one) if everyone else is over 30, but at a school prom may consider their peers to be only those from their own school year group, or even form group.

One of the aspects of modern teenage life that may be hard to understand for parents is the power of the media to create and manipulate a virtual peer group, which can exert an enormous amount of pressure in its own right on young people to look a certain way, behave a certain way and respond to others in a certain way. Included in this virtual group may be the latest boy band/girl band, young actors and actresses, 'fashionistas' and models, sports people – particularly footballers – and their partners, as well as the latest crop of reality TV stars. How these people dress, how they behave and their attitudes and opinions on life in general in many ways dictate the popular culture young people follow and adhere to.

## WHO ARE YOUR FRIENDS?

One of the big differences between your young person's life and your own teen years is that they may have many virtual friendships with others they may not have met face to face, some of which may be extremely intimate in terms of sharing information or pictures online.

This is an excellent exercise to do with your young person. Each of you begins by making a list of 10 people you know and spend time with. Now classify them into:

- A true or best friend (put a 1 beside their name)
- A good friend (put a 2 beside their name)
- A casual friend (put a 3 beside their name)
- A close acquaintance (put a 4 beside their name)
- A casual acquaintance (put a 5 beside their name)
- Someone you know (put a 6 beside their name)

Now share your criteria for each category. What constitutes a 'good' friend as opposed to a 'casual' friend? Does time come into it? What about trust? Or intimacy and shared experience? Does it have to be someone you have met or spend time with face to face? Are your categories based on the same principles as each other or different ones?

## THE 'RULES' OF FRIENDSHIP

Having friends is very important to young people, and the number of people they can list as friends will matter a lot to some. Many friendships are based on shared interests, or a liking for each other, while others are based on pack hierarchy and rules. In extreme cases these can become gangs with set codes of conduct, but in most cases they are less formalised.

Virtual friendships can be difficult to categorise as they may often include large numbers of people that your teen has never met but feels they know quite well. It may also include people they do not like very much, in much the same way as a real-life friendship group. However, unlike face-to-face friendships, it can be difficult to maintain online friendships with some individuals while withholding information from others. Such behaviour can be seen as manipulative and divisive by the group.

Membership of any set or group is bound by often unspoken rules, and these may be different for boys and girls.

## BOYS AND GIRLS COME OUT TO PLAY

Not everyone is comfortable talking about boys and girls behaving in different ways, but there may be significant differences in the way they conduct their relationships, largely – though not solely – related to gender. These behavioural characteristics tend to be amplified in single-sex environments.

Girls tend to play with emotion: including; excluding; sharing; supporting; comforting; hurting; exchanging secrets and gossip; excessive shows of feeling and the development of passionate friendships. Some people observing this behaviour (and in particular men) may view it negatively; in reality it is an important developmental process – women are, after all, the people who tend to keep families and communities connected to one another.

By 'exercising' and developing their relationship skills they are trying out different behaviours and seeing how they feel; and in the process they eventually develop levels of understanding and empathy far exceeding those developed by most males. All this emotion and social manipulation is a learning phase and through practice they grow into open and emotionally available adults.

Boys tend to compete physically, materially and verbally with each other: there will be competitive exercise; team building; hitting and pushing; and general argy-bargy. At times this competition will become intense, as when playing computer games. Even how much they spend on their trainers can become a competition. Through their numerous wins and losses they come to their own understandings about the nature of social groupings and form solid and reliable friendships and strong trust bonds that may be far greater than those between girls.

## LOYALTY AND GRASSING

Loyalty to a friendship group is usually expected by all young people. This means not saying or doing anything that would put anyone in a bad light to those outside the group. (Having a go at someone inside the group, with other group members, is fine though, and is often used as a method of control.) Talking about friends can be so taboo that even extreme behaviour can be covered up – 'grassing a mate' being considered the biggest of all crimes.

It's a good idea to discuss boundaries on 'telling'. Ideal opportunities for this arise through the media – perhaps in a high-profile court case where someone has probably covered up a serious crime to 'help' a friend, for example during an assault. Other people may not have taken part in the crime but did nothing to either stop or report it. Many schools now talk of being a 'telling school', where both good and bad issues are openly shared and explored in non-blaming ways.

## WHAT YOUR YOUNG PEOPLE
## LEARN FROM YOU

How you manage your own friendships will have a big impact on how your teenagers do the same. They will make judgements about what is acceptable, and what makes them feel uncomfortable, based on how they watch you behaving. For example, are you loyal to your friends or do you break confidences? How do you resolve problems with them? Do you talk them through face to face or complain to everyone else? Are you reliable or do you let friends down at the last minute?

Another factor that impacts on young people's ability to make friends is the treatment they receive at home; self-esteem has a huge impact on how friendships are made. If teens are openly teased or ridiculed at home they will find it hard to have the self-confidence to believe they are likeable – and hence able to make friends.

## GROUP DYNAMICS

As we have seen, most school year groups break down into a variety of smaller sub-groups: the 'in crowd' (or 'Alphas'), the 'almost there's' (or 'Betas') and the 'also-rans' (who have a range of sub-groups and names). Most young people are very aware of both which group they belong to and which one they aspire to be part of.

A problem may arise if your young person is on the edge of any group, tolerated rather than accepted, and hanging on for dear life. This may be particularly hard to understand when they are aspiring to be part of the Alpha group when they would be so much more accepted, respected and acclaimed within another set. They may be the butt of the Alphas' jokes, but would still probably rather be part of this group than not. If they are unhappy about this position they need help to behave assertively with the existing group, as well as in considering the choices of friendships available and their comfort versus standing.

> 'I met someone who had spent a season working as a chalet girl in a French ski resort. Having watched groups come and go, she came to the conclusion that there was one factor that was guaranteed to produce a great party atmosphere during the holiday. Her conclusion was that there had to be a scapegoat: someone who was the butt of the jokes.' **Mother**

We all know what young people need to say; parents tell me all the time that they have told their young person how to react or how to address their critics. Unfortunately telling a young person how to act or what to say has almost no effect, because when we come up with our solutions to their problems we are using many years of experience they simply don't have. Asking a young person to give a response that might work for an adult will almost certainly leave them open to ridicule or abuse. Not only does your young person lack the experience you have but the people they are dealing with lack the range of social awareness and emotional responses that you are used to dealing with. When we adults deal with problems we use the logical part of our brain, but when young people deal with problems they approach them from a far more emotional area and may in fact overthink problems when attempting to think them through logically.

Whenever we are helping young people solve problems we need to help them find solutions that will work for them, even if they are completely different from ones we might consider effective. To do this we ask clever questions rather than give clever answers. When we ask them to think through their choices, we are enabling them to find new ways of behaving within their own capability as well as creating new thought patterns for them.

Asking a few interesting, reflective, open questions (see Chapter 5) can help them see things differently, as well as helping them 'join the dots' in their own relationship experiences.

Here are a few examples of questions that have proved helpful:

- 'If his behaviour does not change how do you think he will be in five years' time?'
- 'What are the kinds of problems that young women can face if they have friendship problems?'
- 'When you get tired of arguing and let her have her own way how do you think she understands the relationship between you and her?'
- 'When does he show you he is really sensitive to you and your feelings?'
- 'When was the last time you had really good fun together? What happened?'
- 'If instead of getting cross with him when he loses control you sat and spoke to him reassuringly and calmly, how do you think it would feel for him?'
- 'Everybody loses their temper with their friends sometimes but some people seem to be able to stay calm longer than others. Why do you think that is?'

Taking a long-term view, it may be a good idea to encourage your young person to understand that popularity is not everything – and personal integrity may be more important. Do they really want to be friends with people who treat others like that? You could also encourage your young people to question the value of individual friendships versus their cost. For example: 'Is her friendship really worth all the time you spend worrying about whether or not she likes you?' or 'You never know until the very last minute whether or not he will call for you. Would it be worth thinking about contacting someone else to arrange to spend time together, so you have an alternative plan in place?'

If the situation is more serious, and you suspect bullying, turn to Chapter 8 for more detailed advice.

## PRIVACY

One of the areas that parents and teens seldom agree on is privacy. While parents generally maintain certain standards of privacy around their own relationships and behaviour, they expect to know everything that is happening in their child's life, at least until they are 16 or so. Young people, however, expect a growing privacy around their bodies, friendships and behaviour in general from about the age of 11 or 12 (and sometimes earlier).

The development of greater privacy should depend upon previous behaviour. It is perfectly acceptable for a young person to have their own room as a private space, for example, if they are willing to negotiate, agree to and stick to a set of rules. These might include ensuring all used dishes are returned to the kitchen on a daily basis, all laundry is placed in a laundry basket, the room is adequately cleaned once a week, that the young person changes their bedding once a week, etc. There might also be some restrictions on having other people in their room associated with their age and general responsibility. If they break these rules then you are entitled to enter their space.

If they are too young or too careless to negotiate these rules then they are not yet ready to have a completely private space within the home (except perhaps the bathroom!).

Likewise their communications should be negotiated; using social media, for example, can be risky and when they are just starting to use it, adults should not give them complete confidentiality but should monitor what is happening without being too intrusive. For instance, some parents insist that their young person has them on their friends list on Facebook so that they are aware of what is going on.

However, being too intrusive into your young person's life can be devastating for them, as nothing is more embarrassing to a young teen than their parents. Respecting boundaries is a two-way street and if we want them to respect the rules we need to show that we can also respect theirs. Discuss with them the appropriate level of intervention and socialising that helps them feel private and you feel they are safe.

'One Sunday afternoon when I was about 15 a boy came round to call on me very unexpectedly. I quickly suggested that we went out for a walk, encouraging him to go home before we returned to my house. When I got home, my mother had changed into a dress and laid a tea table in the garden – something we never normally did. I was so relieved I had already got rid of him. I hated the way my parents would talk to my boyfriends, it was so embarrassing, and I would go to great lengths to meet up with them away from home.' **Mother**

## FLASHBACK

Can you remember five friends whose homes you liked going to? Why did you like these five in particular? How does your own home compare?

'One friend I had at school would occasionally ask me for tea but the time spent in her home was always extremely tense. Tea would be laid out in the sitting room and we had to eat very politely while the parents walked in and out interrupting with sharp questions and being rude to each other. I remember I was always so glad to get home after these occasions, and would usually run all the way.' **Mother**

## HOW TO MAKE FRIENDS

Forming a friendship with someone is risky. We often get to know someone in a casual context, but moving the relationship on and offering a greater degree of intimacy is a risk – because we may get rejected.

For example, as adults we may meet a particular person in the same place on a regular basis and ask them about the same thing every time (the progress of their house hunt, the weather, their child's asthma), but have little idea of the wider lives they lead. The crossing point is when we try to move the relationship on a stage, and invite them to meet us on our own or to our own home. And for this to happen, one party to the friendship must move it further; someone must assume the risk. If your young people find it difficult to make friends, learning how their parents do it could be helpful.

The question of making friends becomes particularly impor- tant when your child changes school at 11. If this is an issue for your young person, you could start by confirming in his mind that he is someone that others like to make friends with. If he has just changed schools, can you refer to friendships he had in his previous school and ask him how he found these friends? Remembering how he did it in the past may give him confidence in the future: 'James was your best friend in your last school. How did you first meet him?'

It's also helpful to think about strategies he can use to make friends, so it's a great idea to think about how you make friends yourself, and to talk about the process with him.


### FLASHBACK

Thinking back over the past five years, how have you made friends yourself?

- Through recognising, nodding at and finally talking to someone you met on the train going to work?
- Through getting on and off the same bus at the same stop each day?
- In the queue at a sandwich shop?
- Through spotting someone had the same interests as you (e.g. reading the same book, listening to the same music, having a picture you like on their wall at work)?
- Through a group you began going to (e.g. book group, church group, charity organisation, support group)?
- Through doing your shopping at the same time and place each week?
- Through looking at people as you walk along the street rather than avoiding eye contact?
- Through going to an event that was not part of your usual routine?
- Through speaking to someone at an event you both attended?
- By volunteering to help with something?

Most friendships begin slowly with a conversation about a shared action or interest. Get your young person to think of some opening lines, such as 'This queue gets longer every day' or 'How long have you been interested in . . . ?'

## ONLINE FRIENDSHIPS

Most young people today will be members of several social networking sites online. These are important for today's young people as they enable them to keep up with what is happening among their peers in terms of day-to-day 'gossip', cultural changes and social events and outings.

Most adults assume that their young people are sensible online and never post sensitive material (such as semi-nude photos of themselves), accept friendship requests from people they don't know, send spiteful or mean emails or posts – particularly anonymously – or give out information that could be dangerous in the wrong hands – such as the dates when their family holiday will leave their home empty or their phone number.

Unfortunately millions of young people do exactly these things every year because even the most sensible young person is capable of acting impulsively or thoughtlessly on occasion, as indeed are we all. It is important for parents to communicate regularly and honestly with young people about Internet use and to ask them to think through the acceptable 'rules' for their use, rather than listening to a lecture from you about what they should and shouldn't be up to. Creating some kind of agreement between you and your teen based on sensible use will help you monitor their online behaviour and, if need be, restrict it without too much damage. For more information see Chapter 10.

## WHAT TO DO IF YOU DON'T LIKE YOUR TEENAGER'S FRIENDS

The friendship group a young person chooses to belong to may have more influence on their behaviour than almost any other factor. Whether they are academically minded and regularly do their homework, whether they smoke or take drugs, at what age they become sexually active and their patterns of alcohol consumption are all heavily influenced by the group they belong to – although it could equally be said that young people choose friends who reflect their own attitudes and behaviours in terms of risk and boundaries.

The reality is that young people choose to be with these people even if they are risk-takers, or people who experiment, because they too want to get involved. If your young person wants to be with a group you do not like, it may be helpful if you address the issue of why she wants to be with them.

What are the shared values of this group? Can you help her to see risk-takers as foolish rather than glamorous? Or help her to find a set of more appealing values – if she is interested in animals, could you buy her a puppy? Could you work on her love of music and offer to help her get tickets for a concert she would like to attend? If she is good at sport or writing, can you find a relevant group for her to join? If it is the risk that attracts her, can you encourage her to find out how old you have to be to do a parachute jump or make a scuba dive – and encourage her to start saving for it?

Trying to forcibly separate a young person from their friendship group will have little success; we all know that banning anything can make it so much more attractive for a teenager. However, there are simple strategies that may help you influence your young person's choice:

- Allowing them greater freedom when spending time with one friend over another – setting curfews or travel restrictions related to each specific event rather than having one set of expectations can add weight to certain choices they may make.

- Restricting time spent at a friend's house but still allowing that friend generous time at your home can help you monitor behaviour. If you know that a friend's parents allow behaviour you consider inappropriate, such as unrestricted Internet access, drinking alcohol or using drugs, watching movies or playing games with adult certificates, you have every right to stop your young person spending time in this environment.

- Encouraging your young person to have different groups of friends from different settings by enabling them to belong to groups, clubs and organisations separate from school.

- Providing plenty of risk-taking opportunities for your

young person (if they enjoy them) in a supervised and safe environment, such as theme park tickets as rewards, visits to climbing walls, membership of parkour clubs or BMX clubs. Young people who like to take risks need to do so in safe environments – otherwise they will find their own risks to take!

## HELPING YOUR YOUNG PERSON DEAL WITH REJECTION

This is a time to show empathy for their situation, and not to belittle their pain. Try not to dismiss their hurt as 'playground nonsense' or 'girls will be girls'. You could:

- Share your own experience of hurt to help them know you understand something of how they feel
- Keep letting them know 'It's not you, it's them'
- Encourage them to talk about how they feel but don't try to fix it (e.g. 'If I were you I would . . . '). Just let them speak
- If they are happy talking about the situation, ask questions to show that you are really listening
- Provide any comforts they will accept – hot chocolate, a trip to the cinema, a hot bubble bath, a long walk with the dog. But don't try to spend them into a good mood – just provide comfort and diversion from the bad one

## QUESTIONS & ANSWERS

**Q:** I think I know my daughter well but often feel confused. Simple things worry me, like is she sad, happy or in need of reassurance? I wouldn't always be sure of understanding. She also cannot – or will not – articulate her feelings. Should I hold back or be more active? I don't want always to interfere.

**A:** This question illustrates perfectly a growing gulf between mother and daughter, which is inevitable if she is to become an independent adult. Your daughter is choosing not to communicate everything she feels, and you feel confused and left out. Little children are open and pass on everything they feel. As they grow into teenagers they learn to withhold information and feelings, and you, the parent, who has been the main participant in their lives, are left feeling side-lined.

Maybe she does not confide in you because she feels judged or because you try to 'fix it' for her all the time. The most helpful strategy is to reassure her that you are there if she needs to talk to you but to do this without reminding her verbally – which can feel intrusive. Similarly, try to avoid making her feel that your life is empty without information about what she is doing – which feels too much of a responsibility to her. Think how you would have felt if at this age your mother had kept saying to you 'Why don't you confide in me any more?'

Days out and a chat in a coffee shop can be great equalisers, a time to both chat without either taking the lead. Let her share your thoughts and the ups and downs in your own life and she might feel more willing to share hers, but whatever you do, don't fire questions at her.

Little attentions to detail that show you care may be appreciated. For example, you could offer to have a friend to stay after a party she has been looking forward to. This way you offer her the opportunity for intimacy and chat without insisting it must be with you. You could also make time to do things together that signify she is growing up – maybe taking her to the cinema on your own, or out for lunch. If she does not want to talk, you could keep a conversation going by telling her stuff – or just by being quiet together, which is the sign of a very relaxed friendship.

You may also need to look at your own friendships – whom do you have to talk to on a daily basis now that your daughter is withdrawing from you?

**Q:** My son started at his new school six months ago and has had real difficulty making friends. How can I help him?

**A:** Some young people do find it difficult to form relationships and it can be particularly hard for a parent to watch if this causes distress.

Deal with the obvious things first. Is there something about your son that causes isolation: the way he dresses; his personal hygiene; his unfashionable haircut; or his way of speaking? Young people are very quick to pick up the signals put out by their peers and even small distinctions may cause isolation and rejection. He may not want to completely change his behaviour but you could encourage him not to talk about his particular passion all the time in front of his friends, for instance, if it is a source of teasing.

Most groups of young people have well-established pecking orders, and the young people themselves will be very aware of their relative positions. It will be the more popular members of the class who decide who are the untouchables, and their sidekicks who reinforce these positions. Much of this will blow over, but if your son needs help in steering a course through these difficult early days, suggest he tries the following strategy.

Help him review the behavioural responses he is using at the moment and to explore (by examining the reactions in others to them) if these are reinforcing (rather than discouraging) the behaviour of the other kids. So, if your son usually responds angrily to teasing, perhaps he could think of another way of reacting, perhaps by keeping his temper and shrugging his shoulders? Or if he usually looks upset, he might decide to smile sweetly; if he usually walks away, he might experiment with standing his ground. Remember to ask, don't tell – and help him reflect on the solutions he comes up with and how effective these are.

Can you help him make links with classmates outside school

hours? If your son is the butt of jokes, other classmates probably won't want to hang out with him at school – but they may do outside. Can you facilitate this, perhaps with a visit to a cinema out of town? Alternatively, can you encourage him to join a hobby-based club where he will make new friends unconnected with school? This can be a strong confidence-building strategy.

**Q:** My son seems to want no friends. He's a real loner. How can I encourage him to make relationships?

**A:** A child who is a loner is a real worry to parents. A habit of remaining alone can be hard to break and it can impact on future work and life patterns. It is harder to make relationships as you get older, and if you have not practised the skills as a young person you may be always at a disadvantage in relating to others.

Ask yourself if your son is behaving this way because he genuinely doesn't want others around, or does he have low self-esteem which is getting in the way of forming friendships? You could encourage him to join hobby-based clubs or to attend events such as trade fairs. Internet chatrooms related to his interests may also provide a vehicle for communication; it's better to have online conversations than no communication at all. (Naturally a clear discussion of 'rules online' is required here – see Chapter 10.)

**Q:** My 16-year-old daughter spent much of our expensive summer holiday texting a friend who had just left her school. They won't be together in September so it's hardly a relationship worth investing time in. I felt so annoyed that she avoided contact with her family and wasted the time abroad.

**A:** Did she really waste the time, or just use it differently from how you had anticipated? She certainly made a different decision about how to spend her time from what you would have chosen, and is being criticised for this.

By chatting to her friend she is probably exploring what she is seeing and feeling and may well be taking in more about her summer holiday than you imagine. The friend she is texting may also be more of a prototype than a single relationship, so don't feel that just because this particular girl is changing schools all the effort is wasted. Whenever you feel swamped by your family – in close proximity all the time with none of your usual familiar escape mechanisms around you (your friends, your own room, your music system) – receiving a communication from the world back home, and particularly one that is just for you, can be very consoling.

The bottom line is that we can't live other people's lives for them. Maybe you need to think about developing your own interests and communicating with other members of the family rather than getting stressed about how someone else is spending their time.

Q: I have tried to encourage my son to bring friends home with him. He won't. I want to know more about who he is involved with and to meet them.

A: And presumably that's why he is reluctant to bring them home – you have answered your own question! Most young people reach a stage where everything their parents do embarrasses them, and maybe that's the stage he is at right now.

The way you talk to his friends, the familiar nicknames you use, the food you serve, the way you dress – may all be pored over and commented on by those who come to his house. A visit to someone's home is a very intimate thing to offer and he may fear that it will just provide ammunition for teasing – and maybe he does not feel ready for that kind of scrutiny just yet. Remember how you felt about your friends and their parents when you were the same age? Back off –

don't pressurise him. If he does invite people home, keep well out of the way. You could suggest he invites someone over when you are out.

**Q:** My daughter always says that she is the only one with a strict deadline to get back home after an evening out.

**A:** And I bet there are a few more daughters saying exactly the same thing. Casting your own parents as totally unreasonable – and different from everyone else's parents – is a familiar negotiating tactic for teenagers.

If you do feel that she has a point, you could contact other parents to find out what they have agreed to. You could start by asking her if you should do this: 'Shall I just check with Sarah's parents to see what they have to say?' If she does not want you to ring, you have probably exposed an inconsistency, but leave it at that rather than make the call anyway – that way she emerges with some dignity.

Alternatively, you could be prepared to negotiate with her. Remember that saying 'No' to something you feel strongly about is fine. And don't assume that the rules are always resented. 'Rules = love' is widely understood by teenagers. Your daughter may be complaining in public but subconsciously glad that she has a structure to fit into within which she feels safe and loved.

**Q:** My son's best friend comes from a family that has far more money than we do. We can't keep up. Should I discourage the friendship?

**A:** This question says something about your own attitudes to wealth that is rather unsettling. Have you passed this on to your young person? Encouraging him to drop a friendship due to unequal resources would be a pity, and a poor value statement for how people are viewed.

All families have different resources and different priorities; some spend heavily on meals out, others have expensive holidays, others spend a lot on clothes and entertainments – and of course some do all these things. Try to encourage your son to see that the number of things you get bought is not necessarily the same thing as how much you are valued, and if he is really desperate for things you cannot afford, try to work out strategies for obtaining them such as working in his free time locally.

**Q:** My 14-year-old son has formed a friendship with a teacher at school that worries me. They are both mad keen on the painted collectables that build into an army.

**A:** A true friendship is a relationship between equals, where no one is in charge. In a relationship such as the one you have described the adult is firmly in charge; he has more resources, experience and power than your 14-year-old son.

While it's good for a 14-year-old to communicate effectively with an adult, particularly if they share a strong interest, we are all aware that there are potential risks in such relationships and you should be wary of this turning into a secret relationship. Be aware that the majority of abuse of young people occurs within the family and close friend contexts, and that many young people are willing participants – it's called abuse because it's the abuse of innocence and trust.

A teacher should be very well aware of the boundaries in his relationships with young people, and you should be happy for this friendship to continue only if other young people or adults are included in any meetings. Brief chats at school, sharing information or magazines, etc. are great, but trips to this teacher's house unsupervised are not, and no teacher should be foolish enough to suggest it.

**Q:** An old lady in our neighbourhood was recently beaten up by a gang. I am sure my son knows who did it, but he will not say.

**A:** This is a cultural thing; grassing on others is the worst sin for many young people, which is why confidential phone lines exist. Let him know. This is a deplorable crime and he needs to know that he is on one side or the other here; there is no fence to sit on.

The same goes for providing false alibis. Adults may expect their friends to cover for them – 'If my wife calls, tell her I was with you last night.' But, if we set this model of behaviour for our young people, why should we be surprised if they copy it? Kids give each other alibis all the time, but need to differentiate between times when it is OK and times when it is not OK to do so. To give an alibi to someone so that they can take part in something dangerous or harmful may have huge implications for the liar later on – for example if the friend they are covering up for ends up on a drinking binge and no one knows where they are.

# CHAPTER 8

# The 'B' word: rights, responsibilities, fairness and bullying

Bullying is a key issue for parents and teenagers, and something that often comes up at my parenting workshops. The subject is also much discussed in the media, often prompted by teenage suicides linked to bullying. All schools have to have a policy on bullying – how to spot it as well as how to deal with it and prevent it.

## HOW TO SPOT BULLYING

The following are all comments that I have heard during workshops on bullying. Bullying:

- Can be carried out by a group or an individual
- Can be small acts
- Is not always long-term – it can be a single act
- Involves a misuse of power (and the ability to create it from nothing)
- Involves exerting power over another person
- Is the use of hurtful, frightening and unacceptable force
- Is the imposition of will by force, which can be mental, physical, emotional or verbal
- Can be covert or overt

- Is prompted by the need to control
- Possibly masks an inability to communicate in an acceptable manner
- Is a deliberate intention to damage the self-worth of another
- Is done by some people more than others
- Happens to everybody at some time in their lives
- Is particularly cowardly when it is anonymous
- Is not always serious

When I have worked on this exercise in groups, I have found that the most crucial evidence of whether or not bullying is taking place are two things:

- The intention of the person accused and
- The response of the person being bullied

So, where bullying is taking place there is a deliberate (though possibly unconscious) intention to damage someone's view of themselves by the bully, and in the mind of the person being bullied there is a perception of their self-esteem being deliberately undermined.

Bullying behaviour is usually the product of a need to control, a seeking of the moment of surrender at which point the power of the perpetrator is confirmed. This may be achieved by use of physical violence, whether threatened or actual; language; withdrawal of communication and many other methods (which is why it is often difficult to spot). Bullying controls at a very deep level within the individual, who may respond by having their sense of self-worth continually diminished and so feel less and less able to stand up for themselves.

Bullying has many forms, and the following might constitute bullying if there is both intent and loss of self-worth:

name calling

excluding

teasing or winding up

brushing against in a sexual manner

sending texts from another's phone

sarcasm

spoiling work

spitting

biting

preventing others from working

glaring or staring

passing notes or texts

tripping up

pinching

grabbing what you want

demanding

kicking or hitting

'unliking' posts

chanting

damaging property

posting information on social media

refusing to touch others or their things

belittling or degrading

ganging up

stealing

swearing

humiliating

ignoring

exploiting physical weakness

whispering

'dropping them in it'

aggression

sexual harassment

criticising

physical violence

denying choices

gender abuse

inappropriate use of 'publicness'

taking photos without permission

forcing people to join a group

not giving credit

obstructing

mimicking

spreading rumours

racial abuse

verbal intimidation

dares

threats or extortion

frightening

online trolling

undermining

## DISCIPLINE AS A FORM OF BULLYING

Most parents adopt a regime of disciplinary measures/boundaries in order to preserve order at home. This may include set bedtimes, respecting the boundaries of siblings, return times and the age at which they can stay out overnight.

But while discipline is a moderation mechanism to affect the way individuals behave, in some situations the discipline becomes more important than the good order it is trying to promote and an end in itself. This is when the pursuit of discipline can become a much higher level of controlling. Adults are just as prone to do this as young people – the withholding of comfort, food, affection and conversation in order to force acquiescence to a particular issue is the use of discipline as bullying. For example, a wife may refuse to talk to her husband about anything else and withhold all normal communication until there is agreement about a desired loft extension or new car. Similarly, a young person who has been hurt by a friend's behaviour, and then refuses to speak to her, and encourages her friends to do the same, is exerting a disciplinary measure that turns into controlling. In both these instances the resources available (money, time, communication) are being tweaked in order to shape a desired response – and in the process bullying is taking place.

Discipline can also turn into bullying if it is simply too much effort to insist on what is best for everyone because in the process a row would emerge. For example:

- Allowing a teenager to play very loud music in the house because to make a fuss would lead to an enormous row – and even more noise. Everyone is being informed that their rights do not matter in a wider determination to preserve the status quo.
- Allowing a younger sibling to get away with punching his older brothers and sisters simply because he is the

youngest; the older siblings' rights and needs are being ignored in the process.

• Giving in to a teenager who wants something you do not want to agree to because in the process they amass more arguments than you are prepared to fight with. Teenagers know exactly what buttons to press when they want things – and how to manipulate their parents.

Ultimately not everyone's wants and needs are reconcilable; there will be clashes as priorities and moods conflict. A system of discipline and agreed fairness should, however, prevail. For example, a parent's desire to let off steam may conflict with the teenager's right to be spoken to respectfully, but both parties may agree that if the behaviour that prompted an angry response had been avoided, the situation would not have arisen in the first place. On the other hand, a determination to get through the day without a row may mean that unacceptable behaviours are tolerated and long-term unfair patterns set up – which in turn establish difficult precedents for the future.

Parents sometimes struggle to find appropriate sanctions for teenage behaviour, particularly when their teen is taller and stronger than they are. It is important to remember that for a sanction to be effective – i.e. it can act as a deterrent for future misbehaviour – it needs to be established before the rule is broken, not simply applied as punishment or revenge. Parents frequently use the withholding of phones, computers or games as sanctions and are then surprised when either their strategy has no effect – or their young person becomes more uncontrollable than before.

It is important to remember that to a young person communication with their peers may be more important than almost anything. Taking away their means of communication does not simply restrict their ability to chat for a period of time, it excludes them from the most important network they have. When an individual is not participating in their network they may often find themselves the subject of gossip or spiteful comments from their peers, and many young people who engage frequently do so to ensure they don't become the victim of unkind online chatter. To take a young person's phone or computer away from them for a week can introduce fear in them quite beyond anything we can identify with. This may lead to aggression against the parent, rage, violent outbursts where property may be damaged – or even self-harming in some individuals.

In order to maintain fair and effective discipline – discipline which acts to deter rather than punish – it is important to decide in advance with your young person which sanctions will be applied to which actions. In this way they are making a clear choice when they choose to break a boundary that includes the acceptance of the restriction that will follow.

## KEY PRINCIPLES FOR COMBATING BULLYING

### Rights and privileges

A right is something that's inalienable, and applies on a universal rather than an individual basis. Some rights may be culturally specific, but they must apply to all individuals within that culture.

Teenagers are often quick to claim their rights, to cast the things they want to do as their right and to claim it's their right not to do things they do not want to do. Parents may think the same way, particularly if they work long hours to earn the salary that supports their family's lifestyle. But it's important to grasp that one person's rights may impact on someone else's, that compromise is needed, and the insistence on your own rights to the detriment of someone else's may lead to someone else feeling hard done by. For example, a parent's 'right' to peace and quiet at home may mean that their teenagers do not have the 'right' to enjoy their music at the volume they prefer; a parent's 'right' to enjoy gardening may prevent a teenager's 'right' to kick a ball around to let off steam.

In fact, what we think of as rights on a day-to-day basis may just be privileges. If we are trying to discuss with teenagers what their rights are and what are their privileges, it's helpful if we first examine our own attitudes.

## REFLECTION EXERCISE

Which of the following are rights, and which are privileges? Tick either 'R' or 'P' next to each item on the following list, and ask your young person to do the same.

|  | R | P |
| --- | --- | --- |
| • To have a child | | |
| • To have children | | |
| • To choose how your children are educated | | |
| • To own your own home | | |
| • To work | | |
| • Not to work | | |
| • To use your phone whenever you want to | | |
| • To spend time with friends | | |
| • To smoke | | |
| • To be happy | | |
| • To discipline your children as you see fit | | |
| • To vote | | |
| • To live unafraid of harm | | |
| • To divorce | | |
| • To express your sexuality | | |
| • To speak your opinions freely | | |

Now compare your answers. Do you see things in the same way? What are the differences?

In the process of thinking about these issues you can see that grey areas emerge. A young person may consider it their right to smoke if they want to, but how does this impact on the others in the house – or in the car if they choose to smoke in a confined space? Does this conflict with others' rights to clean air? You may think you have a right to say what you like, but this may impact on other people's rights to privacy – or not to have unfair things said about them. And what works in society at large also works in microcosm at family level: there should be respect for everyone's rights, not just those of the earning/contributors, or the eldest of several siblings.

Thinking about the difference between rights and privileges is a good background to thinking about bullying. An understanding of what it is reasonable to stick up for, and what has to be negotiated, and with what energy, helps us to be objective about whether or not bullying is taking place.

## Responsibilities

It's important that young people come to understand that alongside their rights are the rights of their parents and siblings. Having rights comes with the implied responsibility of maintaining those same rights for others too. For example:

- A young child has a right to have enough food to eat to keep healthy. This is generally the responsibility of the parents of that child.
- A teenager has the right to have enough food to eat to keep healthy, and while this is still the responsibility of the parents to provide the food in the fridge and cupboards, it is the young person's responsibility to help with the preparation and management of meals, clearing away and supporting the person who has cooked the meal rather than rubbishing what is provided. To this should be added a long-term responsibility to learn how

to do it themselves so that one day they can function on their own.

- A young child has the right to sleep in a safe place at night. This is generally the responsibility of the parents of that child.
- A teenager has the right to sleep in a safe place at night and while it is the responsibility of the parents to provide a home and a bed, any teenager who is old enough to be out until late has a responsibility to ensure that they lock the door properly if they are the last person in at night, so that everyone already at home is safe.

## Fairness

Young people are very keen on fairness – 'That's so unfair' being a constant cry – but they tend to see fairness as a one-way system; while they expect you to share everything with them, they do not necessarily see themselves responding in kind. You share everything, they don't. Of course there is an imbalance of resources, but time and willingness to help are just as valuable commodities for sharing as money.

Particular accusations of fairness and unfairness tend to arise between siblings, and it is important to explain that there are pros and cons to every position. Elder siblings may resent the freedoms for which they fought hard being handed to their younger siblings without struggle. Younger siblings resent the fact that their elders do everything first, and better – they can never catch up as the elders always run faster, write better and have a special place in their parents' and grandparents' hearts, simply for having arrived first. Elder children may be forced to take responsibility early; younger children may feel that they never fully grow up in the eyes of their families – their nicknames tend to hang around the longest. Gender too plays a strong role in prompting accusations of unfairness; girls are widely encouraged, and from an earlier age, to be more responsible around the home than their brothers. Considerable research shows that parents may begin reinforcing gender stereotypes almost from birth, and that while parents are the most important influences in gender stereotyping (fathers often more than mothers) for the young child, the media and television in particular do a great deal to reinforce and enhance these as the child grows.

## HOW CAN YOU TELL IF IT IS YOUR OWN YOUNG PERSON WHO IS DOING THE BULLYING?

It can be very difficult. There is no set standard of behaviour that will lead you to understand that you own child bullies others – because there are so many ways of bullying (through physical abuse, conversation, the way you laugh, facial expression and so on).

You could, however, watch out for the following:

- How do their friendships work? Do they take it in turns to talk or does your teenager either dominate the friendship or say nothing at all?
- When they are talking to each other in a group and you are able to observe (say in the car), to whom do they defer? Who gets most eye contact?
- Do they switch in and out of friendships very quickly?
- Within a group of friends, do they prefer one exclusive friend and then switch to another, before switching back again?
- What do they say about their friendships? Do they develop hatred for those who have formerly been their friends?
- When you are out together, and you run into some of their friends, how willingly do the friends greet them? Is there immediate eye contact?
- Do they seem to have lots of extra presents on their birthday?

- Do they borrow money and, if so, do they pay it back?
- What does the school say? While every parent may be inclined to defend their young person, the school sees them in a different context, and on a daily basis.
- Is their sharp 'wit' often directed at others? Or do they unkindly gossip about friends or peers?
- Do they often begin statements with 'I'm only saying, but . . .' or 'I'm not being mean/racist/homophobic etc., but . . .'? This usually means they are (at least some of the time) being exactly those things.

## HELPING YOUNG PEOPLE TO STAY CLEAR OF BULLYING

The profile of a young person who is neither bullied nor bullies others may include:

- Able to communicate and express their own sense experiences and feelings
- Considerate of the feelings of others
- Developing a moral sense
- In contact with own sense experiences
- Accepts and understands cause and effect: knows that their actions have consequences for others
- Willing and able to get help and assistance
- Feels accepted and valued
- Understands that appropriate behaviour differs in different contexts
- Able to be assertive
- Has high, good self-esteem
- Able to empathise
- Able to command attention
- Has a sense of their own rights

This can provide us with a set of attributes and skills we can help young people to develop in order to avoid rather than just manage bullying.

---

### 5 top tips for parents for combating bullying

1   **Encourage them to talk about their feelings.** By all means listen to the negative, but give greater emphasis to the positive; encourage them to differentiate between important and unimportant 'negative' news. Talk to them about how you feel to encourage and develop their emotional vocabulary and try to give expression to a wider range than just angry and happy.

2   **Help them to develop their empathy skills.** Ask them to guess how other people are feeling, for example when you see a child crying in the supermarket you could ask: 'How do you think he is feeling? What do you think may be the reason for this?' Encourage them to see more than the obvious reactions – the crying child is not just 'upset', they might be frightened, angry, disappointed, frustrated or just plain tired. Teach them kindness and 'do as you would be done by'.

3   **Help them to develop their interpersonal skills.** Let them know that we all have rights. Encourage them to talk to you by listening without criticism or explanation. Help them to be clear – play word-based description games with them. Reflect with them on friendships, good and not so good, and encourage them to choose friends for themselves. Give time for reflection about their feelings and the things that they and others do.

4   **Help them develop self-esteem.** Let them know that they are valued, even when they have behaved unacceptably. Let them know that their company is interesting and pleasurable.

Help them to identify the things that need to change – rather than just telling them; at the same time help them reflect on their own changing capabilities and skills. Give them time, support and attention.

5 **Help them to get help when they need it.** Encourage them to ask for the things they need and don't just do it all for them. If a school matter arises, ask them if they want you to see the teacher; don't just do it unless it is serious. If there are messages for the school/teacher, let them give them. Give them guidelines about what should and what shouldn't be 'told'. Encourage them to share feelings and other news with other trusted adults.

## WHAT TO DO IF YOUR YOUNG PERSON TELLS YOU THAT THEY ARE BEING BULLIED AT SCHOOL

- Stay calm, even if your heart is racing
- No matter what the circumstances, in the first instance let them know that they did not deserve it
- Listen and respond to their feelings even if the event was small
- Later, discuss future strategies together: next time . . . ; tomorrow . . .
- The strategy should be realistic, non-bullying and within their capabilities
- Tell the school (with the child's permission)
- Talk about it again and again until they no longer wish to, but don't make a fuss of them every time
- If the bullying continues, make an appointment (rather than just rushing in) to see the head of year to discuss a strategy for ending it
- Make it clear to your young person that you would like to hear of any further situations, but don't ask them every

day whether or not they had a run in with the bullying individuals (which may raise their anxiety and awareness levels). Let them tell you if and when they want

If your young person frequently reports bullying by different people, the above list will help but also consider the additional skills they may need to develop. Think too about your responses – do you make them feel better when they report a problem than when they report a pleasant event? With their consent, talk to their form teacher or head of year about strategies the whole class/school could follow.

## QUESTIONS & ANSWERS

Q: My son repeatedly reports that he is being bullied at school. What should I do?

A: The first thing is to find out what he means by being bullied. Is he being physically abused or called names? Teenagers are quick to use the word bullying, but are not always clear about whether or not there is intention to hurt.

It's important to understand that this bullying is your son's problem, rather than yours. And although you may find it distressing to see him being bullied, you have to teach him strategies to cope with it and deflect it, rather than assuming responsibility for dealing with it yourself.

If he is able to identify why he is being singled out, then discuss with him whether it is behaviour that can be changed. Are there strategies he could pursue to avoid the bullies (take a different bus; hang out with different people at lunchtime; walk away rather than stand and take abuse, or react to it; talk to a teacher he trusts about what is going on)? The golden rule here is ask, don't tell – telling him how to proceed may make him feel even more disempowered; he needs to develop strategies that are manageable for him.

Help him to be more assertive: rather than crying or shouting something back, could he say 'Don't say that to me'; 'That hurts'; or 'Would you like to be called things like that?' Assertive (and sporty) kids get bullied less often. Remind him that the bullies are looking for a reaction and if they cease to get the response they are looking for, they go somewhere else to find it.

Q: My daughter is being bullied at school by the daughter of one of our neighbours. Should I tell her parents of the problem?

A: Unless you can be sure how the parents of the bully will react to being told of the problem, think carefully before you say anything. It's very hard to tell someone else that their child is causing problems – the first response of many parents will be to deny there is a problem without further investigation.

You need to be sure that your daughter is telling you the complete story: many young people with a reputation as bullies at school present themselves at home as being bullied by their peers. You also need to bear in mind whether the child accused will be met with harsh retribution at home if they are accused of bullying. The situation could also rebound on your child: 'grassing' may be a bigger sin among her peer group than bullying.

Talk to your child about what she wants to do. Discuss strategies, give support and step in only if she asks you to. Even then, get involved through negotiated boundaries, rather than your child's intended outcomes (e.g. agree you will talk to her teacher, rather than make everything all right for her). If you interfere in the situation without agreeing with her beforehand, you may reinforce her feelings of powerlessness.

Q: My son is being bullied about something both in and out of school. Three of his former friends are targeting our house, throwing eggs at it and sticking notes addressed to him through our front door. He is really upset but cannot bring himself to tell his teachers at school. Should we do it for him?

A: Most bullying takes place away from parental view, so for the three former friends to be as bold in their behaviour as they are might mean they have information about your son that he will go to any lengths to prevent them repeating. Knowledge is power, and for as long as he is frightened of them telling what they know, he will remain bullied.

Can you ask him if this is the case? If he cannot tell you, can you encourage him to talk to someone else about what it is he is afraid of? You could also encourage him by telling him that there is nothing that you could be told about him that would make you stop loving him, or talk about prominent cases in the media if you suspect – even marginally – that one might be relevant to him.

Q: My son seems to be a natural victim. He doesn't stick up for himself at home and I worry he will be further picked on at school. How can I help him?

A: It's often the case that many of those who are bullied at school tend to get picked on at home; in other words they perpetuate the role they adopt at home, providing a payback for the bully in both places.

You say he doesn't stick up for himself at home. Do you mean that others at home are bullying him, perhaps his father or siblings – or even you? While encouraging him to stand up to his family and helping him develop the skills to do so will undoubtedly make the atmosphere at home much tenser in the short term, in the long term you will be helping him formulate strategies to use at school too. And just as at school if his mother tackles issues for him it will make the situation worse, the same works at home, so encourage him to deal with it himself rather than let you fight his battles for him. Think whether or not you are taking too many decisions on his behalf, hindering him making his own choices and thus growing as an independent person.

It is important to note too that telling a young person that they are not being assertive enough or sticking up for themselves enough may well make them feel criticised and more inadequate. It may not be bullying but it may feel like it!

Family meetings would help increase his confidence (see Appendix 1, pp. 333–6), as would the conflict resolution strategy (see pp. 104–5). Similarly, help him to spot the positives in situations rather than just the negatives, so rather than adopting an attitude of 'Oh no, here it comes again' when someone behaves in a bullying way towards him, he can react more assertively and not assume he deserves to be treated this way.

You will be least help to him if you head off to see his school without discussing with him what is going on first. Parents who are constantly up at school complaining tend to be looking at the problem as someone else's rather than one that involves them too. There is much you can do to support your young person yourself rather than relying on school alone to sort things out.

Q: My daughter's school has regular problems of bullying. Having accepted that there is a problem, why can't the school just stop it?

A: It is much harder than you think to stop bullying in a school, although every state school is required to have formal policies on rooting out and preventing bullying. Identifying that it is going on is only a first stage.

If you come down hard on the bully, you may find that things get worse for those who reported it; the bullying goes deeper and thereafter tends to be done in less obvious ways. Schools regularly call in parents to discuss a situation of bullying and what often happens is that the two parties both protest that their young person is the innocent party. Moreover, young people who bully at school have often been victims of the same thing at home; robust behaviour that they have learnt at home is then practised on someone else at school.

Good schools have several options available for pupils who are experiencing problems with peers. For example they may offer confidential reporting systems; a peer mediation service; confidential counsellors, including peer counsellors; and a programme of Personal, Social and Health Education (PSHE) that explores bullying in the curriculum at several ages and stages and includes a strong emphasis on the development of interpersonal skills.

You could also ask yourself whether the selection policy for your particular school encourages bullying. Those who enter highly selective schools, which measure young people on very specific criteria, may produce bullying behaviour towards those who do not sit in the top third of the population. Most schools acquire a reputation for being a particular kind of organisation, and those who do not fit (or just about fit) the mould can feel bullied. Is this the situation at your daughter's school?

Q: My eldest son bullies his siblings. How can I make him stop?

A: You can't make him do anything. What you can do is look at the situation with both the bully and bullied and see if you can encourage them to work on the relationship. Encourage the younger children to say how they feel when bullied by their brother or to try out similar behaviour on him to see how it feels to him to be on the receiving end (in a managed way).

You can also look at the atmosphere at home and think whether you are colluding with your eldest son by encouraging your younger children to give in rather than stand up for themselves.

Look, too, at the needs of your eldest son – happy, well-adjusted children do not bully. Does his self-esteem rely on putting his siblings down? Does he feel you like them more than him? Does he feel you always make allowances for their poor behaviour because they are younger? If you give him more credit for other aspects of his life, will he no longer need the power rush that comes from bullying his siblings?

Can you help them establish guidelines for the future?

- You will not call me by my family nickname in front of my friends.
- You will not go into my room without permission or when I am not there.
- You will not coerce me into doing things I don't want to do.
- I will leave my door closed if I don't want to be disturbed.

All parties should agree to stick to these, and privileges should be withdrawn if the terms are broken. You can also help keep a happy atmosphere at home by emphasising harmony rather than conflict. Encourage them to say positive things about each other by leading in this yourself; negative thinking is caught rather than spontaneously present in most people.

If the situation is very serious and you are worried about physical harming or coercion, you need to take radical steps to prevent the situation arising, for example by allowing your children to have locks on their doors, not leaving them in the house on their own together or giving the child who is being bullied an 'attack' alarm so they can call for help if physically threatened.

Q: My daughter is involved with three female 'friends' who are very spiteful and constantly comment negatively on other girls in the class. She feels she needs to make similar comments in order to remain with them. I feel she is being bullied – how can I help her get out of this situation?

**A:** The first thing to establish is whether she wants to get out of this situation. You have made it clear how you feel about these girls, so is she choosing these friends as an independence statement to separate herself from you – or is she genuinely unhappy about the way they are behaving?

Girls are often accused of being spiteful, whereas experimenting with emotions is what they do – and it is what in the long term enables them to grow into people with empathy. You could ask her:

- How would you feel if you heard others talking about you in this way?
- How do you feel when you say unpleasant things?
- What does friendship with these three say about you as a person?
- Is this a friendship you really want?
- How do you feel about people thinking that you are just like them and have nothing good to say about anyone?
- Even if you don't support what they say, by being with them are you seen as supporting it?
- How will potential new friends regard you while you are so close to this group?

It's far better for her to say that she does not feel comfortable than for you to say it for her. If you are too judgemental it will not feel like her decision to withdraw and she may either resist or feel pushed into it. Similarly, lying for her to get her out of things she does not want to do with these friends prevents her from taking responsibility and may lead to accusations of having her parents fight her battles for her, which is not very good for her morale or her position with her 'friends'.

If she does want to extricate herself, can you help her make links with other people outside school, in order to then have the confidence to make new relationships within school? Ebbs and flows of friendships are possible and although the sudden withdrawal from their circle would be very difficult, over time she might be able to develop a more subtle exit strategy.

**Q:** I am convinced that my son is being bullied by a teacher at school. What should I do?

**A:** If your young person is being bullied by a teacher – and this does happen – then before you do anything, explore the situation with him. Could it actually be the other way around – is it possible that your son has spotted a weak character and, rather than being bullied, he is in fact bullying the teacher, putting them in situations they find very difficult and then manipulating them?

Explore with your son what particular behaviour prompts the bullying, and once identified, encourage him not to repeat it. So, if he has a tendency to answer back, encourage him to hold his tongue; if it is silence that enrages the teacher, encourage him to answer questions more often.

If you are convinced that there really is a serious problem, then the most important thing to do is to encourage your son to log the situation. He should keep track of the instances that he believes constitute bullying. And he should get witnesses; keep a record of who else was there when the bullying occurred and ask them to support him if he makes a complaint. The next stage is to consult someone within the school that they trust: maybe a school counsellor, maybe a teacher, maybe a teaching assistant – someone who is in a position of authority within the school. Your son will probably find it difficult to report a bullying teacher, and the system will probably at first support the teacher over your son – it being inevitable that teachers get complained about. But the bottom line is that if a teacher is systematically bullying, the situation will not get better unless it is tackled.

**Q:** A former friend of my daughter's recently visited the head of year and 'outed' a group of six girls (one of whom was our daughter) as having bullied her. The girl was in floods of tears and the teacher quite predictably took her side. The school took disciplinary action against all six, however much they were involved, and our daughter has been branded a bully. She assures us that her role was minimal; she was with the others but took no part in what was said – although she did allow her phone to be used to make calls to the girl. We feel it is most unfair that our daughter has been punished.

**A:** You have presumably only heard one side of the story. Even if your daughter's role was minimal, she was still evidently colluding in the bullying and the fact that it was her phone that was used shows that her involvement was active rather than accidental. If it was your daughter who had gone to the head of year rather than another girl, would you have concluded that she was brave rather than mischievous?

We are judged in life, not just at school, by the company we keep, and your daughter must take responsibility for the friends she chooses to make – and keep. And if you carry on protesting her innocence when something has clearly gone on, and you do not know the full story, you will encourage her to conclude that your love for her blinds you to her faults – and to play on this in future.

**Q:** Our school places a lot of emphasis on bullying policies but rather than anticipating problems, I would rather they encouraged the young people to get on with each other. I feel concentration on negative behaviour encourages its spread.

**A:** I agree. Schools today measure performance in all sorts of ways, but there is not enough emphasis on how to enjoy life, how to develop resilience so that you can keep your morale up when things do not go so well and how to be happy.

Sometimes just simply pointing out good feelings to a young person can be enough to encourage them to take pleasure in them in future.

**Q:** There's a gang of adolescents on our estate that goes around terrorising people after dark. My son is being drawn into this gang, although I am sure he does not want to be.

**A:** One problem with anti-social behaviour is that we tend to assume someone else's kids are involved. If the kids are local it's our problem, and if our own kids are involved it's more sensible to accept the situation and try to deal with it than to deny it.

So the first question to ask is how do you know he doesn't want to be part of the gang? If you are sure, try grounding him – he'll be pleased to have an excuse to stay in. If this is a problem, he needs to be taken out of the sphere of these people. Try to get him into clubs, sports or groups, theatre or cinema – whatever he will do or try.

If he is resistant to staying at home, perhaps he is not as unwilling to join the group as you believe. If he is choosing to be with the group then he needs to understand the consequences, both for himself and for the victims of this behaviour. Take him round to meet the neighbours and get them to tell him how they feel. He needs to understand that the only people who think gangs are cool are those who are in them.

## CHAPTER 9

# 'Why didn't you remind me?' Self-organisation, self-discipline, dealing with exams and deadlines

Issues of self-organisation (or rather the lack of it) are some of the most familiar battlegrounds for parents and their teenagers. How do you persuade young people to get up in the mornings, to think ahead, or to appreciate that tidying their rooms is their concern rather than just further evidence of a despotic parent?

The issue seems to crystallise around gender: the parents of boys often seem much more desperate than those of girls. While there are many exceptions to the rule, in general girls have been given far more practice in organising themselves, from a far earlier age.

There is an expectation in many families that daughters will help with domestic chores much earlier than their brothers. Parents (and particularly mothers) will often bewail their sons' complete inability to do anything for themselves, but the bottom line is that if they have got used to being looked after without conditions, why would they bother to learn to do it for themselves? If someone is cooking food you like, when you like it, doing your washing and ironing, pushing the vacuum cleaner around your room every now and again, and doing this on a regular basis (albeit with complaint), what would be the reason for taking over from them? This position is sometimes reinforced by the role taken by a male parental partner. If young people see their father not required to help with the domestic arrangements, they will conclude – whether consciously or subconsciously – that this is the natural order of things. And the longer the situation has gone on, the harder it will be to make changes.

You need to promote an understanding that with increased privileges come increased expectations. So if your young person wants increased pocket money, or a clothing allowance for the first time, it is reasonable to negotiate this on the basis of an increased contribution to the overall household. For example, they could offer to mow the lawn or clean the car, to meet their younger siblings from school or help with basic housework – all on a regular, and reliable, basis.

'I have found that when my teenagers have cleaned something, they are far stricter with their siblings about the need to keep it tidy in future than if I do it. They also like their efforts noticed!' **Mother**

It is important to stress that this is not about paying them to do the chore, but more about having increased expectations of them as they mature. If they have been required to do very little up to now they will probably resist this suggestion – perhaps implying that it is an intolerable burden. But it is not unreasonable that as a young person requires further resources, their responsibilities should increase too – and this may even be part of their increasing development. There is evidence from studies in the US that requiring greater investment in the shared home gives young people a greater sense of connection. It also helps them allocate – and hence learn to prioritise – their time. The other side of this is that if they are not ready to take on a greater contribution to the family home, they are not ready for the associated greater privileges. Bear in mind, too, that it is often up to the mother to make changes in this area of parenting; existing arrangements may suit the father very well!

## TEACHING SELF-ORGANISATION

The bottom line with self-organisation is that it needs to be taught: no one organises themselves naturally. Adults have often got so used to being organised that it can be hard to remember that it's a skill that has to be learnt.

With small children it can be as simple as encouraging them to think things through: what will I need today? With teenagers, whose lives can be much more complicated, more developed self-organisational props may be needed.

---

### 6 top tips to teach self-organisation

1 **Put up a board in the kitchen** or hall on which they write down all their commitments.

2 **Most schools give out homework diaries and ask the parents to sign them in the early years of secondary school.** This is a very valuable habit to acquire, so encourage them to write down everything they need to remember and to update it when things change.

3 **Alternatively, buy them an engagement diary or online planner and encourage them to keep it up to date.** Online diary tools can be particularly useful as they issue reminders.

4 **Keep a family diary** and an accompanying policy that no event/commitment/requirement for a lift is considered to exist until it has been first negotiated by mouth with the provider and then noted in the book.

5 **If they forget something they need, avoid running into school with it.** The lesson of how it felt to have forgotten

something important is much easier to remember than how you were eased out of the difficulty by an obliging parent.

6 **Have regular whole family diary checks** where you run through everyone's commitments in a shared space. The noting of priorities in this way can be both an important way of finding out what is coming up – and ensuring that messages about commitments have been fully heard by all.

'One teacher I know keeps a pair of lilac trainers in her office. Anyone who forgets their footwear is required to wear them. They are so vile that few forget!' **Gill**

## HOW TO DECIDE THE ORDER IN WHICH TO DO THINGS

This staged plan was recommended to me by a good friend, who is also one of the best-organised and most creative people I know:

1 At a time you feel comfortable with (maybe last thing at night, maybe first thing in the morning, whatever you prefer), make a list of everything that needs doing in your life at the moment. You should include all kinds of things: personal, professional, mundane and important.

2 Using a highlighter pen, highlight everything that needs doing the next day. You may find that of your long list, only five or six things really need to be done that day.

3 Put numbers against them showing what order you will tackle them in.

4 Tick them off as you do them.

5 Now think about what to do with the remainder of your day. You could tackle something else on the list, or you

could do something that will give your brain a rest and shed new light on the remaining tasks.

6  If you have lots of time, arrange something around which to construct your day; this ensures you use your time, rather than waste it.

A more sophisticated form of prioritising is to become aware of your own body rhythms and to work to maximum effect around these times. For example, some of us work better at night, some in the morning; and there are no moral absolutes associated with these times. Contrary to popular opinion, last-minute revision is often very productive and constantly working on very tight turnaround times is not necessarily the sign of a degenerate character, just someone who finds risk stimulating. We are all individuals.

It's also a good idea to encourage young people to recognise the difference between getting something done and getting it done properly. For example, a piece of work that should take 3 hours but is quickly rushed through in an hour may be adequate but, if given more time, and done to a higher standard, may give far more satisfaction. On the other hand, allocating 7 hours may mean the ideas lose focus and too much irrelevant additional information is included. Learning to match effort to desired outcome is a valuable life skill.

'If I have something important to do, I work back from the time it has to be ready and then establish whether or not I have time for a cup of coffee before I start. My partner does the same thing, but starts work immediately, planning to reward herself with the coffee once she has finished. Two routes to the same end, but neither of us would feel comfortable with each other's. There are signs our teenage son favours my approach, but I am keeping quiet!' **Father**

## SELF-DISCIPLINE

If you are self-disciplined you understand that on occasion you will be required to choose to do things that you don't particularly want to do in order to achieve a greater long-term goal. For example, young people need self-discipline to do their homework or revise for their exams, when they would rather be out with their friends or watching television.

Again, this is behaviour that is learnt rather than innate, and reinforcing good practice is the best way of encouraging them along this path. Encourage your young people to identify the feelings that go with self-discipline. This can be done by asking questions, for example: 'How does it feel to walk into an exam when you know you have done enough revision?'; 'How does it feel to know that you have done your homework – and so that if you do get picked on to provide the answer, you have already got something to say?'

You could also discuss your own organisational habits (and lapses) with them. For example: 'I make lists of what I have to do during the day because I so enjoy striking things off'; 'Finally doing something you have been putting off for ages gives you such a good feeling of satisfaction.'

When things go badly, help them to own the situation and take responsibility for changing their priorities in future: 'It's really good that you've recognised that getting started on your GCSE coursework earlier would have made your life a lot easier in the last couple of days; it shows maturity. Perhaps for the next piece we should help you to draw up a schedule and think about the order in which you do things.'

For particularly important events such as school or formal exams, or projects they are dreading, it's a good idea to help them put a schedule together. Help them to make and chart their progress by:

- Allocating realistic times to revision and putting the whole lot on a wall chart or planner.
- Dividing subjects into bite-sized chunks so they don't feel daunted by what they have to do in any one day, and so their brains are stimulated rather than overwhelmed. So rather than sticking with just one subject for a whole evening, encourage them to change at regular intervals.
- Rewarding themselves with regular treats, such as a cup of coffee at intervals, an evening off every now and again.
- Providing plenty of water to drink and healthy snacks.
- Using highlighter pens so they can see what progress they have made.
- Developing a system for ticking off at a certain stage of progress, e.g. a pencil tick means it's been done once, a line through it means it's finished.
- Pinning a list of what still needs doing in a prominent place and encouraging the whole family to comment positively on progress.
- Reinforcing their efforts, however basic: 'Even though you are tired tonight, if you do half-an-hour on this new subject before you finish for the evening, it won't feel so daunting when you come back to it tomorrow.'
- If they berate themselves for what they haven't done, point out to them that they always have a choice! Always encourage them to be honest with themselves, even if they can't discuss the subject in full with you: 'I don't need to see your revision plan – it's for you, to help you see how far you have got – but do try to be realistic, and not optimistic, about how you fill it in.'

## HOW TO GET THROUGH THE
## START OF THE DAY

First thing in the day, a lack of self-organisation in teenagers can induce immense frustration in parents. So if you have a young person who will not get up when you call him, or takes an age to get out of the house, the following may help.

Let's start with the ownership of this problem – whose problem is this? It's vital to understand that it is primarily your young person's and not yours.

A young person's ability to get up in the morning seems to get worse as they get older; you may have less trouble getting a 10-year-old to school on time than a 14-year-old. But arriving punctually at school is a contract between him and the school. You should support this, but not take the responsibility away from him. Supporting him could include:

- Altering your waking-up routine as they get older, so whereas you would call them a couple of times when they were 10, as they get older give just one call and move the responsibility on to them. Try to avoid chasing or shouting; this is really hard to start with but gets easier with practice!
- Buying them (or better still, allowing them to choose) a reliable alarm clock. If this does not work, offer a second alarm clock to be placed on the other side of their bedroom.
- Encouraging your young person to let you know when there is something particularly important with which he needs some help in, e.g. 'Please wake me up at 7 on Monday as I have my first GCSE that day.'
- Encouraging them to plan their journey, working back from the time by which they must be at school. Encourage them to chart how long it takes to travel there, factoring in the possible delays in public transport, and then leave it to them to get there on time.

- Allowing them to make alterations to the plan as long as they assume responsibility to match. For example, even though you think they should leave at 8, if they left at 8.10 and walked faster, they could perhaps still get to school on time. Just because you choose not to be in a rush, they may not feel the same way.

Breakfast is another vexed issue. By the time a teenager, already running late, gets downstairs, there may be little opportunity for them to eat anything, and perhaps you don't like them going out on an empty stomach.

Again, this is their choice, not yours. Obviously the extent of your influence over whether or not they eat breakfast will depend on how old your young person is, but bear in mind that lots of adults prefer not to eat in the mornings.

If this really matters to you, you could offer a compromise, perhaps a form of food that they can take with them and eat on the bus (say fruit, pure fruit juice and a cereal bar), but bear in mind that once you have offered this, they will not be inclined to get up for breakfast ever again.

At exam time, you may want to be more lenient, and perhaps give them a small pack of healthy foods to take with them – either to eat in the morning as they travel, or in the interval between exams. You may decide to provide food rather than give them money, because at least in that way you can be sure they are eating something that will give energy rather than just fast-food fat, sugar and salt.

'There was a bloke in my first year at university who was put in self-catering accommodation, never having had to look after himself before. He therefore ate what he liked, and existed on a diet of fish and chips, cans of cola and chocolate eggs. Half-way through the second term he did not feel very well. The doctors finally diagnosed scurvy – a disease that is almost unknown in the developed world. One segment of orange a day (or the equivalent) would have prevented it!' **Father**

## EXAM STRESS

Whatever stress behaviour your young person usually exhibits, it will be worse when they are under exam pressure at school. If they tend to lose their temper, then they are more likely to do so now, and will pick fights with the rest of the family at the slightest provocation. The same goes for the child who retreats into silence when under pressure; they may be even more uncommunicative now. Whether they are increasingly aggressive or withdrawn, they are probably not able to recognise why they are behaving that way. Young people find it difficult to say why they are in particular moods; they just *are* feeling bad.

Sometimes the strains can be revealed in more difficult behaviour: shoplifting; suddenly starting to stay out all night; experimentation with drugs or alcohol; vandalism or graffiti. Girls tend to become much more tearful and this may escalate into self-harm, such as drinking too much, developing a food disorder (vomiting can be an effective method of releasing internal pressure), indulging in promiscuous behaviour or cutting themselves.

The symptoms of these more difficult behaviours may appear for the first time when exam pressure looms, or just get worse.

### How to help them cope

It's a good idea to talk with your young person pre-revision about their hopes and aspirations, making sure they have considered their options should they not get the desired grades. They may think you are being negative by asking, but let them know that what you want is for them to have considered all the options. It is important that they see life as going forward, no matter what.

Involve the whole family in helping the exam candidate to cope. Family de-stressing can really help. For example, you could take a walk together, play two- or three-a-side football in the garden, or organise bat-and-ball games during breaks in revision (hitting things safely is a great de-stressor). Along the same lines, discuss family strategies for helping to provide a supportive atmosphere. These could include putting away the games console, restricting the time that the television is on and encouraging the whole family to eat healthily.

Once the revision period has started, encourage the exam candidate to leave their room for regular breaks (at least half-an-hour every two hours) by making a drink or snack and sitting with them for a few minutes. Try to listen to them rather than firing questions at them or chatting. If they don't want to talk, then sit together in silence.

If they behave inappropriately (bully their siblings or shout at you), deal only with the issue and not the behaviour until they have calmed down. Keep calm yourself. When they are calmer (maybe in the morning) talk to them about their behaviour without making excuses. For example: 'I know you are working really hard at the moment, but . . .' Remind them that they are responsible for their behaviour choices no matter what the circumstances. Explain why their behaviour is unacceptable. Outline what would be acceptable: 'It is not acceptable for you to swear at me. I will accept that you are angry about something if you talk to me reasonably but it is not acceptable for you to swear at me at any time.' Make sure they have understood, ask for an apology if it is needed and then let go of the incident and offer support or compassion for their situation: 'I know you are working really hard and I expect you feel anxious. Is there anything I could do to help you? Perhaps I could . . .' This is a 'boundaries apology talk', in other words setting boundaries for future behaviour.

---

4 top tips to help you and other siblings cope
with difficult behaviour from stressed teenagers

1  **Count** to ten before replying
2  **Withdraw** to another room
3  **Criticise** the behaviour, not the young person
4  **Discuss** with the young person why the situation arose once
   the heat has gone out of the situation

---

## Strategies for avoiding exam or work schedule panic

- Create the right space for working, perhaps in a different room, so that books can be left out undisturbed away from the space in which the exam candidate relaxes or sleeps. If your home does not permit this, offer a new and uncluttered surface on which to work, for example a new table top – with good light.
- Wherever they work, respect their privacy (everyone should knock on the door before they enter, other siblings included).
- Discuss with other family members how to support the candidate. You may find younger siblings very supportive if they are involved – they will be taking notes for when it is their turn to study!
- Help them organise themselves to make a revision plan.
- Ask someone else studying for the same exam into your home who could work with your young person.
- Bring in an external tutor (it's often easier to work with someone else rather than your own parent).
- Use the revision facilities offered by the school on the premises (often in the school library).

- Explore the availability of online revision tools, which can be very useful.
- Concentrate on what they do know rather than what they don't. For example, encourage them to use what is in their head and apply it, e.g. answering a question from memory makes them aware that they have more inside their head than they realise.

If panic really sets in, then try to take the young person away from the situation in which the emotion arose. Try a weekend, day or even just a few hours away; attempt to break the cycle of staring at a desk. Once you have made the break, don't talk straight away, silence is fine. Then begin to ask open-ended questions. An open-ended question is one that does not demand a one-word answer. For example, try asking 'How do you feel about the exams?' rather than 'Are you OK?'

Before starting to talk make it clear that you should try to be honest with one another. Also, beware of repeating your own history. What you did when you were at school is not relevant now – particularly if your young person knows that you did well and they are frightened of not living up to the standards you set. If things seem to be getting out of hand ask yourself why it matters to them so much. If their health is suffering, either physically or mentally, talk to your doctor.

## ESTABLISHING GOOD WORK HABITS EVEN WHEN YOU ARE NOT AT HOME

Today most parents work. This tends to mean that once the children are past the legal age for requiring child-care, most arrive back to an empty home. When exams loom how can you make sure they are revising rather than watching TV?

If a child no longer needs round-the-clock supervision, that does not mean he no longer needs parenting. You could consider employing help – perhaps a neighbour or au pair

– to be at home when the young person arrives back and offer toast and support. Similarly, discuss the daily rituals that help them relax and work effectively: for example, watching television for an hour when they get home. Discuss when the best time to get started is, and how to plan the evening: 'If we eat at 7 p.m. and your school advises that you need to get 3 hours' work done a night, when is that best slotted in?' You could also ring from work when they have been home for about half-an-hour and make a point of chatting rather than just checking they are there; how did the day go?

## QUESTIONS & ANSWERS

**Q:** My teenagers have to be at school by 8.30 a.m. If they are late they get a mark against their name and after three black marks they are excluded for a week. They trade on the fact that they know I don't want them to be excluded and invariably ask me for a lift, usually at the last minute. This makes me late for work.

**A:** They have got you sussed! They are holding you to ransom, but you are allowing it. To get out of this situation, ask them to plan their journeys ahead, and insist that in future you will not provide lifts. Making an announcement of future intentions is one thing, sticking to it is another. You need to be clear now about the special circumstances that are bound to arise – young people are very good at negotiating when their interests are affected.

So, what will you do if it is raining? Will you offer them a lift or still insist that they get there under their own steam? What about days when they have heavy sports bags and equipment to carry? What about when they have been off sick – will you offer them a lift the day they return? What if they have left their coat at school the night before? What if they say they are frightened by the other kids on the bus or find walking in the dark scares them?

Most of the above can be resolved with a little planning. A route that is threatening in the dark should be avoided, even if the alternative is slightly longer. If there is a very unattractive crowd on a particular bus, suggest your young person takes an earlier one, travels with someone or sits right at the front of the bus. Travelling to school without a coat may be a much better way of reminding them to take it in future than making things easy and providing a lift. Sports bags can be left in a locker at school – in fact, thinking carefully about what really needs to be brought home from school and what does not is an important part of learning self-organisation.

**Q:** I have tried insisting that my teenagers do their own ironing. But they do it so badly and I feel that sending them out looking a mess reflects on me rather than them. I don't want a young person of mine going out looking like that.

**A:** You can't have it all your own way. Either you are responsible for how they look or they are – you can't make them responsible but set your own standards.

At the moment it seems you care more than they do, and this is probably fuelling their resistance to your standards, but if you do the ironing for them, they have no incentive to look after themselves at all. When they start to get interested in going out in a crowd of self-conscious young people – all of whom take an intimate interest in how everyone else looks – their involvement in the process of how they look often increases dramatically. Then you may find that you can't get access to the washing machine or iron because they are monopolising it!

**Q:** My young people leave getting ready for school until the very last minute so I end up scrambling to find what is missing.

**A:** Again, responsibility needs to be assumed by them, and this will only be possible once you make it clear that you will not provide a fall-back system as you are doing at the moment. Encourage them to think the night before about what they will need for the following day. To help with this, suggest they pin a copy of both their school timetable and their homework timetable on the inside of their locker door and their bedroom door, and that they check at both ends, thinking through what they will need at home/at school each day. Encourage them to prioritise; to think about the order in which they do things. For example, homework that is due the following day needs to be tackled before homework due in the middle of next week. Involve childminders, older siblings and anyone else involved in any arrangements so that they are understood by all.

**Q:** My daughter's bedroom is an absolute tip. How can I encourage her to keep it in better order? She says it is none of my business how she keeps her room and that if I don't like it I should not go in there.

**A:** It is your daughter's space but as this is part of your home, you need to agree the standards by which it will be maintained. Once she has left home, and has independent accommodation, she will have a complete right to keep it how she wishes. For now, you need to agree a workable strategy at home.

Given the scale of some of the problems parents worry about with teenagers (drink, drugs, pregnancy) the state of their bedrooms may seem a low priority, but the fact is that this often confronts you on a daily basis and parental annoyance can get out of proportion.

A tidy approach to life is best achieved if you start early. Show her how to do it by doing it with her at first – if you do it for her she will never learn to put things away.

Provide her with enough storage space to put her things away. Ensure the storage space is of the right size so things fit neatly – bookshelves for books, a rack for CDs, a shoe holder for putting pairs of shoes in and plastic boxes for knick-knacks. Buy a simple labelling machine to show what goes where. Let her decide on all the storage places and make the matching labels.

Encourage her to have regular clear-outs of items that she does not wear or that no longer fit her. Let her decide where these items should go – who they should be given to or which charity shop should benefit. Suggest she cleans and tidies her room once a week and inspect her efforts. Give her a deadline for this – for example, every Sunday evening, and agree a penalty for not cooperating. For example, once a week, at a prearranged time, anything still on the floor will be picked up by you and put in a bin liner – and will then be out of use for two weeks.

Basic hygiene is important. Young people should return all crockery taken to their rooms each evening – or not be allowed food in their rooms – and their waste bins must be emptied regularly.

**Q:** I am forever finding out-of-date notes from school about trips and so on. I then have to try to persuade the school to allow my son to be included in whatever is on offer. How can I help him to be more organised?

**A:** First by not bailing him out each time he forgets to pass on something important. The memory of missing out on something will live in his mind far longer than the repeated instances of you sorting it out for him.

Set up a system for dealing with school notes, say an envelope on the kitchen wall into which everyone must put things that must be dealt with, including bills and statements. Establish a regular time at which you will go through this, say once a week. This not only ensures his paperwork is dealt with, it also provides him with a valuable lesson in self-organisation as you show him a strategy in action.

Encourage your son to go through his bag on a regular basis, including turning it upside down! School bags often have lots of zip pockets and delving inside every one can reveal all sorts of hidden essentials. Washing the bag (most go into the washing machine without adverse effects) is another useful way of ensuring nothing gets missed.

**Q:** My daughter is late for everything. How can I encourage her to be more punctual?

**A:** Being on time can be difficult for teenagers if they are relying on public transport. If they are repeatedly late for an important time (e.g. arrival at school) and travelling on public transport, you may need to suggest that they review their timings. For example, if their usual bus is late one time in 20, they may decide to stick to their arrangement and be late very occasionally – but be on time most of the time. If their scheduled bus is invariably late, they need to consider taking an earlier bus.

By all means help them devise strategies to be on time, but the ownership of the problem must be theirs not yours. Learning to balance effort and consequences is an important part of growing up that in the long run will help them to both plan and prioritise more effectively.

If there are several clashing deadlines for schoolwork, the best strategy is for them to try to negotiate additional time as early as possible. Most teachers will be impressed by pupils who have planned ahead and noticed clashing deadlines, particularly if they attempt to do something about it rather than panic at the last minute.

Being on time to meet friends and family sends out a positive message – that you are valued and taken seriously. You could discuss how it feels when someone is late to meet them – and how they might choose to behave as a result.

**Q:** Up to now a bright boy, it seems my son couldn't care less about how he does at school any more.

**A:** Just because he appears to be completely switched off from academic achievement, doesn't mean that he really is. Withdrawing effort – or emotional engagement with the whole process – can be a coping strategy. Rather than risk failure, the young person decides not to take part.

He needs to talk to someone, you and your partner if possible, or perhaps a close family friend or doctor (who can advise on additional help). For further contacts see the websites at the end of this book.

**Q:** My daughter accused me recently of living out my dreams through her. I feel this is very unfair.

**A:** It may be so, but lots of young people feel like this. They feel they are being channelled into a re-creation of their parents' school days, irrespective of what they want to do themselves. Pressure from parents can seem unbearable, particularly if they know that their parents did well in exams. They are so worried about failing by comparison that they withdraw effort and do nothing.

**Q:** I left school at 16 and have always felt I missed out. By contrast I am paying for the best possible education for my child. Why is he not more appreciative of the sacrifices I am making for his education?

**A:** Remember that the decision to give him the best was your choice, not his. Depending on whom he mixes with, he may come to see this as not a particularly good investment, particularly if lack of a private education was no barrier to your own achievements. Don't expect gratitude.

Money is very important to the young. It's not a good idea

to put a monetary value on the amount you have spent on a young person's education. If confronted with the total they may conclude it is money they would rather have spent on something else – and hearing this first hand hurts!

**Q:** Our son is approaching GCSEs and is behaving in a horrible manner within the family. We want to support him but don't know how.

**A:** This is a good subject for a family meeting. Get everyone together; talk about how you can all show that you appreciate one of you is going through a testing time, and what you can do to help. Examples could include making a family decision to put away the games console until after the exams. This should be agreed to by everyone and applied to everyone; it's not fair for the exam candidate to hear others enjoying what they cannot. You could also make a plan for how much television will be watched, by whom and when, or decide that a long-planned family treat should be delayed – and rearranged for after the exams are over. You could all agree to try to provide an atmosphere of calm in which studying can take place.

**Q:** I know my teenager needs energy, but he seems to be attracted to completely the wrong sort of foods at the moment, and regularly comes back from school having bought chips or chocolate. What should I provide?

**A:** While the desire for comfort eating is entirely understandable (why else do adults often reach for chocolate when they are under pressure?), this is the wrong time to be eating poor-quality foods, which can make adolescent spots and greasy skin worse. What is more, food with a high fat content tends to make you feel sluggish.

But your own eating habits are not necessarily relevant to

your teenager's needs. Young people who are growing need lots of calories. They seem to be starving most of the time; so to tell them that a balanced meal will be available in 90 minutes is no consolation when they are hungry right now.

You could offer toast and tea (rather than chocolate biscuits and high-sugar snacks) on their return from school. This is also an ideal time for a chat over a drink about how the day went. Or you could provide them with their own tin of high-fibre cereal bars and digestive-type biscuits. These tend to offer high carbohydrate values but are generally lower in sugar and fat (but do check the labels – not all are). Provide a two-litre bottle of water every day, and ensure plenty of fruit is available, perhaps as a large tub of fresh fruit salad prepared every day and left in the fridge for them to help themselves at all times.

Q: My child is swotting hard for exams. Should she be allowed to eat when she wants to rather than joining the family for meals?

A: While studying for exams is important, the young person's role within the family should be maintained. Try to compromise by sticking to set meal-times so she can plan her work before and afterwards. Give a ten-minute warning of an impending meal. Discuss with her whether your timetable fits with her personal revision times (would it be a good idea to bring forward the family supper-time by half-an-hour to make best use of the evening?). You could also allow her to leave the table early.

Q: My son likes to study with his music on. How can he possibly concentrate?

A: Many parents find this difficult to understand, but young people often say that loud music makes it easier to concentrate. If you battle over this, accept that while your individual working methods may be different, you can perhaps agree that it is very difficult to block out the human voice when working. It's reasonable to insist that he avoids radio programmes (in particular shows that request instant feedback via phone or text messaging) or tapes/CDs of the spoken word while revising.

You could suggest that just occasionally he tries silence as a background, as an experiment. If he does give silence a chance, try to get rid of the external noise (most houses produce more than you think). If the sound of his stereo is unbearable, get him a set of headphones.

## CHAPTER 10

# 'Is that thing glued to your ear?' The world of the gadget

It is probably fair to say that every generation of parents has worried about the impact of something new on their children, whether this was the advent of cinema, television or the 'gadget' – a blanket term I am using for devices that connect people digitally. For many young people this will be their smartphone, their tablet or their laptop, and with new gadgets being developed at an amazing speed it seems we may soon add glasses and watches to the growing list of devices that can connect.

Perhaps nothing divides generations more than their relationship to gadgets. Only today I had a conversation with a young person who talked about the 'old days', and when I asked for clarification she told me that she was talking of the time when people had to use a dial to work a telephone stuck to a wall. I didn't admit that I grew up longing for such a telephone and spent a lot of time walking to the public phone box at the end of the street to talk to my friends. To a young person today this is tantamount to admitting to using clay tablets for writing.

## THE POSITIVE SIDE OF GADGETS

Before considering the pitfalls and risks of overuse of gadgets, let's pause for a moment and think about the benefits they have brought. The wise parent can easily utilise their teen's love of gadgets to breed better communication within the family by using and synchronising technology. For example you can benefit from:

- An online calendar for better personal administration and better shared information
- Texting to keep each other updated – a text is particularly useful for reminding or listing things they need to do or remember as it can be looked at again and again
- 'Whatsapp' – the members define the group and information can be simply shared, making everyone feel in touch
- Sending photographs to each other
- Skype when abroad or away from home for any length of time. This is a good way of keeping in touch with children living away and with grandparents when they can't spare the time or are unable to visit
- Customising programs to make processes easier
- Writing tools – best-selling novelist Ben Galley wrote novels on his mobile phone
- Free resources, e.g. revision tools

If we think about why gadgets have become a battleground within many families, there is a gap in understanding. Because most parents did not grow up with their gadgets, they do not fully understand how attached young people can become – and it's a worrying trend to see just how dependent some young people are becoming on them.

What constitutes damaging or addictive use depends very much on who is giving their point of view, but mobile analytics firm Flurry defines a mobile addict as anyone who launches apps more than 60 times a day, which is six times more than the average user. Out of the 1.3 billion mobile devices monitored, 176 million users showed addictive habits – an increase of 123 per cent over the previous 12 months; 52 per cent of these addictive users were female.

In the UK, consumers are now downloading 60 per cent more data to their smartphones and tablets than they were a year ago, with a higher proportion of British young people accessing social networking sites than in any other country. We are also the nation who uses more catch-up TV services online than any other. A higher percentage of families in Britain owns a smart TV with Internet connection than in almost any other country, including the US.

For adults who have grown up without mobiles it can be difficult to understand the degree of attachment many young people feel to theirs, with increasing numbers claiming to experience very real withdrawal symptoms and distress, even panic attacks, at the very thought of being without their device. For those parents who do spend time online, it's good to think clearly about the adrenalin rush that we too experience, and which often precedes access – and whether we are thinking clearly when we are online. This is little written about, which is why the following extract struck me as powerful. For those of us who do have mobile devices and use them regularly, the adrenalin rush that precedes each access needs to be thought of in the context of how a young person is experiencing similar things:

> 'Instant messaging platforms force us daily to survive compressed moments of Gothic suspense: the bated breath as we watch a reply being composed, the minor forboding when our friend drops away unannounced from a conversation or inserts delays into the quick-fire rhythms of the chat . . . [On Skype] Can anyone be blamed for feeling uneasy when the pencil drops to the floor after seconds of hurried scribbling, with no message to show for all this hidden busyness? . . . In digital life, besides our chronic concerns of corporate and governmental surveillance, we

are often explicitly reminded that sets of unseen civilian eyes are aware of our movements. We consider booking a hotel online and are told how many others are viewing it too, just as eBay announces that the rare Thundercat has "54 watching".' **Laurence Scott**, 'Death by Skype', *Financial Times*, 2–3 May 2015

## HOW MUCH TIME IS BEING SPENT ONLINE WITHIN YOUR FAMILY?

Here is a simple quiz you can complete with the whole family to see who might have a problem with mobile gadget use (phone, smartphone, tablet, etc.). Simply enter a name or initial at the top of each column and put a tick in the all boxes that apply to that person's habits.

*Our family gadget use*

|  | Name | Name | Name | Name | Name |
|---|---|---|---|---|---|
| Uses their gadgets while talking to family members? |  |  |  |  |  |
| Has their gadget on the table at mealtimes? |  |  |  |  |  |
| Answers their gadget during mealtimes/while eating? |  |  |  |  |  |
| Usually knows where their gadget is and gets panicky if it can't be found? |  |  |  |  |  |
| Has their gadget by their bedside at night? |  |  |  |  |  |
| Lies about gadget use – says they use it less than they do? |  |  |  |  |  |

| | Name | Name | Name | Name | Name |
|---|---|---|---|---|---|
| Has texted or messaged someone in the same room or building? | | | | | |
| Opens apps more than 60 times in a day? (Twitter/games/FB/Snapchat, etc.) | | | | | |
| Has used their gadget to communicate with someone rather than talk to them face to face? | | | | | |
| Has used their gadget in a cinema, theatre, during a lecture, etc.? | | | | | |
| Has chosen not to go to somewhere just because they won't be able to use their gadget? | | | | | |
| Has a name for their gadget? | | | | | |
| Gets irritable if they can't check for messages, etc. for over an hour? | | | | | |
| Uses their gadget on public transport or in the car? | | | | | |
| Uses their gadget in the street while walking? | | | | | |
| Has had a 'conversation' using their gadget with someone sitting next to them? | | | | | |

## Who has a problem with gadget use in your family?

**Anyone with 5 or fewer ticks** – has a healthy relationship with their gadget.

**Anyone with 6–10 ticks** – needs to spend more time with friends and family to talk face-to-face.

**Anyone with more than 10 ticks** – probably needs to try and leave their gadget in their bag or room when at home once in a while and to put some better boundaries on their gadget use.

**Anyone with 14 ticks or more** – is probably heading towards problem use and may need to set themselves some limits or have some limits put in place for them.

If there are any questions that have ticks for everyone, then perhaps as a family there are some rules about gadget use that need to be put in place to improve family communication, interaction and togetherness.

### WHAT TO DO IF YOU FEAR YOUR YOUNG PERSON (OR YOU) ARE ADDICTED TO A GADGET

Let's start by trying to understand why gadgets are so appealing to young people.

Innovation has always appealed to humans. Our large brains enjoy a challenge and the determination to find new ways to achieve our goals is ongoing, whether it's more effective fabrics for sports clothing, more effective ways of growing crops, or – in the twenty-first century – the creation of new ways to access and share information.

The people who design gadgets understand their market well, and the constantly updated models provide more and more features which appeal to young people aesthetically, reflecting modern trends and fashions. The mobile phone has become the Swiss Army knife of today's generation, as young people compare which apps they have and which features are available in much the same way as their great-grandfathers might have compared penknives.

Today's gadgets don't even come with instruction manuals, relying on intuitive interfaces and word-of-mouth help for their use. It's probably fair to say that most adults use relatively few of their machines' capabilities, and may not even know what else their gadgets can do.

For young people, being part of the crowd is very important so anything that is widely revered will be something they desire, whether it's a brand of clothing, a holiday destination or a type of gadget. They may even have strong views about which brand or operating system they want as it defines their social group – so some young people will crave the latest iPhone while others aspire to the latest Android device.

When it comes to using gadgets the most common uses among young people are for game playing, watching porn, music, video clips on YouTube and social networking. There is now considerable evidence that online game playing acts on the brain by giving a 'hit' of dopamine, the brain's 'feel good' chemical, for wins or points scored. This is pleasurable, and the process may become addictive if the young person is not getting the same stimulation in the real world.

Online social networking has other thrills and plays on many of the insecurities young people feel about face-to-face interaction. It is also socially affirming, allowing them to collect 'friends', and even though they may never have met them, they can still share their lives. Having friends equates to success for young people, and the idea that these friends can 'like' the snippets of their life they choose to share with them is very appealing; it can provide constant affirmation and approval, which again fire pleasurable chemical reactions in the brain. Social networking helps young people feel important at a time when they may feel quite alienated from their family and school. They are at the centre of a web of contacts. Girls in particular may find that constant involvement in online gossip via a digital network can create strong feelings of belonging and boost a sense of their importance within their group.

## Is there a downside?

Not everyone agrees that gadget addiction is real or on a par with other forms of addiction. But there is a growing body of concern based on research that indicates that many young people all over the world are now becoming increasingly dependent on gadget use to the point where it is affecting their real-life relationships and health. For example, in China there are a growing number of rehab centres specifically for young people with gaming or Internet addiction.

Many time-poor parents show the same kinds of dependent use as their children, texting or networking constantly while with their families, or using gadgets to work around the clock wherever they are and regardless of who they are with. While many parents are careful to monitor and limit alcohol use, and would be horrified to hear of their child using illegal drugs regularly, they remain tolerant of gadget use, seeing it as an annoying but harmless habit.

Because parents did not grow up with such readily accessible gadgets, and generally use them in appropriate ways, they frequently don't realise the impact they have on their children and young people. There are gaps in our knowledge. For example, there is incomplete understanding about the impact that electronic devices have on young brains, and discussion that even television watching is not recommended for children under the age of two. Bright lights and flashing images stimulate the brain. This can be a good thing, but if overused it can mean that the slower-moving and drabber real world becomes boring and hard to engage with. There is research in the US which seems to imply that the enormous rise in attention disorders noted by doctors has a direct correlation with TV and gadget use in young children. Whether or not this is true, it is known that children who spend a lot of time in front of electronic screens have shorter attention spans and may find slower forms of entertainment such as reading and conversation harder to engage with.

There is also a growing body of evidence from around the world which indicates that young people who spend a lot of time online have poorer emotional intelligence and less-developed social skills in the real world than their peers. They are also more likely to be lonely and to have developed what have been described as 'deviant' values.

For young people who regularly surf the Internet, a degree of desensitisation has been recorded when viewing images of extreme physical or sexual violence, or suffering in animals or humans – presumably due to having already seen many examples. Such material is readily accessible and may be viewed on news sites, posted video clip sites and even on Facebook where pictures of beheadings, murdered children or sexual mutilations are passed around. It has been noted that there is an increase in society as a whole of people becoming passive observers rather than participants in events and dramas in the real world; someone being attacked in the street is frequently more likely to be photographed or videoed than helped.

Young people are particularly vulnerable to developing addictions as their brain is undergoing so many changes during adolescence.

## HOW MUCH IS TOO MUCH?

While celebrating the benefits of online access, there have also been retractions made in recent years, as more and more evidence has been gathered about the negative effects of complete connectedness, 24/7. A story emerged in 2014 in the *New York Times*[1] in which it was revealed that the late Steve Jobs, founder of Apple and the man behind the smartphone and tablet revolution, did not allow his children to use gadgets at all, and sent them to a school that didn't use computers, because he recognised how damaging and addictive their effects could be on the young. He preferred his children to read books and have conversations around the dinner table on history and current affairs!

It is interesting to note that different countries have come up with different ways of dealing with the increasing number of young people exhibiting symptoms of addiction. For example, South Korea blocks Internet signals after midnight to curb late-night game playing, and Taiwan has introduced a law requiring parents to set limits on Internet use for their children. Many businesses do not permit their employees to send email before or after specific times.

Young people may be using many different gadgets (laptop, games console, tablet, smart TV, smartphone, etc.) – and may also be using several at the same time. It is generally considered a good idea to set limits on their use under the heading of 'screen time', as an accumulation of all the minutes spent on device(s), rather than negotiating about each item. The benefit of having a screen time restriction over gadget restriction is that it allows a young person choice, and can encourage them to think about how they want to use their time.

Some families choose to restrict screen time by physical location: young people can use the computer or watch television

---

[1] http://www.nytimes.com/2014/09/11.

in the family room or main living room, but may only have a certain number of hours on a device elsewhere. Access in a public space discourages the more dangerous types of use but still allows for homework, which is often the reason young people give for needing constant access to the Internet!

Time spent online alone, which research has shown is the majority of time online for children, can be detrimental to their real-time social interactions with their families and friends. It can leave them potentially at risk of viewing sites that are unsuitable, engaging in risky conversations or interactions, and being tempted to play or shop compulsively. Many parents think that if their young person is upstairs in their room they are safe, as you know where they are. But if they are alone with a gadget it may mean that all the things that worry you are potentially right there in the room with them.

There is no definitive recommendation for a young person's amount of screen time, though the American Academy of Pediatrics recommends an entertainment screen-time limit of two hours a day. This is far from the current usage, which the UK watchdog Ofcom estimates on average as an alarming 6.5 hours for teenagers.

All experts now agree that TVs and computers in bedrooms are a very bad idea for children and young people, as they inhibit sleep and encourage late-night use. Many parents have restrictions on their young person's Internet use but do not restrict their TV use, even though there are now a wide variety of 'masturbation channels' geared at young men on after 11 p.m. and available on any digital TV, which do not present young women or women's sexuality and sexual behaviour in a positive light.

## WHAT CAN PARENTS DO?

Firstly, accept that any changes to your young person's gadget use or screen time will not be easy to manage. The best way to restrict a young person's viewing is to not supply them with gadgets in the first place – or to do your research and only buy gadgets that come with excellent parental controls that allow you to set timings as well as limits on which sites can and can't be visited. There are several good online tutorials for parents showing you how to use parental controls and restrictions on all gadgets, so no parent has a good excuse for not using these. A couple of examples are given at the end of this book in 'useful websites', Appendix 2.

As well as restricting their gadgets parents can also help by:

- Using a timer to monitor how long the computer has been used for.
- Installing parental blocks on the kinds of site that can be accessed.
- Always complying with recommended age restrictions on purchased games or movies, including those accessed online
- Not allowing your child to join a social-networking site until they are the age required by that site
- Setting limits on screen time – these may be more restrictive for school nights with additional time during holidays and weekends: for example, 1.5 hours per day Sunday to Thursday, 2.5 hours per day Friday and Saturday. Alternatively the time could be cumulative, on a weekly basis, thus allowing the young person more freedom to choose when the time is to be spent and how
- Creating mobile phone and tablet rules for the whole family (including you), such as no gadgets at the table during meals, no gadgets before 8.30 a.m., no gadgets in the family room during shared TV watching, etc. It is good for young people (and everyone else) to learn that even if someone sends them a text message they do not have to respond immediately
- Being more aware of your own mobile use and restricting

it when you are with your family. Let them see that texts and tweets do not need an instant reply

- Setting up a computer for family use in a relatively quiet communal area of your home to be used for homework – provide noise-cancelling headphones if necessary
- If having the computer in a bedroom is the only solution, put it on a trolley that can be wheeled around the home and thus control the hours of use, e.g. moved out of the bedroom when it is time for sleep
- Restricting the use of computers and tablets, particularly after bedtime. If need be, install the family router in your bedroom and turn it off at night
- Taking away, or even locking up, phones at night. Switch the computer off rather than leaving it idle, once a session is finished. This implies finality and that access is over for a while
- If the family has a laptop buy a lock for it and lock it up at night; these can be bought fairly cheaply second-hand

'The son of a friend did very badly in his mock GCSEs and his parents proposed depriving him of his phone. His anguish was so extreme that it prompted further discussions. It was then that it was revealed that he was acting as a "lifeline" for a suicidal friend, who would regularly ring him in the middle of the night to talk about his problems. While they respected the attempts their son had gone to to support his friend, they felt action had to be taken to widen the support network for the friend. They involved the school.'

- Ensuring their young person gets plenty of real-time experience with other people, including you, and with their friends and yours
- Encouraging them to attend clubs or classes outside

school. This is known to be good for developing resilience as well as expanding social contacts and social skills, so try to encourage and enable their participation
- Promoting physical activity, which is both healthy and sleep-inducing. Encourage your young person to be as physically active as possible by doing things as a family such as cycling or running, encouraging them to cycle or walk to school and stop giving them lifts
- Insist that family meals are taken together, at the table
- Plan an outing to something; get on the phone and buy the tickets
- Make sure bicycles are in tip-top condition
- Go shopping for groceries together – say you need help carrying things or choosing what to eat. Get her to cook too; this is absorbing and a source of pride when something edible is created!
- Offer her a subscription to a magazine of her choice, and make sure it really is her choice. Don't say 'Wouldn't you rather have the *New Statesman* – then I could read it too?'

## WHEN GADGETS BITE – GROOMING, CYBER BULLYING AND OTHER UNSPEAKABLE THINGS

### Grooming

For any young person with a regular online presence there are risks involved, and of these the one that most alarms parents is probably that of sexual predation. This affects boys and girls, most of whom firmly believe it could never happen to them. But grooming is a sophisticated and slow process of winning trust, offering affection and acceptance and stripping away moral boundaries that when carried out by someone with an understanding of the adolescent mind is both difficult to spot and often extremely successful. Grooming techniques are not only used for sexual access to young people but also to recruit activists. Social-networking sites are now being accessed by terror groups such as IS to recruit young people who may already be feeling isolated and rejected by society, and in doing this they often use very similar techniques as those who seek to exploit young people sexually.

Parents will need to have frank and open discussions with their teens about online predators and it may help to give them some guidelines, such as these by Safety Net (www. safetynetkids.org.uk):

- Don't post any personal information online – like your address, email address or mobile number
- Think carefully before posting pictures or videos of yourself. Once you've put  a picture of yourself online most people can see it and may be able to download it, it's not just yours any more
- Keep your privacy settings as high as possible
- Never give out your passwords
- Don't befriend people you don't know
- Don't meet up with people you've met online.  Speak to your parent or carer about people who suggest you do
- Remember that not everyone online is who they say they are
- Think carefully about what you say before you post something online
- Respect other people's views; even if you don't agree with someone else's views  it doesn't mean you need to be rude
- If you see something online that makes you feel uncomfortable, unsafe or worried: leave the website, turn off your computer if you want to and tell a trusted adult immediately

It might help to have a copy of the 'rules' by the family computer if you have one. With younger teens just starting out online it is advisable to monitor their use regularly. Making such checks part of the process of online access, as a condition of being allowed to access social-networking sites, of having the gadgetry required or of having their bills met or contract paid for, can be a useful strategy. Some parents do this by becoming 'friends' or 'followers' of their teen, so they can see the list of people and sample the posts for a while until they are confident all is well (although it is probably not a good idea to post themselves). Other parents have regular updates with their young person where they will look at the friends list with them, look at the topics being discussed and the kinds of pictures being posted. It can also be a useful strategy to discuss relevant news coverage with your young people; stories of those who met after talking online only to find out the person they had shared their thoughts with was not as they seemed appear regrettably often.

## Cyber bullying

Cyber bullying is the blanket term used to refer to any form of harassment or spiteful behaviour online. It includes a wide range of things, such as:

- Sending mean or threatening texts, unflattering or ridiculous messages or emails
- Spreading rumours through social media or text
- Pretending to be someone else in order to cause problems – perhaps sending an unkind or rude message to a friend or family member from their phone or by hacking into their online account
- Revealing secrets or private conversations to a whole class or school
- Posting unflattering pictures or messages online without permission
- Circulating information (real or made up) about somebody's sexual behaviour

- Making unkind or unpleasant comments to posts
- Regularly failing to 'like' posts
- Altering photographs to be obscene, unflattering or ridiculous

Trolling is the sending of anonymous messages, usually repetitively and spitefully.

## How widespread is cyber bullying?

A survey by the multinational research network EU kids online[1] recorded that for 2014 in the UK:

- 70 per cent of young people were victims of cyber bullying (an estimated 5.43 million)
- 37 per cent of young people experienced cyber bullying on a highly frequent basis (1.26 million)
- 20 per cent of young people experienced extreme cyber bullying on a daily basis
- New research suggests that young males and females are equally at risk of cyber bullying
- Young people were found to be twice as likely to be cyber bullied on Facebook as on any other social network, with 54 per cent of users reporting that they had experienced cyber bullying on the site.
- Cyber bullying was found to have catastrophic effects upon the self-esteem and social lives of up to 70 per cent of young people

Interestingly the number of young people who admit to ever having cyber bullied someone themselves is very small. Many incidents of online bullying may in fact involve both parties in passing or posting unkind or spiteful material, with each

---

[1] http://www.eukidsonline.net.

party feeling that the other person is the only one doing something wrong, as they 'started it'.

If your child reports cyber bullying to you, deal with it as you would any form of bullying (see Chapter 8) – by letting them know in the first instance that they don't deserve it and that you are wholeheartedly on their side. All the same principles apply – 'ask, don't tell'.

- Stay calm, even if your heart is racing
- Listen and respond to their feelings even if the event was small
- Later, discuss future strategies together: next time . . .; tomorrow . . .
- But the strategy should be realistic, non-bullying and within their capabilities
- Tell the school (with the child's permission), if the perpetrator is a fellow pupil
- Talk about it again and again until they no longer wish to, but don't make a fuss of them every time
- If the bullying continues, make an appointment (rather than just rushing in) to see the head of year to discuss a strategy for ending it
- Make it clear to your young person that you would like to hear of any further situations, but don't ask them every day whether or not they had a run in with the bullying individuals (which may raise their anxiety and awareness levels). Let them tell you if and when they want

Whereas your first response may be to take their gadget away, this needs much more careful consideration. Removing their gadget, or closing down their online account, will only make them hide any future bullying from you. But discuss how often they access their messages/networking sites – and how it feels to see themselves written about; spotting an adrenalin rush can help them shape their response and see the issue in perspective.

## Case Study

The mother of a 14-year-old found his school friends had been discussing his relationship with his 18-year-old sister in a chatroom. He did not tell his mother himself, she found out because her daughter became involved and it was referred to during a family row. The discussion implied that there was a sexual relationship between the siblings. Horrified, she realised that these comments had been posted during a time when all those involved were in the care of the school (during the after-school home-work club) and she therefore immediately made contact with the school.

The school took her concerns seriously, spoke to those involved and suspended them for a week, but then considered the matter dealt with. The mother, however, was not satisfied and wanted more serious action taken against those who had posted the comments – who by then were back in the classroom, and continuing to taunt her son about what she was doing. She contacted the head teacher directly, and when this did not deliver the further action she thought was required, she got in touch with the school governors. She said she felt it was important that all concerned with the school should know what kind of establishment was being run, and that other families should not be compromised in this way. The school, however, would not offer any increase on the punishment that had been imposed, and responded very badly to the storm she was creating; ultimately she felt she had no alternative but to withdraw her son from the school.

This case study shows an obvious difference in thinking between the mother and the school. To the school this

was an act of bullying that had been dealt with suffi-
ciently; to the mother this was a shocking defamation of
her family that should perhaps have even been taken
through the courts.

Young people don't behave like adults and to view
their behaviour, and in particular the way they talk, in the
same way is often unhelpful. Of course any bullying is
wrong but the way in which young people can get under
each other's skin simply highlights their immaturity – they
use a vocabulary that is highly colourful and obsessed
with all things sexual (just try standing at a bus stop at a
time when secondary school pupils come out, and you
will see what I mean). Treating the content of the bullying
in the same way as one would for an adult is unhelpful as
such sexual language is extremely widespread. Bullying
should always be addressed and never excused, but
getting hung up on how young people talk to each other
is pointless. Hopefully the school is already working with
all its pupils about appropriate and inappropriate
behaviour and the line between banter and bullying, and
after such an incident a good school will ensure the pupils
involved have some individual or small group sessions too.
Taking a young person away from their school and their
friendship group should only be done if there is no
alternative, and always with the young person's agreement, otherwise it can feel like bullying by the parent.

## QUESTIONS & ANSWERS

Q: I am absolutely appalled by the continuous use of mobile
phones in public places. Of course there are times when it's
important to get a message to someone quickly, but I have
heard so many very personal calls, including people sharing

lewd gossip or ringing their bank and giving banking details – the other day I heard someone pay by credit card on a crowded bus, including passing on their card number and code. I know that when I was young there were no mobile phones but now it seems there are no rules and no such thing as privacy – both for the person using the phone and the person sitting next to them. What do I tell my children about using phones in public?

**A:** It's because these gadgets are new that parents like you don't have any firm rules to offer their young people. Given there are no established rules, it's a good idea to fall back on basic etiquette, and what parents can teach their children about respect for others, the notion of personal space and how to behave in public. For the modern parent this will incorporate the use of gadgets.

Not giving out personal details on a mobile device in public would come under the heading of safety. This should be discussed with children from a young age, with the information changing in character and complexity as your teenager develops. Not only should they not be giving out bank details, it is also unwise to share their address or number, email address or details of plans where anyone else can hear. They might also need to think about security when texting in crowded places.

**Q:** My son is like any other teenager – glued to his mobile phone. Most of the time I just put up with it but what really annoys me is that he still looks at it and fiddles with it when I am talking to him. He thinks I am overreacting when I insist he leaves it on the table and gives me eye contact. What do you think?

**A:** If he is actively texting someone else while you are talking, then he cannot truly be listening to what you are saying and his behaviour is not acceptable. However, if he is simply looking at and fiddling with the phone it may well be that he finds it comforting to have something else to look at while listening. Many teenagers, particularly boys, find eye contact at close quarters or when discussing anything they might consider personal (such as their behaviour or attitude) extremely diffi-cult. He may find the simple distraction of the phone in his hand helps him to listen.

**Q:** My daughter is 14 and we have let her have her own phone since she was 9. At first she was thrilled but now it has become a point of honour with her to have the very latest model and these come along very quickly. I have told her that she must keep her phone for at least two years as I have two other children and I cannot afford to keep replacing perfectly good phones. She feels this is desperately unfair and says that all her friends have new models except her. Am I being unkind?

**A:** I think this is a problem for many parents today. Phone and gadget companies have realised that people want the latest model so they are bringing out upgrades and updates regularly. If your daughter is so ashamed to have anything but the latest model then I suggest you talk to her about how she can pay for upgrades. As she is only 14 this probably means that her work and earnings potential are both low, but perhaps she could start doing some babysitting for local families or neigh-bours, sell some of her old or unused items on eBay, or ask for money for all her birthday and Christmas presents to save up for a new model. You could offer to help her by saving the money for her and perhaps offering to add a certain amount yourself – so for example you might suggest that you will add £50 for every £100 she manages to save. This will either help her to become better at budgeting or will cure her of wanting upgrades so frequently.

**Q:** One day recently, by accident, my son left his phone at home and I couldn't resist the temptation to look – I know his pass code from watching him enter it many times before.

I looked through his browsing history and his texts and I was absolutely horrified, I cannot believe that this is the same boy that I see day in day out. He has been looking at some really disgusting hard porn sites, looking up all kinds of drugs information, watching videos of beheadings and executions, sending pictures of his penis to girls I have never heard of and posting some extremely lewd comments online. I don't know what to do about it: to challenge him means I have to admit that I looked at his phone, but to do nothing means letting him carry on this way.

**A:** As your son is 16 it is not against the law to look at his private material but, as I think you have just realised, it is not a very good idea. What you have seen is a snapshot into the brain of a 16-year-old boy; his curiosities and habits are not at all unusual even if they are disturbing. What is different is that in the modern world his thoughts can be translated into actions very easily and his curiosities can be satisfied very graphically.

What is clear from your question is that you have no parental settings in use on your son's phone and this is not a good idea. Of course he will still be able to see the same pictures and sites on the phones of his friends whose parents also don't use the parental settings. Every phone these days comes with such settings, and insisting on their installation will make clear to him where your boundaries lie.

You will need to decide whether you tell him you have looked at his phone. If you do tell him, he will undoubtedly feel violated, but at the same time it will make him more careful of his phone use if he thinks you may look again. Either way, I suggest that if you are paying for his phone contract you make the stipulation that some degree of parental control is placed on his use.

**Q:** My 14-year-old daughter regularly uses our home computer for her homework. Recently she had to write a book review and completed it in a matter of minutes. I questioned her and she told me that she had found a review of the book online and had simply copied this as her own work. When we talked about this she told me that everyone at school does the same thing and that it is an acceptable practice. I'm sure she is wrong, because what is the point of homework if all she is doing is copying and pasting someone else's views?

**A:** In some respects she is right. Many people are doing much the same, including teachers when they design lesson materials. Young people often prize the ability to access information online and many are tempted to equate this with doing the writing themselves.

Teachers are, however, generally pretty adept at spotting what is a student's own effort, and what is not – largely from the different writing styles which can end up sitting side by side in the same piece of work. It's also not uncommon for several members of the same class to download identical material – which obviously can't be original to everyone! Some schools (and all universities) use software which can match content, and spot if it comes from somewhere else. Students are regularly warned that they will be caught if using unedited or unreferenced text, and many are.

How such a situation is dealt with at school may be troubling for you, particularly if you remember sweating your way through essays the hard way. If your teenager is caught downloading information without referencing where it came from, she may be asked to repeat the task and her teacher will scrutinise what she submits more closely in future – although there may be no punishment for a first offence.

The wider question here is what makes reuse acceptable and what is simply copying. Cutting and pasting in order to get something done as quickly as possible is not a good solution.

If your daughter has not really engaged with the material she has included and cannot defend the content's relevance, then she is probably learning little – and her satisfaction in the work may not be that great.

It is, however, worth bearing in mind that as students get older, they are taught to use quotation as a legitimate means of illustrating their argument or providing background information, and the accompanying skills of scanning quickly, sourcing effectively and referencing fully are likely to be very useful to her in future. In any case, generations of school pupils have completed homework by copying chunks of text from books. The cut-and-paste of today's young people is arguably simply an updated approach, incorporating technology.

Instead of recriminations, and if she is willing, why not show her how to use the Internet to access a variety of sources and help her put these together into a logical argument; to see what else has been written as evidence that can be gathered to extend her thinking – rather than text that can be downloaded whole. Remind her that not everything that appears on the Internet has been checked, and that even if she gets away with it now she may look dishonest in the longer term if a review she presents is subsequently shown to be someone else's work. In the process, you will be building her skills and her long-term satisfaction in the work she completes. She may even be impressed that you can do this!

# CHAPTER 11

# 'Money, money, money'. How much, how often, how to get some and how important?

Giving young people an allowance every week or month, or a set amount of pocket money, has rather fallen out of fashion these days as many families simply give out money as and when it is needed. Giving an allowance or pocket money is a good strategy because it encourages young people on the path towards a sensible attitude to money, and good habits in handling it. It's also enjoyable for them to have a bit of cash to splash out on things without needing your say so.

It's good to encourage young people to understand how much things cost and that money requires choices – as it can only be spent once. Even quite little children can enjoy a small amount of money, and through spending it on what they like, on a regular basis, they can feel independent and responsible. Understanding that you can't have the comic if you have already spent your pocket money on a large bar of chocolate is a good lesson in handling money sensibly later in life. Of course, this will only work if you don't give in to their whingeing and buy them the comic anyway!

By contrast, not having any money to spend when your friends do, can be difficult. Things that we are denied in childhood have a habit of showing up on bank statements in later life.

## FLASHBACK

Do you remember a time when you were young when you really wanted something that your parents said 'No' to?

- What was it?
- How did it feel to be told 'No' – and how did you react?
- What did you do about it?
- Did you get the item in the end? How?
- Did you learn anything from the experience?
- How did that experience and others like it affect how you are with your kids when they ask for something?

'Every Sunday my son sings in the church choir and in the interval between the service and the rehearsal that follows, they have a short break. Most of the group have a small amount of money to spend and they go off together to the local shop and choose something to buy – perhaps a drink, a bun or some sweets – or sometimes pooling their funds to buy some food from one of the coffee shops that is open at that time. The choosing often takes most of the time, and sometimes the children select different items and share them in an impromptu picnic.

'There is one young man who never has any money, and this puts him in a difficult position. He has either to pretend he is not interested, or cadge a share from the other boys. At first the others shared with him, now he gets teased and avoided – and must feel isolated. While I can understand that his mother may be concerned for the state of his teeth, he is missing out on the camaraderie of the group and this seems a pity.' **Mother**

## HOW TO CALCULATE AN ALLOWANCE

How much money a young person receives usually depends on family circumstances and peer pressure. You will be told the optimum amount ('everyone else gets at least £x'); you have to decide both what is sensible and what you can afford.

To establish an allowance, get your young person to make a list of all the expenses incurred during the given period, for example a magazine or newspaper, perhaps a visit to the corner shop for sweets or something similar on Fridays. Then discuss the entertainments to be included: maybe a trip to the cinema once a month and going swimming too. Are clothes to be included or not? What about transport? Travelcards for getting to school or college are generally free but will you cover additional transport costs, depending on how good public transport is where you live. Perhaps there needs to be a distinction between essential fares and those that could form a supplement to the allowance if the decision was made to walk instead. What about top-up cards for their phone? Once you have agreed a total, try to make sure it is paid regularly (directly into a bank account is a good idea) and stick to it. Try not to provide extra unless it suits you both, e.g. 'I will give you £5 if you wash the car for me.'

If your young person decides to save up some of this money for something they really want, they are learning to budget and you should be pleased. The same goes for reaching the final week of the month and having nothing left for bus fares; walking instead will focus their mind on making the money last next month! But this will only work if you let them learn – if you give them a lecture followed by more money, it will certainly happen again. It's not a good idea to let them 'borrow' from next month either. They will learn about credit quite soon enough.

Most banks and building societies offer 'starter accounts' to encourage young people to sign up with them for life. Why not suggest that your young person shops around to find out the best deal on offer (often a combination of a better rate of interest and associated freebies)?

Once offered and accepted, an allowance should be paid regularly. In the heat of an argument, it's tempting to cancel it as a punishment but this just emphasises the young person's lack of power. You are angry and can take away their spending power; they on the other hand feel just as strongly but can only shout and slam doors. If the wrongdoing is particularly serious, you could take their bank card away until the situation is resolved. But another sanction is probably better, such as grounding or imposing a curfew.

## WHAT TO ASK FOR IN RETURN

It is good practice to relate money received to increased responsibilities. As children get older the number of cash handouts they receive should naturally reduce (otherwise they will be asking all the time) and the introduction of a regular allowance should be linked in return to an increase in responsibility. So an increased allowance should be offset against a greater commitment to the family, perhaps doing the washing up or mowing the lawn on a regular basis. The regular handling of chores encourages young people to take a pride in their work – and understand what is involved in running a home.

A larger allowance, say for clothing or entertainments, should be in return for greater responsibility: 'If you are old enough to buy your own clothes, then you are old enough to collect your younger sister from Brownies every week.' You could try linking a clothing allowance to additional clothing responsibilities – washing or ironing, hanging up, etc.

The young person will, of course, agree as they want the money, but they may later fall down on their part of the bargain – in which case they are not old enough for either.

You could then choose to suspend the allowance or make an interim agreement, say some money towards clothes tied in with always putting dirty clothes in the laundry basket and putting away clean clothes when left on their bed. It is important, however, that they don't see their allowance as payment for doing chores; rather that the two go hand in hand – greater responsibility and increasing financial responsibility.

## WHOSE MONEY IS IT ANYWAY?

In theory, money that is given belongs – immediately – to the person to whom it is given. A 5-year-old given 50p to spend at the corner shop will resent it if the accompanying adult tries to dictate how it is spent. A teenager told how to spend their allowance will naturally react in just the same way – as would you if your boss told you how to spend your salary.

It's good to take an interest in what they buy; to help them spot gaps in their wardrobe rather than buy duplicate items, but the ultimate choice is theirs. Encourage them to save up for things they really want, and share their pleasure when the item comes home.

It's fine to lay down conditions on how an allowance is to be spent before you award it. For example, 'This money must not be used for alcohol or tobacco'; 'I don't expect your phone top-up cards to come out of this amount.'

Of course it is much easier to insist on these things with a 12-year-old than a 16-year-old, but a valuable opportunity for restating the principles on which an allowance is given comes up each time your young person wants a rise: 'Your birthday is coming up and we will talk about a rise, but can we just go through what does and does not come out of your allowance?' However, if this is the only money they get you'll need to be aware that they may lie and agree, even if they fully intend to use it on a night down the pub.

'My daughter recently wanted an expensive hair straight-ener. It was more than I was willing to pay and she decided to save up for one. She spent nothing from her allowance for two months and put all her Christmas money towards it. We went through lots of websites looking for the best model and she sought advice from friends on which one to buy. I have enjoyed watching her make a careful purchase and she is delighted with the result. The whole family has now been "straightened". I feel that her pleasure was so much greater than if we had just gone out and bought it for her.' **Mother**

## STUFF AND MORE STUFF

Many modern teenagers have a great deal of 'stuff', made up of clothes, books, music and movies, and the ever-present gadgets. It is a good idea to encourage your young person to discard items regularly, perhaps when replacing them with a newer version. This way their cupboards are not so full and they have more respect for the items they have. Giving cast-offs to charity is a good way of helping others but they may prefer to sell replaced items online. If they are doing so encourage them to tick the box that allows some of the proceeds of their sale to go to charity too.

Many young people will want to upgrade their gadgets regu-larly to the latest versions – a practice that manufacturers encourage for obvious reasons. If you choose to buy a phone, laptop or tablet for your young person, make it clear to them that upgrading is their responsibility not yours. Of course they will want the latest model, but living with a two-year-old phone will not harm them and if they want to buy a new one the responsibility for raising the appropriate cash is theirs. (There will, however, be some negotiation needed when an item breaks down or is lost and there is an incentive from the retailer to upgrade at the same time.)

## WORKING

One of the ways young people can get more of the things they want is to find some paid work. This is not as easy as it sounds. Many of the roles traditionally taken by their parents at the same age are now taken by adults on daily contracts, and wider legislation of the employment market has also affected the availability of casual labour. There are, however, still paid jobs around if they are willing to do them. Some parents worry that if their young person works their studies will suffer or they will miss out on social and relaxation activities, but the opposite is possibly true. Working has several benefits for a young person. It can promote:

- Improved time management
- Better understanding of money and the value of money in relation to effort
- Increased determination to do well at school, often because they realise 'I wouldn't want to be doing this all my life'
- Appreciation of the value of their leisure time – which they are less likely to waste
- Depending on the work they do, and the people they meet and talk to, a greater awareness of roles and situations they don't know

Young people cannot legally work until they are 13 unless they work as actors, models or in the performing arts, in which case they need to have a performance licence.

In the UK the rules for the employment of young people state that they are not allowed to work:

- Without an employment permit issued by the education department of the local council, if this is required by local bylaws

- In places like a factory or industrial site
- During school hours
- Before 7 a.m. or after 7 p.m.
- For more than one hour before school (unless local bylaws allow it)
- For more than four hours without taking a break of at least one hour
- In most jobs in pubs and betting shops, and those prohibited in local bylaws
- In any work that may be harmful to their health, well-being or education
- Without having a two-week break from any work during the school holidays in each calendar year

There are also special rules which only apply during term times and school holiday times.

## Term-time rules

During term time children can only work a maximum of 12 hours a week. This includes:

- A maximum of two hours on school days and Sundays
- A maximum of five hours on Saturdays for 13- to 14-year-olds, or eight hours for 15- to 16-year-olds

## School holiday rules

During school holidays 13- to 14-year-olds are only allowed to work a maximum of 25 hours a week. This includes:

- A maximum of five hours on weekdays and Saturdays
- A maximum of two hours on Sunday

During school holidays 15- to 16-year-olds can only work a maximum of 35 hours a week. This includes:

- A maximum of eight hours on weekdays and Saturdays
- A maximum of two hours on Sunday

## Local rules on the types of work children can do

Local bylaws list the jobs that children *can't* do. If a job is on this list, a child under the minimum school leaving age can't do this work. Local bylaws may also have other restrictions on working hours, conditions of work and the type of employment.

Contact your local council's education department or education welfare service for more information.

## THE BUDDING ENTREPRENEUR

While not all young people want to go out and find work, most would be very glad of some additional money from time to time, and this gives them a good incentive to become creative and find ways to work from home. The Internet provides a lot of opportunities for creating a small business online using one of the many online marketplaces such as eBay or Etsy. Vintage clothing, up-cycled household items and handmade jewellery are just three examples of creative money-making opportunities. One young woman buys old glassware from charity shops and paints on woodland animals before selling them for ten times the price, and a young man combs the markets and charity shops to find rare vinyl records which he sells to collectors online.

With a bit of effort and inspiration, and perhaps some help from friends, any young person can begin to earn extra money if they're willing to work hard. However, if you are going to encourage your young person to sell their old and unwanted items, there need to be some procedures in place to ensure that the process is managed legally and that they only sell things that belong to them! Initial success in selling may cause them to look more widely at their home as a source of further disposable assets, and if in the process they start stripping your home this can cause big problems, particularly if the items have a sentimental value or belong to their siblings. By all means encourage them to clear out their own belongings but they may need some rules, such as:

- If selling an item that is shared among the family, or between siblings, they need the permission of all involved before going ahead; there needs to be a discussion about who is to get the income, and how it is to be shared. For example, does the person who is managing the sale get a bigger slice of the proceeds?
- Parents will need to stand as the account holder for online sales mechanisms, and need to ensure that their young people are advertising items honestly and managing their sales fairly.
- All costs of their business should be met by them. They cannot expect you to pay for postage or raw materials unless this is by agreement or a loan.

Some young people do extremely well from home-run computer-based businesses, and as long as their earnings are below the tax threshold they will not be liable for tax. Bear in mind, however, that if you accept the money into your account, and then pay out the earnings to them, your tax position may be affected.

There is no legal age limit at which a young person can open a bank account of their own; the local management of the bank will decide whether an account can be opened, and if so of what type. Each type of account will have restrictions, however; for example, young people are not normally legally responsible for their debts so they are unlikely to be granted an overdraft. However, if they are over 14 but under 18, they can enter into a credit or hire purchase agreement if an adult acts as their guarantor. A young person under 18 applying for a credit card will have their application turned down.

## QUESTIONS & ANSWERS

Q: Should I have to pay my daughter to baby-sit for her younger brothers?

A: About the age of 14 young people acquire a value to other people – as cheap labour. Employers are only required to pay the minimum wage to 16-year-olds and above, and your young person may decide to take a paper round or – usually more lucratively – offer to baby-sit for neighbours.

Baby-sitting your siblings is often harder work than baby-sitting other people's children. If she is turning down a booking in order to baby-sit for you (and thereby forcing a regular customer to look elsewhere), it's not unreasonable for you to pay her for this service. But given the family link, perhaps you could negotiate a lower rate.

Q: Money has gone missing from my youngest child's room. We suspect his elder brother. What do we do?

A: Stealing from family members is a common problem. If the money is left lying around, the opportunities are there, and the loss may not even be noticed – or believed ('Are you sure it's not there, you must have lost it'). Taking money from parents is similarly tempting and the amount in question may mean much more to your young person than to you.

Try to talk about the problem with your young person. If the taker is not short of money, then this is a sign of something being wrong. Young people who are taking things that don't belong to them, and who understand what they are doing, are not happy. Of course there are some grey areas like finding money lying around, or 'keeping the change' as part of an errand, but if they are taking from shops or others they are expressing some degree of disturbance and may need help.

If the problem persists, have a lock put on a drawer, or in extreme cases, on a sibling's room, to deter theft. This is because everyone has the right to their own things and you have to give the sibling the right to protect their belongings and feel safe in the ownership of their property.

**Q:** My daughter borrows money from her friends. Should I allow this?

**A:** This can be difficult to stop. But first ask yourself why is she doing this? Are her needs outstripping her allowance or is she just bad with money?

Borrowing money is not a good habit to get into and you need to talk to her about how she is spending what she has and what the extra money was borrowed for. If she is in need of more money, you could negotiate on the basis of extra help in the house or extra responsibilities. You could explain the long-term difficulties of borrowing to fund a lifestyle she can't afford (magazines aimed at young people include advertisements from debt consolidation agencies as well as regular articles on credit problems).

It's also important to recognise the message that young people pick up from society in general. The stigma formerly associated with debt has gone and young people constantly see the offer to save money by taking credit. They see their parents using 'plastic' for everything they want to buy. A whole sheaf of store cards can be easily obtained and huge amounts of credit available in one afternoon on the local high street.

**Q:** My daughter spends her allowance as quickly as she gets it and is always asking for subsidies for extra outings and clothes. How can I encourage her to take a more responsible attitude to money?

A: There are two things you need to be clear about. Firstly, how is her allowance worked out? Have you agreed what it should cover and is this reasonable to both of you? Secondly, do you give her more when she asks for it?

If her allowance has been negotiated, and awarded, on a fair basis, there should be no need for subsidies, and none given. If you stick to her allowance she will have to make choices about how she spends it, and that is the best way of learning a responsible attitude to money.

Talk through her problems. Maybe you should give her two instalments, rather than one lump sum. Perhaps you could 'hold on' to some to help her save, but these should be her choices and not yours. If you help her to own her feelings, it can also be a very strong learning experience.

Q: My son's friend has been offered £50 for every A* GCSE pass he gets. Should I do the same?

A: This is really difficult. There is rampant reward inflation going on in schools – I heard of a 10-year-old child offered £1,000 if he passed his 11+, and many others have got new games consoles or bikes for similar effort. The problem is that offering money in return for academic achievement puts pressure on the child – it's a form of bullying by the parents. The pride in passing at a high grade and the sense of achievement should be sufficient reward; money won't make them any more motivated.

On the other hand, financial rewards for *not* doing something are easier to live with – and work towards. A cash bonus (or air flight to a popular destination) for not smoking by the time you are 18 can work well.

**Q:** My 14-year-old daughter's phone was stolen (or possibly lost) and while I have some money from the insurance to replace it she is asking for a much more up-to-date and expensive phone, like the ones her friends have. I have suggested she has the upgraded phone for her birthday but she feels this is dreadfully unfair.

**A:** Your suggestion for a compromise sounds perfectly reasonable. Of course she will not be happy about it because she is not getting everything she wants. Give her the two choices clearly stated – either a replacement phone of similar value to the one that has been lost, or an upgrade to a more expensive phone as a birthday gift.

Upgrading her for losing her phone could be a very dangerous practice, as she will probably want several upgrades during her teen years and she may decide that losing her phone is a good way to get one!

# CHAPTER 12

# 'You're not going out in that!' What they want to wear, what's appropriate and what is not

M ost teenagers want to wear the right brands, and these are expensive. Every parent knows that. In fact, the assumption that teenagers want expensive branded clothes often originates with parents rather than young people. Parents of teenagers may assume that their young people want them, simply because they see so many of them and teenagers seem to know all about them. But whereas most teenagers can recognise the coveted brands, it's far from being the case that they routinely expect to be bought them.

If you want proof of this, look in high street shops. You will find they are full of bright, cheerful, attractive clothes for teenagers – at a wide range of prices; and it is not only the most expensive shops that are full of would-be customers. To young people the *quantity* of clothes they have can be as important as *quality* represented by certain brands. It's also worth noting that pursuing a more idiosyncratic look is becoming much more popular too, and the number of vintage shops (themed second-hand shops specialising in older clothes) is growing.

'I can still remember my first Afghan coat. It smelt absolutely awful, particularly if I got caught in the rain, but I just adored it.' **Mother**

'I remember the swishy feeling around my legs when I wore my very first long dress. What a pleasure.' **Alison**

It's important for parents to grasp that clothes for teenagers are about belonging – and not necessarily about the product itself, or keeping up with the latest fashion. Clothes are a very powerful way of showing that you belong to a particular group or club. Adults often respond the same way, and can be very aware of the prestige achieved by owning certain goods. You might consider whether you have passed on your own 'designer desire' to your young person? Do you covet all the latest gadgets, high-spec cars and expensive labels? If none of these excite you, the chances are that your child is as happy to buy clothes in cheap shops as they are to have designer gear.

Clothes have always been something that people aspire to – the concept of 'best clothes' for special occasions exists in every society. Clothes have long been social markers of belonging and, today, with the narrowing of differences between accents and lifestyles, they have become even more important. Clothes define which group you belong to and at what level of intimacy you find yourself: leader, part of the inner circle, or hanger on.

'I can still remember my first "going out" outfit, from when I was about 13. I had a very faded pair of blue jeans, which I had bought from a friend; a black shirt from Dorothy Perkins with white zig-zag stitching on the collar, and a dusky pink cheesecloth smock on top; all accessorised with some cheap beads that I had bought on a market. I don't think I have ever felt so pleased with any outfit since – it really made me feel good.' **Alison**

## 4 top tips for debunking designer desire

1 **Encourage your teenager** to make choices about what they wear. Rather than giving in and buying everything they ask for, offer an amount of money that may be spent as they wish. The same amount of money may buy just one top with the right brand name, or a complete outfit from another store. Try to ensure that the choices made are real choices, for if you give in the following week and buy the expensive trousers as well you are seriously undermining the rationale you encouraged them to develop. Look at the amount you are spending over a longer period – are you disguising a move towards a totally branded style of dressing through lots of little stages?

2 **Explore cut-price solutions** in designer outlets such as TK Maxx, charity shops, vintage clothing stores and eBay. The move to always have the latest means there is often a lot of merchandise available at knock-down prices.

3 **When the 'right' items are bought,** don't knock their pleasure; most of us have items of clothing that we are really proud of and love to wear. If an item is a present, ensure you come away with the associated carrier bag and free stickers; try not to rationalise away the desire for these items, they really do enhance the experience.

4 **Allow them to enjoy what they buy** and compliment them on their choice. I've seen my son glow with pleasure when a sales assistant commented positively on what he has bought, and it's a good idea for parents to try to do the same. And the more specific your comment, the more they will like it: 'I like the red stitching' rather than 'It's really nice.'

'I resisted designer trainers for a very long time. Now I have relented, what I have found is that my normally slap-dash and forgetful son has taken care of them in a way I would never have anticipated. Because he is proud of them they are never lost, get changed out of before playing football in the garden with his brothers, and are kept clean. He has finally demonstrated that he values something, and while I wish it was something more worth valuing, I am grateful for this development.' **Mother**

## WHAT CLOTHES SAY ABOUT YOU

It's a really good idea for parents to encourage their young people to think about the message that their clothes send out about who they are; to help them make choices about how they dress. Don't assume that it's only girls who need advice – boys can find the business of thinking about what to wear just as demanding. Some boys never learn to be confident with clothes; spending the whole of their adult lives buying replicas of the same clothes they had when they were teenagers – often in navy blue! If you don't know where to start, the following may help.

### 9 top tips for encouraging good clothes sense

1 **Encourage your young people** to think about which colours enhance their complexion and which shapes suit their bodies. Not all colours and styles suit all bodies! We accept this is true for us, so naturally the same applies to teenagers.

2 **Encourage them to think about what is appropriate.** What fabrics and styles are suitable for what kinds of occasions?

3 **Encourage them to think about how clothes make them feel.** How comfortable are they in particular styles and fabrics? Are there some clothes in which they feel more or less confident?

4 **Help them spot their personal tastes:** what kind of styles they tend to choose and which colours. Encourage them to think about why they are making these choices and to explore whether or not they are happy with them.

5 **Help them to become canny shoppers** and think about how long what they buy will last. For example, some acrylic mixes may look good when you buy them but degenerate very quickly when they are washed. This may be acceptable for a high fashion cheap buy, but not for a classic or more expensive item. Show them how to read the label inside clothing that specifies what it is made of, and get them to remember past experiences – how did something of a similar fabric respond to repeated washing last time?

6 **Help them to see that managed well, the clothes we are particularly fond of will last much longer.** Show what constitutes good management (reading the care label, washing at the right temperature, etc.). Let them manage this process themselves – it can deliver surprising satisfaction.

7 **Help them to think about the impression they are making** and to wear the kind of clothes to assist in the process. For example, the kind of clothes you would wear for work experience would probably be different from what you would choose for a night out with your friends.

8 **Help them to think about the practicalities of what they have chosen.** Low-rise jeans may be a nuisance if they are planning to go with their mates to the park and play football but ideal if they are going to the cinema. Very high-heeled shoes may be a real problem if there are long distances to be walked.

9 **A good rule of thumb is not to draw attention to more than any one part of your body at any one time.** So a bustier worn with trousers may look really attractive; team it with a very short skirt and the effect is totally compromised.

Having offered your advice, bear in mind that your views will probably be far less influential than those of their friends. Think too about when you give your advice. When you are getting ready for a deadline and everyone is stressed is not an ideal time to point out that you consider what they have chosen totally unsuitable. Instead, can you have a chat about clothing when there is less emotion in the air? A good time is when an invitation is received, or during the week before a big night out.

## HOW MANY CLOTHES A YOUNG PERSON NEEDS

Mothers of daughters in particular often lament the amount of clothes bought by teenagers. They can be profligate and wasteful, and do not wear everything they buy.

For a teenager, having lots of clothes to choose between may be very important; they may even represent new 'skins' to wear. Having a lot of clothes may seem wasteful to you if you prefer a very simple wardrobe, but money can be spent in different ways, and there is no implicit moral superiority in spending on one very expensive T-shirt rather than five cheaper versions that cost the same amount in total.

To many teenagers shopping can be a major hobby, but it is about far more than just buying things. For teenage girls in particular, shopping is about socialising, and learning about textures and colours. Shopping also tends to be a communal activity; buying in groups reassures you that you are buying the right things and that others approve of your purchases – and reconfirms you as part of the group.

You could encourage a young person with lots of clothes to have regular clear-outs – say sorting out all the items that have not been worn in the past six months. It's commonly said of adults that we wear 10 per cent of our wardrobe 90 per cent of the time and the same is true of teenagers. Help your young person to spot the cathartic pleasure in passing on things you do not need, to see growing out of things as a positive stage in their development, and get them to suggest where they should go next (to a charity shop, to the recycling bins or passed on to someone else who may appreciate them).

## HOW MUCH FLESH TO REVEAL

How much flesh (or underwear) to show is another vexed issue for parents. But attitudes about which there was general agreement when you grew up may have changed dramatically.

The next time you drop your daughter off at a party or for a group get-together, look at what everyone else is wearing, not just your own daughter. Styles of dress really have changed, and what would have once only made an appearance at a fancy dress party is now worn by almost all teenage girls, every time they go out. Yet, ironically, the vast majority of teenage girls are very conservative dressers; they get huge satisfaction from appearing almost identical.

'I have noticed that when my daughter brings a group of friends back to our house after school on Friday, the first thing they do is go upstairs and change from one uniform into another – they re-emerge wearing identical coloured tops, hoodies and jeans. And they take note of the precise details that make each item of clothing slightly different. At 10 my daughter could describe all her female classmates' shoes, now she can do the same with the style of appliqué on everyone's top. A friend's daughter has quite a different approach. She buys all her clothes from charity shops and takes pride in looking different. At 13 this is a tremendously brave thing to do.' **Mother**

## BODY ART: PIERCINGS, HAIR COLOURINGS AND TATTOOS

One of the biggest changes in fashion is that it's now quite normal to change the look of your hair, skin and various other parts of the body at an ever earlier age. It's ironic that many adults spend a lot of money on changing the look of their own hair but resent their young people doing the same thing. The difference is that teenagers now experiment with colouring and styling that their parents usually only took up much later on.

Problem hair is not worth sweating over – it grows out. Be aware that particular hairstyles have icon status, especially among groups of boys; they are a way of stating your tribal allegiance at a glance. The rules from their school may, however, help reinforce particular standards around which they make decisions.

The law on tattoos and piercings gives a parent some starting points, and again school rules will probably provide another. It is illegal for anyone to give a tattoo to a person under 18 years old. There is currently no national legislation in relation to piercings but most local authorities will have some restrictions. The most widely used would be the need for written parental consent for under 16s, but you will need to check what it is where you live. Citizens' Advice can help, or phone a local piercing shop and ask. Not all schools will have restrictions on piercings either, but if they do these should be found in the school prospectus or established by a call to the school office.

Body piercing in 2015 has no greater stigma than ear piercing in 1970; it's a matter of changed taste. Most piercings will close if you leave them anyway. Tattoos of course remain permanent. Point out how it would be to have the same picture on the wall for ever. Your young people may be turned off the idea in any case by the fact that it's increasingly popular for their parents' generation to acquire them too! Encourage the use of washable 'tats' first.

---

### 5 top tips for safer dressing up for girls

1 **Suggest she wears a coat on top of her outfit.** This is easier said than done; teenage girls tend to resist coats. Even if she does agree, most girls like to leave the front flapping open, so suggest she does the buttons up when she is on her own.

2 **If she still resists,** consider letting her choose a gorgeous coat that she does not want to take off.

3 **Alternatively,** a large kagoul, or wet weather top, is easily hidden in a bag and can be pulled out at the last minute. A much bigger version, perhaps one borrowed from an older sibling or cool friend, may be more acceptable than one her own size.

4 **Encourage** her to take clothes to change into at the party, taking care to change back again before she comes home.

5 **Discuss** the situation with her along with her friends. Teenage girls tend to be much more rational with each other's parents than they are with their own.

---

## THE FLEXIBLE WARDROBE – BORROWING AND LENDING CLOTHES

In most families there will be a certain amount of clothes borrowing going on, from the sharing of socks to wearing favourite outfits belonging to others. There are many parents who feel quite flattered when their young person wants to borrow their clothing items, but when that borrowing becomes the 'stealing' of an expensive or favourite item feelings can change and tensions mount. Siblings can be upset too by unauthorised borrowing, particularly if their clothing is not properly cared for or is never returned.

It is a good idea to discuss the rules for wearing or borrowing clothes belonging to others during a family meeting at a time when no one is particularly outraged by the behaviour of another so that the discussion can remain calm and non-blaming. In most families there will be some items that can readily be shared – these might include tights, socks, scarves, etc. – and others that have clear ownership and should never be used without permission. If the rules are broken then some penalty might need to be introduced: for example, a fine or providing a service for the family or aggrieved person such as tidying their bedroom, ironing their clothes, or clearing up the kitchen every evening for a week. It is important that the penalties are decided upon before any incident occurs when everyone can think clearly and without bias.

You might also want to discuss what happens if clothing is borrowed and damaged unintentionally. Does the borrower have to replace the item or is it put down to bad luck and a life lesson for the lender? Ideally when someone asks to borrow an item the lender should let them know any conditions, such as 'Yes you can borrow it just for tomorrow but if it comes back damaged in any way you'll have to buy me a new one.' This way everyone is clear. Note the time limit here too – sometimes a young person given permission to borrow an item once will see it as permission to borrow it any time they choose!

## QUESTIONS & ANSWERS

**Q:** My daughter pushes her school uniform regulations to the very limits. She twists the waistband around at the top of her skirt to turn it up as high as possible, and although she wears the regulation tights, they are full of ladders and holes. How can I encourage her to be more law-abiding?

**A:** You can't, although you could set a weekly budget for how much you think she should spend on tights, give her this as an allowance and get her to buy her own in future. Maybe the chance to keep the money she saves when she does not ladder her tights might encourage her to take more care in future!

School uniform is a natural boundary for young people to push against. And while they will often concede that a uniform has its advantages (it makes getting dressed quicker, it means their own clothes do not get spoiled), the desire to personalise it by varying from the quoted norm is a very natural one. Why not let the school enforce the degree to which pupils conform to the rules rather than you?

**Q:** I don't like the way my daughter dresses when she goes out at night and worry that she is sending out the wrong signals. What can I do?

**A:** This is a common concern: parents worry that their children are sending out the wrong message and at the very least that they will catch cold. There are two issues to tease out here and one or both may be relevant to you.

The first suggestion is to think carefully about why a particular outfit attracts such a negative response in you. Does a short skirt and crop top remind you of a style of dressing that was an unattractive stereotype from your own youth? Or does the style she has adopted make you feel she looks 'too grown-up' or more grown-up than you are ready for her to be? Being honest with yourself about the origin of your own negative feelings is a very good starting point.

The other cause for concern may be that someone else is noticing her style of dressing. A short skirt and bare midriff is seeking attention from men, and your daughter is probably perfectly conscious of this. But young men, in her own age bracket, may have different views on her appearance from older men, who may have very different associations for her style of dress. She probably doesn't even notice anyone more than five or six years older than herself.

It's very important to alert her to the messages she may be sending out, but equally vital that this chat does not take place when the outfit is on and she is trying to escape through the front door – this is far too volatile a situation for a sensible discussion.

Instead, when there is less emotion in the air, try to draw her attention to how her style of clothing may be seen and explain the risks she may face as a result. A particularly good time to raise such an issue is when there is a prominent news story, and sadly there are always some to be found. Another good time for such a chat is when she gets an invitation; you could talk about what she is planning to wear alongside the intended travel arrangements. Going out with her friends in a group, and being taken there and back by parents may be low risk, but if she has to walk home or take public transport the risks may be greater.

Q: Why won't my daughter wear a coat when she goes out? I am terrified she will catch pneumonia.

A: Parents often complain that their young person refuses to wear a topcoat (or anything warm) when they go out. Teenagers seem to be impervious to cold; they would rather freeze than look wrong. This often starts with much younger children, who hate the inconvenience of a bulky or heavy coat, and are very sensitive to the feel and look of what their parents choose.

Before she goes out, encourage your daughter to think through what is happening during the time away, how the change in hours/season will affect the temperature, and what she may later wish she thought of; talk through the safety issues. If she still decides to drop the coat, provided it is not a life-threatening situation, stick by her decision. A memory of how cold she was will be far more persuasive in the long run than a dim recollection of how you saved the day. Easy-to-pack fold-up coats are particularly useful, as are improvisations – my daughter was about to go off to a Halloween party recently and would not wear a coat. We quickly made a cloak out of a black bin liner, which she went out wearing quite happily.

**Q:** My son won't wear anything that does not have a major brand name on it. Why is this so important to his age group?

**A:** This is a beguilingly simple issue that masks much more serious undertones. If you can afford it, why not give into your son's demands for some designer gear? His protests that without it he will be laughed at or 'left out' go straight to a parent's heart, and may remind you of similar situations you faced as a child – and buying it together may be an experience that gives you both pleasure.

Teenage boys are very aware of pecking orders; they tend to view the world as a club to which you belong on a variety of different levels. Who you are seen with and what you are seen wearing may be tremendously important and reveal who your friendship group is and perhaps even your place within that group. Brands can thus be used to mask insecurities.

The problem is that it is all too easy for brand-based ranking systems to produce much more unacceptable forms of behaviour: sneering; putting people down; exclusion; and even physical violence. Equally, ostentatious brand sporting can make the young person very vulnerable; boys wearing all the right brands are good prospects for muggers – the chances are that if you are suitably dressed there will be a mobile phone worth taking and a wallet of the same quality.

In the long term, try encouraging your son to notice and value differences in other people and be aware of people who are individuals and are respected as such: for example, certain sports personalities. You could also encourage him to broaden his interests and therefore his friendship base. Help him to get a sense of identity that is not based on being part of the crowd and to learn how to value difference, and you will be encouraging his emergence as a mature adult.

**Q:** My 14-year-old son borrowed a jacket from his 17-year-old brother a couple of weeks ago when he was going to a party with his friends and wanted to look older. My elder son let him have it with very good grace and promptly forgot all about it until yesterday when he wanted to wear it. When he asked his brother to return the jacket it turned out that he had left it at the party and as far as I can make out has made no effort to get it back. Needless to say my elder son is furious and there have been a lot of shouting matches going on.

I feel that it is an unspoken agreement when borrowing something that it will be returned or replaced but my younger son insists that it was not his fault and he should not be penalised for it. What should I do to restore peace?

**A:** Your younger son was responsible for this item from the moment he borrowed it and he does not seem to be making enough effort to get it back. I understand that the party might not have been at a friend's house and he may not know the party-giver personally but he needs to make every effort to get the jacket back. You can help him by talking through with him his reticence to do so up till now. Perhaps there is someone he knows – or even you – who might be able to approach the party-giver on his behalf if he is shy or unwilling to do so?

Unless it has been definitely established that the jacket has gone and cannot be retrieved this would seem to be the appropriate answer to the problem, and if your younger son still refuses to make things right the jacket should be replaced from his own money or clothing allowance.

# CHAPTER 13

# 'Shh, don't tell my mum . . .'
# Sex, fancying, dating and keeping safe

These days sex is used to sell everything from cars to tooth-paste. It is overt and everywhere: on posters in the high street and online, in playground language, in toys (a bosomy Barbie is now marketed at the under-7s), on television well before the 9 o'clock watershed, in shops – indeed, not to be having a prominently displayed sexual relationship seems to mark individuals out as losers. When your children reach their teens it seems even more prevalent, and many parents have mixed reactions. One-half of the parental brain may feel that it's all too early, and you want to hang on to their innocence for as long as possible; the other half that you want to equip them with the information and skills that will allow them to make and act upon informed choices, and to decrease their vulnerability.

In fact, one may also question how innocent children are – from an early age they are very sensual creatures, playing openly with their genitalia 'because it feels nice' long before society has taught them not to do so in polite company. Children do have erotic feelings, but they don't understand them, and they quickly learn not to display them in front of others.

Our children are also growing up in a world where porno-graphy is more explicit and more readily available than ever before, where music lyrics and associated videos leave little to the imagination and are designed to be highly provocative in order to be watched as many times as possible by their target market, children and young people.

It is surprising too how often parents are completely naïve about how much their young people know about sex. During workshops on parenting teenagers, it's not uncommon for me to hear parents remark that their (say) 14-year-old daughter has absolutely no interest in sex. This is very unlikely. It is much more probable that the young person has avoided conversations that have anything to do with sex or relationships, because they have concluded that their parent(s) will find them embarrassing.

## WHY SEX AND RELATIONSHIPS EDUCATION IS IMPORTANT

Sexual competence is associated with openness about sex within the home and family, and early and consistent provision of sex education in schools. It is characterised by being able to:

- Maintain friendships with both sexes
- Discuss problems with friends of both sexes
- Communicate effectively with a sexual partner/potential partner
- Think about, plan and implement safer sex strategies
- Negotiate the use of contraception
- Agree the status of a relationship
- Fully understand terms such as coercion, consent and pressure in relation to sex and choices of behaviour in relationships
- Discuss the meaning and importance of sex within the relationship

This is all very well, but in the process of working towards this ideal, adolescence can be an exhausting time for young people and their parents.

Many parents would wish it to be less complicated: the fallings in and out of love, the break-ups and make-ups, the sheer turbulence of it all – particularly when they remember how they felt at the same stage, they hope their young people may avoid what they went through. But while it may be tempting to long for your young person to achieve stability in his or her love life, to find a steady boy- or girlfriend and have a less high-octane emotional life, in reality the turbulence is all part of discovering how relationships work and, in the long term, of finding a partner in a caring, committed relationship. The discussion of relationships with your peers is also bonding; if you pair off too early you can find it difficult to form both same sex and other sex friendships. Adults who 'settle down' very early often feel later in life that they have missed out, and this can be a cause of both personal and relationship breakdown.

## SEX IN CONTEXT

While sex appears to be the major plot strand in every television drama, film and hot news story, one of the most important things for the emerging sexual person to hang on to is a sense of their own value. Young people need to understand that they should only have sex when they feel ready for it, when they want it and their chosen partner does also, and when it is appropriate.

Most parents – and eventually their children – wish to see their child express their sexuality within a long-term, loving and committed partnership. One of the most important ways in which parents can set a context for the happy sex life of their children is by showing the place that intimacy occupies in a sexual relationship. How to behave in a relationship is learnt – and so all parents should be aware of what they are teaching their children through their own behaviour. This will prepare them to look and work at their own relationships, and themselves raise a child who has two loving and involved parents.

Of course your young person will be very embarrassed to see you and a partner holding hands in the street, but hugging each other in front of the children at home is a very valuable thing for parents to do. Public expressions of affection in a relationship that the teenager must acknowledge must once have been sexual (because they exist!) are helpful in allowing a young person to see sex as part of a shared physical intimacy.

---

### 5 top tips for encouraging good relationships

1  **Show affection to your partner and friends.**
2  **Talk through problems and issues,** including those about aspects of the relationship between you.
3  **Steer clear of** 'men are . . ./women are . . .' statements and jokes.
4  **It does no harm** to argue in front of your children as long as it is not too often, not too vitriolic and that you make it up and apologise to each other in front of them too!
5  **Be aware** that there is no time when you can argue with your partner and the children will be unaware of it – they may not know the details but they will hear or pick up on atmosphere. Dare to be honest with them but don't involve them, expect them to take sides, make them feel insecure or that your relationship is unstable or rocky.

---

Along similar lines, it's valuable for young people to see that there is a part of their parents' life that is separate from the family; parents do well to keep a room that is their own private space, and not part of the family space. So, if it's possible, it's a good idea to keep your own bedroom a private area – a zone the children to do not routinely enter as they get older. Even if the family television downstairs is switched on to something they do not want to watch, and you have a television in your room, they should ask permission before going into your room and installing themselves there.

For a young person to see joy, affection and mutual encouragement in a relationship between adults is very helpful. In the process they begin to understand that parenting is not just about paying bills!

## HAPPY SEXUAL RELATIONSHIPS ARE MORAL ONES

Before you start talking to your own young person about morality it is important to think about where you yourself stand. Your attitudes and beliefs will be shaped by your own upbringing, the situation you find yourself in now and the extent to which you are informed about world events.

Cultural, religious and family standards make it difficult to give precise recommendations, but in general a sexual relationship is a moral one when it is part of a long-term, caring and mutually supportive relationship, and both people want to have a sexual relationship with each other. And while the equal safety of both people is addressed, so is the equal pleasure.

### REFLECTION EXERCISE

Think about where you stand on the moral issues listed below. Place a score between 1 and 5 next to each statement indicating how strongly you agree or disagree with it – 1 is the lowest and stands for completely disagree; 5 is the highest and stands for totally agree.

Consider asking your young person to try the same exercise, but do not insist on them sharing their answers with you unless they want to. If they are willing it might lead to some interesting discussions on morality and perhaps safety too.

| | You | Them |
|---|---|---|
| Cheating is OK if you don't tell or get caught | | |
| Swapping intimate photos is a laugh | | |
| Girls should carry condoms | | |
| Abortion is an easy option | | |
| It makes no difference if someone is gay or straight | | |
| The better you look the better-looking partner you get | | |
| Porn is harmless | | |
| Sex is no big deal these days | | |
| Serious relationships are for when you're older | | |
| Marriage for life is old fashioned | | |
| One-night stands are harmless fun | | |

## SEX AND SEX EDUCATION

Young people need to know the biological as well as the emotional facts, and a surprising number of adults emerge with only a vague idea of how the body works in relation to sex. For example, boys as well as girls need to know about periods – why they happen, how often, what are the side-effects (e.g.

possible irritability and pain). Girls need to know about erections, 'penis management' and wet dreams. Both parties need to know the biological layouts of their bodies and the names for them: for example, where is the uterus and where are the testicles?

It's a good idea to seize opportunities to talk to your young people about sex, as and when they arise. Seeing a pregnant woman or a new baby in the street may spark a conversation, as may stories in the media or plot lines in soaps. It's sensible to answer the questions they ask and if necessary to ask them questions to clarify what they want to know, rather than launching into a huge lecture on all aspects of sex and relationships. The rule of thumb is little and often, and by doing so you will be providing the information they are ready for and their understanding will grow at a natural pace. If your child does not ask you anything about sex, is it because they think you will find this embarrassing? You could try asking a general question to find out if they would like to know more. Most children and young people are fascinated by the story of their own birth, and telling them about this may start a valuable conversation.

## Why it is important that parents talk to their children about sex – rather than leaving it all to teachers at school

It's true that public programmes of sex education are starting at ever-lower ages in school. The Sex Education Act 1994 made the provision of sex education compulsory at secondary schools and it was strongly recommended that primary schools should have programmes in place too. Personal, Social and Health Education programmes (PSHE) are a valuable way of exploring sensitive issues including sex and sexuality. Many people worry that telling young people too much too soon will make them want to experiment and try things out. However, evidence from around the world seems to indicate the opposite is true. Young people who have thorough, open and frank sex and relationships education are less likely to experiment and more likely to wait until they feel mature enough to handle the complexity of a sexual relationship and to take care of their physical and emotional needs within it.

There are many good reasons for talking to your young person yourself about sex rather than leaving it to teachers. Firstly, you help support their self-esteem, and help them value themselves in relationships. A mature attitude to sex helps them make responsible choices, and takes care of both their partners and themselves. Secondly, you support their moral well-being. The choices they make in this area will live with them for ever – you cannot turn the clock back. Thirdly, you increase their personal safety. Having a strong sense of self-worth in a relationship enables a young person to insist that a sexual relationship only proceeds once they feel ready and that it is safe (a condom is used). This helps avoid HIV and other sexually transmitted infections – as well as pregnancy.

Finally, while there are many instances of good practice, there are also many teachers who do not feel comfortable tackling the subjects of sex and sexuality in the classroom. In any case, your child may be happier asking a question in the privacy of their own home rather than in front of their peers.

'I find long car journeys are a particularly good time for sensitive talks. There is no eye contact – and you can stare out of the window if you want time to think before replying. Apparently one of my sons referred to being told the facts of life by me as "The M4 chat".' **Father**

## Talking about sex

Most of us seldom talk about sex except in jokey, sexy or medical situations. Even the vocabulary may sound weird to us – too clinical or too medical.

### FLASHBACK

For most of us our first knowledge of sex is a 'flashbulb memory' – one that stays in our minds for ever, like our first day at school, or where we were when we heard about the death of Princess Diana.

So, remember the first time your parent(s) talked to you about sex. How old were you? Where were you at the time? How did you feel? How did they behave and what did they say? What would you have liked to happen? To be younger/older? To ask questions? To see pictures? To run away?

What we tend to remember is how embarrassed our parents were. How does your experience then relate to how you talk or don't talk to your own young people about sex? Those of us who found out at school or from friends may well have hidden the fact from our parents – we ended up protecting their innocence!

'I remember finding out about the facts of life in the playground, from a girl who had an elder sister and consequently knew much more about everything than us. I was too embarrassed to ask my parents about it. About a year later my mother sat me down to tell me. I pretended that I was hearing it all for the first time.' **Antonia**, aged 14

Today, most parents want their children to be broad-minded and accepting – in particular when dealing with sexual orientation

– but find it hard to talk about it to their young people. The best way to encourage an acceptance of difference in your young people is to talk to them about it, no matter how uncomfortable it feels. It's not what you tell them, it's the talking that counts, so if you don't know everything, don't worry – ask or look up relevant websites on the Internet together, or look at a leaflet to find out. Young people who can talk openly about sex are less likely to start sexual activity young and are more likely to negotiate the use of contraception when they do choose to have sex.

There is the additional bonus that when you do tackle issues that are difficult to talk about, you gain feelings of both liberation and satisfaction – and an accompanying self-knowledge. Try – it will get easier!

## Getting the vocabulary right

Your sex is something you are born with, a set of genitals and other defining characteristics that make you out to be either male or female. Gender on the other hand is assumed, it is a choice about how you live your life, and works on a sliding scale – for example girls can be described as 'tomboys' or 'girly girls'. While these terms are frequently not helpful, and may disguise the fact that people display different behaviour in different situations, they do reveal how much latitude there is in the living out of gender. A person's sexuality is how they express their sexual self, for example as a heterosexual, homosexual or bisexual.

The word 'gay' is widely used as a term of abuse among young people in a huge variety of different situations, often as a general putdown, or to imply something is naff, wrong or stupid, and usually when absolutely no sexual reference is intended.

Yet being gay is about so much more than whom you choose to have a sexual relationship with; it refers to how someone relates to the world, their career choices, preferences, hobbies and relationships with other people, and the use of the term 'gay' as a putdown seriously affects the self-esteem of young people who have a growing awareness that they are themselves gay. With the high rate of suicide attempts among young gay people this is very important. These are not someone else's young people, but ours.

Using words inappropriately should be avoided and it's important to tell your young people how much offence they are causing, however unconsciously, by doing so. Taking a word they value (a footballer's or rock star's name for example) and over-using it to mean something bad often gets the point across.

## WHAT ARE WE AIMING FOR?

Before you think about trying to raise a sexually well-educated person, it's worth thinking about some goals. You might consider how you relate to each of these qualities before you think about where your teenagers currently sit. A sexually well-educated person:

- Is aware of their own sexuality
- Is comfortable with their own sexuality
- Is comfortable with the sexuality of others
- Is broad-minded
- Is tolerant
- Is well informed
- Is well balanced
- Knows and understands about bodies
- Knows about contraception
- Knows where to get contraception
- Is able to get contraception
- Knows when sexual expression is appropriate within a relationship
- Knows the difference between love, sex and lust

- Practises safe/safer sex
- Is prepared to organise safe/safer sex
- Is able to please/be pleased in a sexual relationship
- Is aware of sexually transmitted infections
- Is aware of HIV/AIDS

## WHAT HAS CHANGED SINCE YOU HAD SEX EDUCATION AT SCHOOL

If at school you had lectures on different forms of contraception, or read leaflets at a Family Planning Clinic, you will probably remember that the main aim was to avoid pregnancy at all costs; each method's statistical success rate was very important.

Today, condoms are preferable to all other forms of contraception because they protect the young person against more than pregnancy – sexually transmitted infections and, of course, HIV can have life-threatening consequences. Other infections are not killers but can have life-changing implications: left untreated, the sexually transmitted infection chlamydia can leave someone infertile.

Repeated health surveys have shown how quickly the HIV virus has spread in countries where condoms are seldom used, leading to the HIV/AIDS pandemic. Surveys of sexually active young people in the UK repeatedly show high levels of infection with chlamydia, which would seem to indicate that they are not using condoms and are exposing themselves to the risk of contracting infections and viruses.

Young people should equate sexual contact with protecting themselves from the very first sexual experiences, so encouraging condom use for sexual contact should be part of every parent's care for their child.

## SEX IN THE COMPUTER AGE

Parents will regularly say that sex is something that never changes, but perhaps this thought needs updating. For young people growing up today, sex is being presented very differently than in previous generations. By the age of 11 most young people will have seen some pornography – and don't be fooled into thinking this is the kind of pornography that was around when you were young: those magazine images would now be found quite often in advertising. Modern pornography is frequently violent or aggressive, routinely shows a range of sexual acts performed without intimacy or sensitivity and features just about every possible fantasy scenario. It is primarily geared at men and is designed to assist in masturbation. While porn has always been a way in which young people, and particularly young men, explore sex, modern porn may lead to aggressive and unrealistic expectations of partners and, as young women are also watching, may lead them to believe that 'being good at sex' is more important than intimacy or pleasure.

It is important that we talk to young people about porn and the differences between sex portrayed with the intention of stimulating, and real-life sex – which can be funny, embarrassing, clumsy and less than perfect. They may also need to understand that porn as an industry is frequently exploitative of its performers, particularly the many very young people who take part in order to make a living.

Porn can also become addictive as it may enhance masturbation, allowing for a quicker and more powerful surge of pleasure hormones in the brain. For young people with such an addiction, real-life relationships can prove unsatisfying and hard to maintain throughout their lives, so it makes sense that we not only talk to them but that we restrict their access to porn wherever possible: by making sure we put parental locks on phones, tablets, laptops and computers and talking with other parents to help them do the same. Having television sets in bedrooms is also a very bad idea. Not only does it inhibit sleep but it also allows young people unlimited access to late-night masturbation channels on ordinary digital TV.

Another of the big changes is the phenomenon of sexting – the sending of messages or photos of an extremely sexual nature to another person. Sometimes young people use sexting as an introduction to someone they are interested in; many girls and young women tell me that they have received photos of a young man's penis before they have even had a conversation with him. This may seem shocking to many parents but it is rather like an electronic version of the 'I'll show you mine if you show me yours' that children have always engaged in.

Obviously there are risks here. When a young person sends a sexually explicit image to someone they do not know, it may be circulated or posted online. An open and frank conversation about sexting, and in particular about sending images, should be part of every young person's sex and relationships education in school, but as coverage of this is somewhat patchy, it's probably best not to rely on the school to tell your child how to keep safe. Any image sent online still exists somewhere, even if the recipient deletes it, and such images can ruin a young person's dreams of a good career if they come to light. Today employers regularly look online to find out about prospective employees, and such pictures have a habit of resurfacing. Sending an image or film clip to a partner may also leave a young person open to ridicule or abuse if the relationship goes wrong. There are many incidences of celebrities having their private photos hacked, and these provide valuable opportunities for parents to have a conversation with their young person.

Parents often ask if they should check their young person's phone or computer – while this may be distasteful, letting a minor (under the age of 16) know in advance that you might make occasional checks could mean they are more careful about their usage. Once they reach 16 their gadgets are private, although parental controls should be applied until they are

18. However if you do look at their electronic gadgets, be warned that you are likely to read or view some things you will find shocking; your parents would have been just as shocked if they had been able to see inside your head as easily as you can see inside their phone or computer.

## FANCYING, DATING AND HOOKING UP

Young children may refer to friends as their 'boyfriend' or 'girlfriend'; slightly older children may dance together at parties, and announce they are 'going out', but not actually go anywhere. The term 'going out' signifies a relationship based on attraction rather than just friendship.

Many young people start going out in mixed-sex groups, say to the cinema, and within these groups couples may start to pair off – sit together or hold hands – while the rest just 'swarm'. It's a good idea to encourage these groups at first. There is safety in numbers and much of the early relationship angst and trauma can be reduced or even overcome by allowing young people to mix freely with each other and learn more about the feelings and motivations of others. The choices made about their education (single-sex or mixed-sex schools or classrooms) can impact on how comfortable your young people feel with all people their own age; stereotypes about the other sex and their behaviour can persist and block communication.

Some families have strict rules about how old you have to be to go out with a boyfriend or girlfriend on your own, and though these have merit with the very young, one consequence of these rules is often that young people make detailed plans to avoid detection if they are breaking them. This may mean that they do not have access to sources of help and support they need to help them make sense of their feelings and desires, attitudes and concerns.

Before they start one-to-one dating, make sure you have

had enough practice at talking with them about sex and relationships to ensure that you can address the changing nature of their involvement in attraction-based relationships without embarrassment. By far the biggest issues to discuss are consent and alcohol! As in your day, the two often go hand in hand and the statistics for young people today make sad reading. The majority of first intimate sexual contacts between young people still happens when liberal quantities of alcohol have been drunk, and a high percentage of young women both claim that they wish their first experience had not happened when it did and that without the alcohol it would not have happened.

All young people need to know and understand that all sexual behaviour with others is wrong unless there is informed consent – in other words the person needs to be clear about what they are consenting to. Silence does not count as consent; it has to be clearly given without pressure and it can be revoked at any time – a 'yes' one day is not a 'yes' next time, and a 'yes' early on does not take away a person's right to say 'no' later on in the experience if they feel uncomfortable or change their mind.

When they are dating, try to support and not to put down their relationships. If you tease them, they will tell you nothing in future. If you offer to collect from parties, they want you to do just that, not chat to their friends. If they are travelling home on their own, ensure that they have strategies should the unexpected happen. For example, if a promised lift does not materialise, do they have enough money for a cab, a strategy for how late they can call you – and a mobile phone that works?

There are advantages to starting to date a bit later. Whether you like (or accept) it or not, 'dating' is a time for exploring relationships and boundaries – including sexual relationships and sexual boundaries – in a practical rather than an academic sense. Starting to date later (15 or so) rather than earlier (12 or 13) will probably mean your young person has more, rather than less respect for their own sexuality and self, and will therefore take better care of themselves as a consequence. Young people who start one-on-one dating early are not guaranteed to start having sex early but there is an increased likelihood that they will. It is probably a good idea to discourage one-on-one unsupervised dating for as long as possible – regardless of the 'all my friends' plea. However, just because they are not talking about a boyfriend or girlfriend just yet doesn't mean they are not having sex or sharing sexual experiences.

There is a well-established sub-culture of 'hooking up' these days, which means anything from a casual date to oral or penetrative sex. Many young people prefer to be part of a crowd within which individuals spend time together or pair off as they wish without anyone having a commitment or responsibility to one individual over another. Young people's parties can often be places where they go to hook up with someone they may or may not want to spend time with outside a group setting. Not all young people enjoy this behaviour and it can lead to heartbreak and disillusionment if they find out that someone they thought they were 'going out' with saw them just as a 'hook up'.

As soon as they start going to evening parties or gatherings, it's a good idea to encourage your young person to talk to you about how people behave there. Even if your jaw wants to drop to your chest, play it cool and avoid judgement. Use the things that your son or daughter observes and experiences as opportunities to explore with them their attitudes and self-worth.

When they do start to date for the first time you can encourage responsible dating by expecting your young person to introduce you to his or her date in advance and agreeing to be picked up at the end of the evening by you or the other young person's parent. Show interest without any bias and don't try to grill them about their own behaviour; show kindness and concern without curiosity.

> 'After a whole year of writing his name on all my books and hanging around the car park where he parked his Vespa, I finally got asked out by the school heart throb! While feeling overjoyed and excited by the enormity of it all I was terrified – I'd barely gone out unsupervised with friends let alone a boy – but my mum was great. She bought me a short grown-up dress, new shoes and tights and even some make up and, owing to the fact that my older siblings didn't tease me unmercifully, I'm guessing she had a word with them too.' **Gill**

## HOW TO GET SOMEONE TO GO OUT WITH YOU

It can be very painful for parents watching a young person droop about the house longing to ask someone out, but not being able to summon up the courage to do so.

The first thing to bear in mind is that even though you can see a solution (i.e. your son or daughter asks the young person in question out), this is their problem rather than yours, and you could start by considering whether they actually quite enjoying the drooping; nurturing an unrequited love may be all they want at the moment.

If he or she does look for advice, you could suggest the following – but do bear in mind that it has to be them that makes the first move and not you:

- Could they find out who his or her friends are and get to know them? Perhaps one of them could drop a hint that your young person likes them? Many relationships begin on the basis that one party really likes the other, the other finds out and, having not particularly noticed the other before, is keen once they find out they are fancied!

- Find out what his or her interests are – are there clubs or interest groups they go to on a regular basis? Could your young person go along too?
- What route to school does the object of their affection take; does it overlap (or can it be made to overlap) with theirs at all?
- Could they invite him or her (or get someone else to invite them) to go out in a group of friends, perhaps to the cinema or bowling?

Encourage them to think about how their flame might show they like them back. Boys and girls can find each other very hard to read. For example, avoiding eye contact and looking at anyone in a group apart from them might be a strong sign that they fancy him or her – but it could also mean they find them unappealing! Sooner or later they'll simply need to ask, and the method used by most young people is to ask a friend to ask ('My mate fancies your friend, is she/he interested in him/her?'), rather than face the humiliation of asking in person.

Try not to ask your child for progress reports on how it is going, and don't be angry if the route home from school is taking much longer or they are coming home an illogical way in the hope of meeting their crush. Don't you remember doing similar things?

## WHAT TO DO IF ALL YOUR YOUNG PERSON'S FRIENDS ARE STARTING TO PAIR OFF – BUT NOT THEM

Of course many young people are not even interested in dating or hooking up until they are older, but may want to be considered attractive all the same.

'I wouldn't touch any of them [the boys at school] with a bargepole, they are all so immature and sex-obsessed but it really upsets me that no one is ever interested in me. What's wrong with me?' **14-year-old girl**

The real issue here is how to support your teenager's self-esteem when it is being battered by not being selected.

Deal with all the obvious practical things first – personal hygiene, clothes that give confidence – and then encourage concentration on keeping a wide circle of friends. You could also encourage your young person to talk to people they meet – rather than saying nothing or submitting to group practice when meeting new people (leave all conversation to the leader and observe them exchanging knowing glances that exclude others). Both sexes tend to be nervous and maybe glad to find someone of the other sex who will talk to them – and often an initial sympathy can encourage a possible partner to take the next step in a relationship!

'When I was at school there was a boy in the sixth form who didn't seem particularly attractive – he was rather overweight and had quite a few spots – but he always seemed to have lots of girlfriends. "He's so funny" was the general verdict.' **Mother**

They may need to think about the kind of signals their more popular peers are giving off that are different from their own in order to understand their choices. Unfortunately many may have to choose between popularity and their principles for a while, although in time the more principled young person will probably be more dateable than their peers.

## BECOMING SEXUALLY ACTIVE

While the media is full of stories about young people who are having sex at a very young age, in practice most young people become sexually active around their sixteenth year – with many waiting considerably longer.

Most young people become sexually active long before their parents are aware of it, so it's important to talk to them about contraception and the impact of sex on relationships far earlier than you suspect they need it. Some parents may find this embarrassing because they did not have the opportunity to talk to their own parents about these issues. While there are sources available for wider reading, and teenagers will get information at school, a good starting point is a folder of practical information, held somewhere where everyone knows to find it, that all family members can access.

The obvious consequence of involvement in sexual relationships is the risk of pregnancy. Research shows us that the earlier a young person starts having sexual intercourse, the less likely they are to use contraception. It's also true that no form of contraception is 100 per cent effective, so even young people who are doing what they can to avoid pregnancy, may still find themselves facing an unplanned pregnancy.

## WHAT TO DO IF YOUR TEENAGE DAUGHTER SUSPECTS SHE MAY BE PREGNANT

Depending on when sex took place, there may be time to take the morning-after pill. Provided it is taken within 72 hours of sex, this is a relatively straightforward method of preventing a pregnancy developing – the pill delivers a high dose of the regular 'pill' (either progesterone, progesterone and oestrogen or oestrogen alone), which prevents a fertilised egg from implanting in the uterus. The morning-after pill is now available free in certain pharmacies, and from GP clinics that offer contraceptive services, your GP and walk-in NHS clinics. A quick check on Google or call to a GP will give you local information. Information on how to get the pill should be part of your general information file (see Chapter 2) and discussed with her.

This method of birth control is not to be relied on for the future, however. High doses of hormone are dangerous if repeatedly taken, and only condoms offer protection against HIV and sexually transmitted infections too.

If she is pregnant, the most important thing is to help your daughter make up her own mind, so that she feels supported. What choice she makes will affect your life too, and so you have a right to explore possibilities with her, but the ultimate decision remains hers.

Abortion is often presented as an easy option, but the reality is that it is not straightforward emotionally. The physical scars may heal (although a slight risk to long-term fertility from abortions remains) but the emotional ones take much longer. Abortion should never be considered as the light answer to a big problem. It may be helpful for her to see a counsellor, to talk about the situation with someone not emotionally involved (see Appendix 2 for how to find one).

## WHAT TO DO IF YOUR SON HAS FATHERED AN UNBORN BABY

Again the most important thing is to make the young man feel he is supported, loved and able to communicate his feelings, whatever has happened. 'Getting someone pregnant' is a two-person process and he should be encouraged to face his responsibilities (which may be financial as well as emotional), rather than just walk away or deny it – at the same time acknowledging that the decision over the fate of the unborn child will most probably be more hers than his.

The decision about what to do in this situation should

ideally be made together – perhaps with the other set of parents involved too – although be aware that anger and name-calling will not help. Marriages and planned partnerships based on an accidental pregnancy, at a young age, statistically have a very low chance of turning into successful long-term relationships.

## QUESTIONS & ANSWERS

**Q:** My daughter was recently dumped by her boyfriend of three months. She is devastated. How do I help her cope?

**A:** Firstly you should take her unhappiness seriously. You should deal with the pain itself rather than the context of the emotion – thus you should take it as seriously as if a friend has just rung to say her 15-year marriage is over. Teenage relationships are important to them and should be treated as such – so don't be tempted to use phrases like 'There are plenty more fish in the sea', comment that you never liked him anyway, or belittle her pain.

Allow her to cry; sit with her and listen to her talk about her misery while you eat ice cream or chocolate (or whatever else feels appropriate) together under a duvet on the sofa. Give her your time rather than tell her that she will soon be over it. Encourage other members of the family to empathise with her, and be sensitive. Little brothers whom you fear might be tempted to tease can usually be brought on side by explaining that they will be probably be feeling the same at some time in the future – this makes them feel more grown-up.

**Q:** My son has just found out that his girlfriend is two-timing him with his best friend. What should he do?

**A:** This is a very difficult situation because it kills on two levels: his trust in both his girlfriend and his best mate. Of the two, the loss of the best mate may be the more devastating to him, as it deprives him of the person he would most likely talk to. With boys, this situation can be further complicated by the need to retain face and not to show that he minds.

Encourage your son to say how he feels and to tell you even if he cannot yet bring himself to discuss the situation with the others involved. Tell him that it's OK to feel lots of things – intense anger, sadness, hatred and depression. Encourage him to take out his frustration on inanimate things: the gym, kicking a football, running hard. Talk to him about breaking trust, how that makes people feel and what can be learnt in the process.

Deep down, he may be worrying that she left him because he was not good enough for her, so encourage him to dwell on the positives that come out of such a situation. You could encourage him to concentrate on the fun that they had while they were together. You could also ask how he looks at both his friend and his girlfriend now, and what he thinks other people will make of the situation – have they emerged with any credit? He may find his wider circle of friends and acquaintances are very sympathetic to his position and think well of him. At least he has now had a girlfriend, and being able to talk about 'your ex' may change his relationship with his peers.

Q: My daughter is really keen on this lad in her class. The problem is that I am sure he knows it too and feels that she is throwing herself at him. How can I encourage her not to make herself look cheap?

A: Telling her that she is 'making herself look cheap' may isolate her from you right now. If she is really keen on him, and doesn't believe that females should wait to be asked out by males – and most young women today don't – you risk looking out of touch by making such comments. What looks blindingly obvious to parents often looks quite different to young people. Courses of action that we see as leading nowhere, or worse, are part of their learning how to handle situations, and it would be more helpful to encourage her to talk about what she has tried and what has not worked, than to criticise what she has already done.

Help her see that she is worth going out with, but also look at things from the young man's point of view. If someone is interested in you, and you give them a hint, they will probably take it up. Repeated trying makes you both feel bad.

Q: My son was dumped by his girlfriend, but I've heard him saying he dumped her. Should I encourage him to be honest?

A: This is an age-old situation and his friends may collude in his self-deception – or tease him about it. Whatever he says in public, help him to own his feelings and if he looks sad, try to be supportive. Ultimately though, this is his business not yours. You are his parent, not his best friend.

Q: I am horrified by the sexual explicitness of teenage magazines. Should I ban them?

A: The problem is that if you ban them, they become more exciting and your young person will find other ways of getting to read them – perhaps reading them at friends' houses.

Instead, why not buy a copy of the magazine and discuss it with your young person, concentrating on articles of interest and adding a wider dimension. For example, an article about how to give a boy a good sexual experience raises the question of whether the girl should be entitled to one too, and whether being known as someone who is technically adept at sex is a helpful reputation to have.

Q: Problem pages in teenage magazines lay a lot of emphasis on how to give pleasure in a sexual relationship. Is this something I should talk to my daughter about?

A: Think back to your own adolescence. Would you have wanted your parents to talk to you about sexual gratification and techniques? Most of us would have found this excruciatingly embarrassing. Besides, what is the height of sexiness for one person may prove laughable to someone else.

Parents can comfortably leave this aspect of a sex education to a young person's contemporaries, advice sources and later experience.

Q: My son has festooned his walls with pictures of naked women cut from magazines. Should I object?

A: Your attitude to your son's decorations depends on you – so if you are embarrassed by what you see, and this is an area of the house you are routinely in, then you should discuss what would be appropriate. An alternative might be to allow the posters to remain but ask that from now on he cleans up his own bedroom. If the room is shared with a sibling, then their opinions need to be considered too.

Q: I found my teenage son looking through the drawers under our bed. I was very embarrassed.

A: Ask him what he was looking for. If he was looking to see what contraception looks like, volunteer to show him.

Curiosity about sex is entirely natural and should be encouraged. Young people are fascinated about how the bits fit together, with the hidden organs of the female giving rise to particular curiosity. So give your daughter a mirror and encourage her to examine herself; allow boys of 10–11 to look at a sanitary towel or tampon and experiment to see just how much liquid they can hold. Allow him to open up a condom when he expresses curiosity to find out how it works. He will be fascinated and then move on. Knowledge makes him feel grown-up and equips him for dealing with his peers – those who don't know what things look like can find life difficult at school.

Q: I am a single mother raising a son without the support of a male partner. Having brought my son up to treat women with respect, I now find he routinely looks at pornography and is developing a casual vocabulary for both women and sex that really disturbs me. What have I done wrong?

A: A woman bringing up a boy on her own may well find her teenage son's attitude to sex unappealing. The teenage boy's response is in part biological, part developmental and part cultural. In a sense, flexing his biceps and being provocative is a way of developing some distance from a parent he has been very close to – something that is essential for his healthy future development – and does not necessarily mean he will turn into a sexually depraved adult.

However politically correct are the attitudes with which we raise children, there may be a difference between the way young males and females regard sex and fantasise about it. For large numbers of males the ideal is 'dirty sex'; sex from the waist down with only the genitals touching; a 'blow job' by a big breasted woman. They fantasise about explosive sex with no emotional context or long-lasting attachment, quick and powerful. Girls' fantasies tend to fall into two kinds. The majority fantasise about sex in a context of emotional involvement; they are often much more romantic, perhaps fuelled by literature and media geared towards female markets. However, many young women would refute such an image of female sexuality, and there is a growing trend for young women to be more forthright and sexually extrovert than young men – just look at the music videos being made by females these days.

But you should take comfort from the fact that, as the proverb says, 'the apple does not fall far from the tree'. Even though he may be trying to establish his independence right now by expressing opinions he knows offend you, there is a world of difference between fantasy and reality (for all of us), and in the long term the views he has been brought up with may be closer to his eventual opinions. Wait and see how he treats a real-life partner and you may be very proud of him after all.

**Q:** Should I allow my teenage son or daughter to bring a partner home to stay the night in my house?

**A:** The most important considerations here are how old your young person is and how mature they are. Sex with a young person under 16 is illegal for both sexes, so that should generally be the age limit for overnight stays in the same room. Of course even if one is in another room or on the sofa there is a possibility of 'corridor creeping', so asking permission to stay over should be obtained by the partner's parents too. This may even mean phoning them if you are unsure but this should never be done without the knowledge of your young person and their partner.

Bear in mind that if, when asked whether a partner can stay the night, you are uncomfortable with the idea, it's fine to say no – indeed, your young person may be looking for you to do this, i.e. having a ready-made and face-saving excuse of 'my mum won't let me'.

Nor does the request for a partner to stay the night necessarily mean they are wanting to have sex. For many young people a decision to sleep together is just that – taking intimacy a stage further than is possible during the day.

If you are unhappy about them staying the night together in your house (and your feelings are just as important as theirs), you might consider allowing the partner to stay when you are away from home or allowing your teenager to stay away from home at the partner's house. Bear in mind, though, that if they want to stay the night with a partner elsewhere, and they are over 16, there is relatively little you can do about it; your approval or disapproval may make a difference, but will not necessarily be the deciding factor. Remember, too, that young people create the possibility for sex in all sorts of unlikely places; it's not unheard of to find it taking place in school lavatories, in sports changing rooms, as well as that traditional location 'behind the bike sheds'.

> 'My wife and I were always very permissive about allowing boy and girlfriends to stay at our house. We took the view that whatever our young people were going to get up to, they would be doing it anyway, and we would rather they were doing it somewhere safe and warm.'
> **Father**

Q: What if my young person wants to bring a partner of the same sex home for the night?

A: All the same issues arise as with the previous question. If it is your house, your views have to be considered; asking for your consent may just be the first stage in letting you know how they feel.

But do ask yourself how you would react if the partner your young person wanted to bring home were of the other sex; i.e. if the relationship were clearly heterosexual. Even if you are unwilling to allow what your young person wants to occur under your roof, do try to discuss it with them. 'I am willing to admit that I am prejudiced, but would like to talk about how this situation makes me feel.' Honesty is the first step to intimacy.

Q: A friend suggested I should provide a box of condoms somewhere accessible for my teenagers. Isn't this just encouraging promiscuity?

**A:** Providing access to condoms will not make someone have sex if they don't want to, nor will not providing them make someone stop having sex if they want to. And access to a large box of contraceptives is unlikely to produce a response of 'I must use these up' among your young people.

What providing easy access to condoms does do is reinforce a responsible attitude to sex, and remind young people that each sexual contact is an opportunity for someone to become pregnant or acquire a sexually transmitted infection.

A large box of condoms placed in a convenient place (say the bathroom cabinet) that can be accessed in private is a good idea. I'd recommend a large box not because I recommend as much sex as possible, but because access is then private – a small packet is more embarrassing as it is obvious to all if something has been taken. In any case, just because your teenager is taking them, does not mean they are actually using them – they may be getting familiar with them, showing them to their friends or taking them for use by a friend who has less easy access – in which case you are doing them a good turn. Condoms, like all contraception, are available free on the NHS.

**Q:** I feel differently about my son experimenting with sex to my daughter. Am I being unreasonable?

**A:** However equal we try to make the sexes, the environment in which they grow up can make negotiating sex seem very unfair. Your daughter may view her sexual future in terms of maintaining a good sexual reputation, not becoming pregnant nor acquiring a sexually transmitted infection, while your son may be trying to appear knowledgeable and powerful, not to lose face, to be perceived as good at heterosexual sex (whether or not he is actually practising it) and to develop a successful masculine persona (for example through frequent sexual encounters).

If you have boys and girls in the family be aware that there are different issues, but try not to make different rules. So by all means talk with sons and daughters about the dangers and risks associated for each sex and the different (and sometimes unfair) expectations and roles within relationships, but at the same time treat them as equals. So if your 16-year-old son is allowed to spend time in his room with his girlfriend, your 16-year-old daughter is entitled to the same treatment.

**Q:** I don't like the relationship that has developed between my teenager and her teacher. What can I do about it?

**A:** The tabloid newspapers are full of stories of inappropriate sexual relationships – between old men and young girls, mature female teachers and their teenage charges, and abusive relationships between members of the same family. Some of these are prompted by the close physical proximity between the parties, others by the Internet. If you suspect an inappropriate relationship between your teenager and a teacher, then your response will probably depend on how old your young person is.

If the relationship is in a school context, a young person under 18, having an inappropriate relationship with an adult, is an immediate cause for concern and you may need to make immediate contact with the school to discuss your worries. There are child protection issues here that need to be discussed – and fast. Within the context of school, the law has now been changed so that it is always an offence for someone in a position of trust (e.g. a teacher) to engage in a sexual relationship with a young person in their care, even if over 16.

**Q:** My daughter's best friend spends hours in Internet chatrooms and my daughter wants the same access. Should I let her?

**A:** Cases of sexual grooming that begin in Internet chatrooms are difficult to spot in their early stages. The details of recent cases have become well known, and many parents have reacted with horror at both the amount of time paedophiles devote to grooming young people for inappropriate relationships (18 months before a first meeting is not uncommon) and the extent of time some teenagers spend in Internet chatrooms (in a recent case, a 14-year-old girl was spending up to eight hours a day online).

It's not true that inappropriate friendships on the Internet put young people in danger from strangers. By the time a relationship has developed online, it no longer feels like they are talking to someone they do not know. Often people seeking out under-age partners (girls and boys) will begin by befriending and showing affection and care for a young person. They are very good at what they do and can spot vulnerable youngsters easily. The process of grooming, whether for sex or, more recently, for terrorist affiliations, slowly builds a relationship with a young person until they feel that the groomer is the only person who really cares about them, understands them and desires them – either physically or ideologically. They are then vulnerable to suggestions which, if made in other ways, they would have rejected easily.

An obvious response is to say that the young person should not have this much access online, but if both parents are working and tired in the evenings, and the computer is in the young person's bedroom and they are quiet, it's tempting to let the situation run on. So while limiting the amount of time your young person is online is the starting point, it's also important to try to put something else in its place: perhaps family time, outings, sports activities, a walk or run, games evenings, no-TV nights or just simple conversation. Try to teach them how to enjoy themselves in ways other than using the Internet – given that a survey recently reported that many adults find the computer better company than their family, this could be quite a challenge for parents too!

It's also very helpful for parents to talk through with their young people the dangers of using the Internet. Young people need to know how predatory Internet users frequently use false identities online or pretend to be much younger than they really are. You should encourage their cynicism: never take information provided online at face value. An ideal time to do this is when there are relevant stories in the news. Parental controls on the Internet are quite workable – you can buy programmes that limit access to pornographic sites.

# CHAPTER 14

# 'Off my head!' on drugs and alcohol – safety, moderation and dialogue

Drug-taking must be seen in the context of the world we all live in. Accurate information on what is available, how drugs affect the body, the highs they can produce, what are the risks and what are the harm-reduction strategies that protect your young people and their friends are all essential if they are to take responsibility for what they are doing.

By encouraging them to take responsibility for their actions, and having the confidence and self-esteem to decide for themselves what they want to do, rather than issuing blanket directions on non-use, parents encourage young people in the right direction. It is worth pointing out that rather than just treating the drug-related behaviour, rehab clinics spend a lot of time discussing with clients why they feel the need to take the drugs they use; in other words what circumstances in their lives have led them to treat themselves, their future and their relationships in such potentially damaging ways. Most parents worry about the use of illegal drugs, but be reassured that, in the long run, most young people who do take an illegal drug stop using them of their own accord. However, legal drugs continue to be a real danger, with alcohol, the commonest of all, contributing to just about every circumstance a parent worries about.

The good news for parents is that after many years of active and detailed strategies across all areas of health and education, drug use of all kinds is steadily going down among young people.

## SPOTTING THE POTENTIAL RISK-TAKERS

The parents of most teenagers worry about them forming bad habits, and getting into bad company. Drugs are a particular concern and 'What are the danger signs to watch out for?' is a question that often gets asked at my parenting seminars.

While it's true that there are things that might indicate drug use, there is no definitive list. A better approach may be to look at the circumstances surrounding young people today – their decision-making processes and those who influence them – and to think about why they might want to get involved. This leaves you in a better position to talk to your young people about the choices they make, better able to assess the risks associated with those choices, and to discuss how to reduce them. This starting point is important.

Many parents believe that by giving their young person information and talking to them about the risks involved they are doing everything they can to protect their young person. Unfortunately young people are far more likely to use their own experience and the information of friends and others they consider reliable than the word of parents or teachers. Acknowledging that they are the ones making the choice and helping them to explore for themselves through reliable outlets what the outcomes of those choices might be will increase their confidence and skill.

Parents' notion of risk is often not real, being based on often rather lurid stories they have come across in the media. And while they are aware of the physical risks, young people between the ages of approximately 13 to 16 will be far more interested in the social risks of going against their peer group or young people's culture. Ultimately, the choice about what they then do is theirs, but helping them identify the disadvantages to their social standing of drug use may be helpful.

It's popular to talk about 'addictive personalities' and scientists have attempted to match gene structure to this. But probably each one of us gets addicted to something – it might be nicotine, but it might be soap operas, magazines or computers. These things give us feelings we find attractive, a sense of security – and stop us thinking about what worries us. Every time we indulge in a pleasurable or risky activity we get a small hit of 'feel good' chemicals in our brains. In young people the receptive areas are rather numbed for a while, and consequently young people might need bigger and bigger stimuli to activate them – or even to resort to external chemical means.

So, rather than just thinking about whether your young people are developing an addiction for drink or drugs, parents do well to think about both their own and their young people's attitudes to risk-taking in general.

Risk-takers seem to be born rather than made. Certain children will always try to climb higher, swim deeper, pedal further – and thus, when they reach adolescence, they may take on far riskier activities to get the same feelings. Spotting that you have a risk-taker in the family is fairly easy, and if you do, you need to try to communicate effective strategies for harm reduction or provide opportunities for that risk-taking behaviour to be satisfied in healthy, well-supervised ways.

## DRUG EDUCATION – IN AND OUT OF SCHOOL

All schools are now required to have a programme of drug education for their students. However the quality and effectiveness of these may vary enormously from school to school.

It's a good idea to find out what your young person's school has on offer and when different elements of the programme are delivered. This way you can ask them about the things they are learning not as a parent but as someone who wishes to know more themselves – a student even.

If you feel that the drug education programme is too weak or is not encouraging the students to examine their own attitudes enough, then do have a word with the drug education coordinator (usually the PSHE coordinator for the school, whose name and role will usually be available on the school website) and let them know. Parent power goes a long way in schools these days. Through a programme of skills development, attitude exploration and unbiased information young people should:

- Understand the risks and range of possible side-effects of different drugs
- Know that some drugs are legal and others illegal, and that just because something is legal does not mean it is harm-free
- Know the limits of what they are taking – a bottle of vodka or whisky drunk neat in one go will kill them
- Know that allergic reactions to drugs and bad experiences are possible and can have life-threatening consequences, particularly if they are alone or with friends who don't know what to do
- Understand that dehydration (and sudden rehydration) can be as harmful as a drug itself
- Know how to spot behaviour that implies drug use
- Know what to do if someone collapses
- Have explored strategies for reducing risk of harm in a range of scenarios and settings

## WHAT PARENTS DO NEED TO WORRY ABOUT – LEGAL HIGHS AND DRINK AS WELL AS 'DRUGS'

Parents tend to concentrate their worries on illegal drugs, forgetting that there are equally dangerous substances openly available to young people in their own homes. Alcohol is a very dangerous drug that society tolerates; were it to be invented today it would probably go straight into the class 'A' category, along with heroin and crack cocaine.

Alcohol increases an individual's self-confidence in the first instance, and takes away inhibitions. Too much alcohol is a factor in most teenage pregnancies, unplanned (and usually unprotected) sex and sexually transmitted infections, and a huge proportion of domestic violence, rapes, car accidents and fights. Cannabis makes users more likely to flop in front of the telly or listen to music than engage in predatory sex or physical aggression. So it's not whether a drug is legal or illegal that makes it dangerous. Of all the millions of cannabis users there has been only one death in the UK directly attributable to taking too much;[1] too much alcohol in one go can, and does regularly, kill young people.

Parents often have preconceptions about shady drug dealers hanging around the school gates, or targeting specific socio-economic groups, but in reality most young people will get substances from their friends, who in turn will get it from older siblings, friends of their siblings – or even their parents. Today there are also new patterns of substance misuse that are very widespread with young people and involve the use of a range of legal substances such as nitrous oxide (laughing gas) and a range of products using herbs or synthetic chemicals. They are frequently marketed as plant food, bath crystals or

---

[1] Although long-term use is considered to be as dangerous to health, or possibly more so, than cigarette smoking.

fertiliser and are labelled as 'unfit for human consumption' as a way of getting round the drug laws. They are easily bought in high street shops specialising in young people's clothing and drug paraphernalia – commonly known as 'Head Shops' – or through the Internet. Even well-known outlets like eBay sell gas canisters which are marketed in small cans and sold ostensibly for cream whipping machines. Legal highs are the newest and most worrying form of drug misuse as many young people equate legal with safe. Deaths from these substances have been rising steeply in recent years as deaths from other drugs have declined dramatically.

## ENCOURAGING SENSIBLE ALCOHOL USE

Encourage your young people to understand the effect that seemingly innocent drinks have on their bodies. The products most commonly drunk by many teens, particularly girls, are alcopops, which taste sweet and not noticeably of alcohol. They also seem to favour drinks with a high alcohol content such as strong ciders and vodka, which is sold in large bottles relatively cheaply in high street supermarkets. Encourage your young person to look at the alcohol content of various drinks at home and relate these strengths to the impact on the central nervous system. This doesn't have to be about 'hard facts'; it is far more powerful to talk about the social implications of alcohol use. So for example one drink might relax the drinker, after two they might feel more uninhibited and talkative – ready to laugh and enjoy themselves, but after five or so they may be becoming obnoxious – swearing, arguing, shouting and showing little regard for others' feelings.

One of the biggest problems with alcohol and young people is that for many being extremely drunk is seen as funny. Helping young people see that losing control is anything but will help them control drinking far more than messages about future cirrhosis or dependence will. Try watching some clips of extreme drunken behaviour on YouTube together and encourage them to be critical rather than amused.

Many people feel that by drinking with your young person, you teach them responsible drinking habits. In Europe young children regularly drink with their parents. But as well as teaching them how to handle alcohol, are you also passing on your own bad habits? Do you reach for a beer or a gin and tonic as a relaxation strategy? Is offering a guest alcohol the first thing you do when you greet them; i.e. it is seen as essential to conversation? Do you really need to keep a large stock of beer or wine in the house?

Examining the environment in which your teenagers are growing up, and the evidence they see of drink as both a social prop that boosts the enjoyment of any occasion, and something that provides release from tension, may be helpful to everyone in the family.

---

### 7 top tips to help prevent teenage binge drinking on an evening out

1  **Encourage** them to have something to eat before they go out; with food in the stomach, alcohol reaches the blood stream more slowly.

2  **Give them a little extra money** to allow them to buy drinks at the bar during the evening rather than binge drink outside the venue before they go in; discuss this strategy with your teenager's friends' parents so that they are pre-prepared too. (But be aware that they may just spend this on an extra bottle on the doorstep.)

3  **Give them a couple of alcohol-free drinks** (in equally attractive bottles) to take with them and drink outside.

4  **Encourage them to drink long drinks;** adding mixers will reduce the harm.

5 **Arrange to meet them at the end of the evening** rather than allowing them to walk home.

6 **Encourage them to look out for each other** and to notice if someone has had too much to drink; good friends stay with each other when one of them is in difficulty and don't just abandon them.

7 **If they do come home the worse for drink** show strong disapproval – you'd be surprised how often young people will state 'my mum will kill me' as a reason not to drink too much.

The management of many clubs will also take parents' concerns seriously; after all if they have parental approval their door takings will rise, and the extent to which they have to take responsibility for those within their premises is highlighted by prosecutions. 'Chill out rooms' in nightclubs are just such a response to serious concerns about what goes on within their walls.

## SMOKING

While smoking is decreasing among the population as a whole, smoking rates among young people continue to be high, with girls smoking more than boys. The reasons are complex but 'peer culture' may be one of the most powerful.

Kids who smoke look cool to other kids. They demonstrate an independence young people find appealing and show themselves (at least when they are young) as risk-takers who walk on the wild side. What is cool at 13 is very definitely not cool at 30, but by then the habit may be too hard to break.

Encourage your young person to think about what really is cool from quite a young age, and to consider smoking and smokers (let's face it, they smell of it) in this light. Encourage health and smelling nice, a good complexion and sweet breath, to say nothing of more money in your pocket.

One of the reasons why so many girls smoke is related to weight and the belief that smokers stay thinner than non-smokers. This is dangerous ground as many illegal drugs can reduce appetite as a side-effect too. Young people need to know and understand about nutrition and a healthy diet. So encourage your daughter to join a gym club or fitness class, or go swimming with her regularly. These activities will tone her body and improve her appearance – rather than having a fag, which will make her smell, ruin her health, and make her skin and hair dull.

## WHAT SORT OF DRUGS, AND HOW AVAILABLE THEY ARE

Let's start with the basics. The sheer availability of drugs today may be surprising to those who have not been very aware of a drug culture since their own youth.

Broadly speaking, drugs fall into three categories, which share effects on the body or mind.

### Depressants

The term doesn't apply to depressing the mood of the user but to the central nervous system. These drugs slow down the heart rate so the breathing usually slows down too; they reduce physical (and emotional) feelings of pain, slow down many body functions such as digestion and the immune response. Body temperature is lowered and users may sleep. They are the one category of drugs that have the potential risk of fatal overdose as too much will slow the heart down until it stops. That is why a mixture of two drugs from this category is particularly dangerous as it may lead to an unintentional overdose. This is also the category of drug where tolerance and physical dependence can build quickly. Users frequently need to use more and more of the drug to get any effect, and sudden withdrawal from the drug once the body has become used to it will cause physical symptoms and could even be dangerous in a heavy or long-term user.

The benefits to the user are that they may feel removed from care or deep anguish such as grief, sleep well, lose inhibitions or self-criticism (as the drug depresses the 'guilt and shame' responses in the brain).

The dangers include death by overdose, physical dependence – needing the drug to get by so it can take over a person's life – hypothermia, damage to the organs of the body as the metabolism is compromised, such as liver disease, constipation, poor circulation and breathing problems. They may cause anxiety and paranoia and a reduced awareness of risk.

Drugs in this category include barbiturates, alcohol, morphine and heroin.

## Stimulants

Simulants, on the other hand, have many opposite characteristics. Stimulant drugs increase the heart rate and consequently users may breathe faster. They may increase the amount of energy a person expends – making them very lively or quick. Thinking may become faster and quicker too and a quick rush of adrenalin to the brain may make users feel powerful or invincible. The drugs act on the body rather like the fight-or-flight response and so may slow down many processes such as kidney function.

The benefits to the user are that they feel very warm, alive and energetic and may feel very powerful and on top of things. In the past such drugs have been used for weight loss as they burn up a lot of energy, though this is no longer legal (but it is still an attraction for some).

The dangers include heart problems in anyone with an

underlying heart weakness, as well as increased blood pressure and the problems associated with it. Because of the feelings during use, these drugs can develop a psychological dependence very quickly – users may feel marvellous with the drug and awful without. There is a real come-down period for these drugs as the energy expended by dancing all night or going without sleep for four days does not come from the drug itself but from the user's own energy reserves. There is also a danger of overheating or exhaustion, particularly in a hot club.

Drugs in this category include amphetamines or 'speed', cocaine and crack cocaine, nicotine and caffeine. The last two of course have far less obvious effects because of the relatively low quantities taken. Taken at high doses in concentrated form the effects would be very apparent.

## Hallucinogens

The third major drug category. These work on the brain mainly, although many of the drugs will have components of the previous two categories in them. Hallucinogens affect the way the receptors in the brain receive and process information, creating a misfire in some cases or set everything going at once. Put simply, a sound may trigger not only the sound receptors but also those associated with taste, colour, sight and touch, giving the user a seemingly profound or enthralling experience. Hallucinations are not usually in the 'seeing something that isn't really there' category – rather an altered perception.

The benefits to the user are that their sensory experiences are heightened. Music may become enhanced, food may taste better, conversation may be more meaningful, jokes more hilarious, emotions more sincere and overwhelming.

The risks of this category include an increased risk of accidents as the user's perception of both objects and danger may be altered. The drugs may induce anxiety and paranoia and in susceptible people may trigger or contribute to schizophrenia. There are indications of possible permanent damage to the brain function in some circumstances and cannabis is famously associated with short-term memory loss.

Drugs in this category include LSD, cannabis and magic mushrooms. Ecstasy also belongs partly in this category and partly in the stimulant category.

By far the most commonly used drug is alcohol. The most common illegal drug for the teenage population is cannabis. By the time they are 13 or 14 your young people will probably know how to get hold of it, who in their class at school is an occasional user, who is showing signs of dependency and who is experimenting with something stronger. They may have already seen classmates returning from lunch showing signs of recent drug use. They are also offered it in the street, quite openly.

Parents tend to approach the drug issue from the position of both potential personal victim and protector of the vulnerable. As potential personal victim they are scared of the rise in burglary and street crime, which threatens them personally and which the media report as constantly rising to feed drug habits. As protector of the vulnerable they are frightened by the idea of drug 'pushers' approaching their young people and creating a habit where none was sought.

But most drugs supplied to schoolchildren are on the basis of 'pulling' rather than 'pushing'. For example, someone may announce that they are getting hold of a tablet of E (a stimulant/hallucinogen) for use at the weekend, and their friends will ask if they can get one for them at the same time. Other young people obtain drugs through older brothers and sisters. Most young people are curious about drugs and will try them at some stage of their teenage years, in the same way that they are curious to have their first sexual experience. What parents and teachers need to do is prepare them for this, so that young people make informed choices about the risks they choose to take. They need to understand the effects of different substances, and in particular the co-factors that can lead to harm. For example, a lower body heat due to the combination of alcohol and wearing skimpy clothes during cold weather can produce hypothermia.

## DRUGS AWARENESS FROM YOUR TEENAGERS

There are drugs awareness courses available to parents, and books and many good websites to look at (see Appendix 2 for details). Ironically though, most teenagers already know more about drugs than their parents, so whereas parents may be trying to get informed in order to explain risks to their teenagers, the latter almost certainly know more than you do already. That does not mean you should not try to find out more, or that just because the relevant information is with someone in your family, it will necessarily be shared with you – young people have very strong notions of loyalty and do not willingly break confidentiality. It is also fair to say that their sources of information are not always accurate and a lot of what they know may fall into the 'my friend said' category – neither more nor less accurate than the headlines in the newspapers.

So for drugs awareness it's a good idea if the starting point is to ask your young person what they already know about drugs, and to share information – rather than trying to tell them what they already know! There are many excellent websites now for young people and adults alike. Look through these with your young person and ask them which sites they find most useful and accessible. Bite your tongue when it comes to horror stories, if they think you are already biased they are unlikely to talk easily with you on the subject.

'My 15-year-old son admits freely that he knows who in his class is regularly smoking dope, and who provides it.

That does not mean he will tell me – or his teachers.'
**Father**

'The slang names for illegal drugs seem to change all the
time and date very quickly. I find it's far better to ask
my 15-year-old son for the current name than imagine
I will have heard it yet.' **Mother**

## OPEN THE DISCUSSION

It pays not to overreact and to remain open to discussion. Telling
your young person that Ecstasy can kill is not believable given
that they probably know that thousands of people take it each
weekend and are still back at school on Monday mornings.
Telling them that Ecstasy damages brain serotonin-receptors,
which in the long term might reduce an individual's ability
to feel happy – so you become more and more dependent on
drugs in order to feel pleasure – may have more impact.

Along similar lines, scare stories about marijuana leading to
heroin use may have less effect than discussing with young
people how passive it makes you feel, and the long-term effect
it has on memory. This may hit home at a time when they
are trying to fill their brains with information prior to exams.

'As a kid you tend to do exactly what you're told not to,
and maybe if my parents had constantly warned me not
to smoke and threatened me with cancer and damnation
I would have tried a bit harder with Pete's Embassy Number
Ones. As it is, I know that Mum – an ex-smoker – would
have disapproved loudly if I'd taken smoking up as a
covert habit, but it was never cast as the original sin.'
**Andrew Collins**, *Where Did It All Go Right?* Ebury, 2003.

## DRUG USE AS AN AUTOMATIC PROGRESSION

Another popular parental view of drug culture, particularly from those whose own experience of drugs is limited, is that it is one long slippery slope, from occasional use of cannabis to dependency on heroin.

Of course there are instances of this happening – most heroin addicts began as occasional cannabis smokers – but there is also a lot of evidence that young people gravitate towards particular types of drug in order to match the experience they are seeking, for example:

**Alcohol** (a depressant with some stimulant-like qualities) is a popular drug for those who feel angry or who want to 'let rip'. It enables those who find it difficult to show their anger to lose their inhibitions.

**Cannabis** (a depressant) helps you feel relaxed and peaceful. It heightens awareness and is particularly attractive to those who like nothing better than listening to music and having deep conversations. It does, however, inhibit action, and is not so attractive to a 'party person' who wants to dance.

**Cocaine** (a stimulant) makes you feel on top of the world and very sure of yourself. It therefore appeals to people who may be having problems with self-esteem or working or studying in a very competitive atmosphere where they frequently worry about whether or not they are good enough.

**Hallucinogenic drugs** with a high amphetamine content – such as Ecstasy and other 'dance drugs' – speed you up and make you feel bright and colourful. Those who want to intensify experiences they feel in nightclubs will be drawn to these.

**Heroin** is a major painkiller and is used by those who want to blot out the world. Its medicinal version is diamorphine and is closely allied to morphine, which is used in easing severe pain. Heroin creates a warm isolated bubble between you and the rest of the world.

## 12 top tips for parents: young people and drugs

1  **Be aware of the messages** and attitudes you are passing on to your child. Do you resort to alcohol or drugs to quick fix your feelings or moods? When you have a stress headache do you rest and relax or take a pill?

2  **Have real conversations** with your child about drugs – no matter what age they are. Ask questions. They probably know more than you already. Telling them things won't do any good – but by all means talk to them about where they (and you) can get reliable information.

3  **Teach them how to make choices.** Let them see you weighing up options, finding out more before making a decision. Learning how to make choices is not automatic. Use the word 'choice' often – everything we do is at some level a choice.

4  **Actively encourage their self-esteem at all times,** even when you are angry with them. Be generous with praise even if they squirm; when things go wrong criticise the behaviour, not the person. Let them know that you love them and are proud of them as often as you can.

5  **Help them develop self-motivation skills.**

6  **Encourage your young person to plan ahead,** asking them 'What will you do tomorrow after school?' Have a family wall planner or calendar with a space for them to write in their important things. Don't constantly remind them of things they have to do; let them learn by

experiencing the consequences. Remind them once and then post a note on their memory board and leave it at that. When they are bored or can't think what to do ask them (rather than you) to suggest options. Turn off the television sometimes.

7 **Help them develop assertion skills.** Encourage them to talk about their feelings, not just their experiences. Talk to them about rights: their own, other people's and yours. Encourage them to have their own opinions even if you think they are daft. Be assertive with your child (by not giving in) but without being aggressive, bullying or being manipulative.

8 **Don't be afraid of creating rules and boundaries and sticking to them.** Rules and boundaries = love to teenagers, even if they don't realise it until later.

9 **Check that your young person is receiving good quality drug education.** Keep a folder or box file at home for leaflets, help-lines and websites for all kinds of things and make sure you have good information about drugs and first aid in it. Ensure the whole family know where the file is, can get at it without asking, and help to update and add to it.

10 **Let them have access to good information online.** Most parents will have blocks on their young people's Internet access – but this may prevent them getting good information too. Once in a while, sit with them at the computer and search for some good sites – there are lots for young people. You might even ask them to help you find out!

11 **If you suspect your young person has been using an illegal drug,** don't panic. Losing your temper and reeling off all the possible (or imagined) dangers of drug use will alienate not help them. Talk calmly, try to get at the truth and deal with it. Talk about quantity and not substance – how much and how often may be more relevant than what.

Make sure they understand and know the risks and penalties – how and where to get help. Stick to boundaries, for example: 'If you ever bring cannabis into this house again, even if it is just looking after it for a friend, or have anything on you that suggests you have been smoking cannabis, you will be grounded for two weeks and have your allowance cut for a month. Is that clear?'

12 **If you suspect your young person is developing a potentially risky habit,** encourage them to get help. Most available services will expect a young person to refer themselves – parents can't do it for them. However, many agencies dealing with minors can make referrals to a range of services. For example, the school, police and social services can refer young people for support.

## QUESTIONS & ANSWERS

**Q:** I suspect my son is using cannabis. What should I do?

**A:** Firstly, don't panic. Shouting at him about the mess he is making of his life will not help, particularly if he is still high. The vast majority of young people who try illegal drugs (and the majority will) experiment with cannabis; they do so 'recreationally', at parties or in clubs. And for most this is not problematic.

The occasional use of cannabis can lead to more cannabis, and if its use then becomes a strategy to cope with daily routines such as getting to sleep or relaxing, this can lead to a habit that is hard to shake. Cannabis can also have long-term effects on memory and energy levels, and as it produces lethargic behaviour in many, perhaps teenagers should be out having fun with their friends rather than sitting stoned in a dark corner listening to music. If the cannabis use is sporadic and social – say at the occasional party – you may not be too concerned, but a regular or increasing habit at home may require more attention: perhaps help from a drug counsellor or your GP.

Drug counselling services are available locally for all young people; some are better than others. There are drug advisory services that you can consult (see Appendix 2), and several offer support to the parents of those with problems. But remember that to have any effect, the young people must desire change themselves; you can't change their behaviour on your own.

**Q:** I know my teenage daughter smokes cannabis at parties. Should I let her smoke it at home?

**A:** No, not if you don't want her to. It's important to establish boundaries, and allowing your young person to smoke it at home will inevitably increase the amount smoked overall. And the potential for damage increases with the amount smoked. It's also against the law to have cannabis in your home and allow its use.

The same goes for allowing your young person to smoke tobacco at home. The more permissive you are, the more the young person will smoke and the greater the long-term damage to their health. There is a lot of evidence that the earlier they start smoking the greater the long-term risk of heart disease, cancer and other serious health problems.

**Q:** I've always thought it's important to be with those you trust when you smoke cannabis. I am still an occasional user myself, so why not smoke it with my son – in the same way that we have a beer together occasionally?

A: Let's be really honest about what is going on here. Is this about enjoying an experience with your son, or looking cool? Are you trying to share something with him or just demonstrate that you are not past it?

The wider issue is that this is a very dangerous precedent to set, and by doing so you are trying to be a friend to your son rather than to parent him. The debate about whether or not to offer alcohol to young people is not straightforward, but it remains true that while alcohol is a legal drug, cannabis is not. By smoking cannabis with your young person you are demonstrating that it is an acceptable form of recreation. This is dangerous and will undoubtedly increase the amount they eventually smoke, and the more they take in, and the earlier the age, the greater the long-term damage to their health.

Q: I have never tried drugs and worry that my inexperience makes me unable to offer my teenager advice in this area.

A: You may not have tried illegal drugs, but there are probably almost no adults who have tried no drugs of any kind – for example coffee, tea, prescription drugs and alcohol. The effects of these can be just as powerful, if not more so, than illegal drugs.

People with little knowledge always assume that because a drug is illegal it's going to blow them away. Small quantities of illegal drugs may be hardly noticed when taken – it's as much to do with how and how much is taken as to do with what.

There are websites you can use to find out more (see Appendix 2). Why not explore the subject with your young person? Sitting side by side in front of the computer, impressing you with how much they already know, and guiding your research, is a status-enhancing thing for them to do.

**Q:** Should I tell my young person about the dodgy situations I got into as a teenager under the influence of drink and drugs?

**A:** Try to concentrate on the learning outcomes rather than the horror stories. For example, you could advise that drink can make you less careful about whom you have sex with – and the risks you therefore take of getting a sexually transmitted infection – rather than the details of your drunken night in 1980.

**Q:** I had too much to drink at a party that my teenagers were also attending. I feel so embarrassed. Should I pretend it never happened?

**A:** This is an ideal opportunity to show them how to handle mistakes. Tell them that you feel embarrassed by what you did, that alcohol impairs your judgement and can make things feel fine when they are not. Try not to make it a family joke, as this reinforces the view that drinking too much is funny. Always refer to it seriously as an error of judgement you regret.

**Q:** My son got drunk at a family party. Two years later his relations still refer to it whenever they see him. What can I do – he does not want to come to the next one.

**A:** Most teenagers get drunk at some stage; indeed a memory of the hangover that came afterwards can be a very valuable warning lesson on the dangers of not being in control of how much you drink.

So, if they are going to get drunk, in terms of where to do it, your son got it absolutely right – in a safe environment, surrounded by people who care for him and who could be trusted to act in an appropriate manner if the situation got out of hand. He also got drunk in a social environment – secret drinking alone is more worrying. But the problem for him now is that the memory lives on.

One strategy you could take before the next such occasion is to initiate a conversation about it with your relatives, whether individually or as a group. You could say that your son has grown up a lot in the last two years. Just because he had too much to drink on that occasion does not make him a life-long alcoholic. He needs to be allowed to move on from this – otherwise he will not want to attend family gatherings at all. And that would be a pity.

Q: When they go out for an evening, my daughter and her friends take alcohol with them and drink it outside, before they go into a nightclub. I've seen young people lined up on the pavements, drinking outside clubs, and this worries me.

A: This is very common behaviour among young people. Given the high price of drinks inside most clubs, many young people 'pre-drink' or 'tank up' before they go in.

The problem is that they are then taking large amounts of alcohol in a short space of time – rather than absorbing it slowly over the course of an evening and so cannot stop once they feel themselves getting affected. This can also bring trouble once inside, where she may find herself taking risks she would not normally take because her judgement is impaired. And the friends will not be able to watch out for each other because, having drunk together, and at the same rate, they will all be in the same state.

Your daughter needs to be aware of how she appears to others when she enters the club. There are a lot of people waiting to target young women just like her intentionally. She needs to see how her safety and her alcohol consumption are linked, and to make sensible choices.

**Q:** My 13-year-old daughter went to a party recently and the parents of the host had provided neat spirits, mixers and alco-pops – with no adult supervision at all – they were upstairs watching television while the party went on downstairs. One child ended up drinking too much and being rushed to hospital. My daughter does not want me to complain but I feel really shocked.

**A:** I bet you do! Alcohol is a dangerous drug – drinking a bottle of vodka could kill an adult, let alone a child – and providing large quantities unsupervised is asking for trouble.

At 13 you may want to offer a fruit punch with a cider or wine base – in very limited quantities – but all alcohol must be supervised. If they are older you may want to provide beer but the access should be controlled at all times.

If you find it difficult to control who is drinking what in your own home (many will sneak in small bottles of spirits), then you may prefer to have a party in a 'neutral' location such as a local hall. There the rules and their enforcement are delegated to someone else – and to a teenager it's cooler to say that the management won't allow things than that their parents won't. You could get someone to act as a bouncer, to check on what is being brought to the party, as well as how much individuals are consuming.

Young people do not behave like adults at parties; they do not 'social drink', they down quantities in order to enjoy them-selves. If you are not prepared for this, don't have a party. And as for the parents who offered large quantities of drink to under-age drinkers, they were acting *in loco parentis* and exposed themselves to huge risk.

**Q:** My sister's son has been accused of supplying his classmates with drugs. He insists he only got E tablets for them from the same person who was supplying them to him. What should she do?

A: Unfortunately for him he was supplying them. The law does not differentiate between getting them for friends and selling them to strangers.

Find out precisely what he is accused of and get legal representation. He will probably be playing it cool but if this is his first offence he will undoubtedly be scared. She needs to get through this with the minimum amount of personal and family damage, and the best way is to concentrate on getting through it together rather than immediately casting blame. So while he has to realise he has done something stupid, save the discussion until later. Reassure him that he is loved and valued, even when he behaves stupidly. This is not the time for any of his family to disown him.

Q: My son was found drunk and disorderly and taken back to a police cell for the night. Should I have gone in to collect him right away?

A: It's not a bad lesson for teenagers that, while you love and support them, you cannot – and frequently will not – wave a magic wand to make all their troubles go away. If he was unlikely to come to any harm, and you wanted the experience to be particularly memorable, you could have left him there for the night – although the consequences for your relationship could have been quite strong. The police can also be a useful gateway to treatment. Self-referral to services (e.g. treatment for drink and substance abuse) is the norm, but the police are able to refer young people, as can social services and the criminal justice system.

Once things have quietened down a little you might engage him in reflection about that incident and what, if anything he has learnt from it to take forward with him. We often assume young people learn from experience, but sometimes they need to be encouraged to reflect and make conscious the learning provided.

He might be encouraged to think about:

- The amount and speed of his alcohol consumption
- The opinion of others – if friends or family were present
- Factors that led to his 'disorderly' behaviour
- The role of friends – why didn't they look out for him?
- The potential consequences of being picked up by police in the future.

**Q:** It's all very well telling me to have a discussion with my son about drugs but I feel before I do that I need to be well armed with facts. Where do I get a straightforward fact-sheet?

**A:** It sounds to me that your idea of a discussion and mine are very different. Do you really want an information sheet, or a cudgel of facts to beat him into submission and to make him see it your way? The risk if one side arms themselves is that they feel empowered – and any meaningful dialogue goes out the window. If you want to state your case and draw up the battle lines, go for it. But what your son needs more than anything is a sensible mature adult to help him and support him as he makes his own decisions in the minefield of drugs. By stating your position so clearly you will alienate him and shut down any real dialogue now and in the future.

The 'facts' about drugs are nothing like as clear cut as you might like to believe. Alcohol is by far the most dangerous drug in everyday use and yet it is legal; more young people die every year being driven to school by their parents than die of Ecstasy. Nor does 'knowing the facts' necessarily change behaviour: smokers see 'smoking kills' on every packet they buy.

The truth about drugs is that decisions taken in the moment may affect a young person for the rest of their lives. Therefore they should resist the desires of the moment and think things through carefully; weigh up the pros and cons; and do all they can do to reduce the risks presented by the behaviour they eventually choose.

# CHAPTER 15

# 'Bor-ing!' Hobbies, pastimes and obsessions

It's a good idea for parents to reinforce the value of hobbies and pastimes that involve spending time with other people, preferably cooperating – or at least communicating – with others rather than just occupying the same space.

Who chooses how teenagers spend their free time? While parents tend to maintain that the choice is up to the teen, reminding their young people of all the things they can do today compared to what was available in their teenage years, how young people actually occupy themselves is often dictated primarily by what is supported at home, in both a positive and negative sense, with young people responding accordingly.

Once they reach their teenage years, many young people react against their parents' interests, quite intentionally. This is part of the process of growing up rather than a deliberate desire to hurt – they need to separate from you and to make their own identity. Finding a way of separating often depends on the way you have raised them. If you have been very permissive they may respond by becoming an 'old fogey' (think Saffy in *Absolutely Fabulous*!); if you have been very strict they may become rebellious. If you take an interest in their hobbies they may react against that and decide to be interested in something different.

While this may be disappointing in the short term, particularly if there are things you have enjoyed doing together in the past, take comfort – ultimately the experiences of their early years will stay with them. They may not want to share with you right now, even an activity that you have previously enjoyed together – and you may have the odd experience of watching them do things you told them about, or showed them how to do, with their friends. But looking further ahead, maybe you can pick up shared interests together again in future. In the meantime, it's a good idea for parents as well as young people to look at making new friends to pursue your hobbies with, rather than relying on your young people.

How they occupy their free time may also be influenced by gender; boys and girls often behave differently. For instance, boys are often attracted by competition, and activities are chosen to supply that. They will pursue sport, computer games, collecting, role-play scenarios and tend to choose television programmes that reinforce the feelings these activities induce (sport, physical competition, ordeals). Meanwhile, girls of the same age may be fantasising about life as or perhaps with someone else – perhaps a rock star or actor, or someone in a television series whose style of dress, and even way of talking, they copy in precise detail. They will read all they can about their idol's lifestyle and hobbies, and talk about them to their friends.

In the long term, most young people grow out of these fixations. However, an enduring obsession with an idol, a 'love addiction' where the young person's grip on reality recedes and they start to believe that the enhanced reality with their choice of idol is actuality, can be a sign of mental illness. Many celebrities have been plagued by fans who turn into stalkers.

## FLASHBACK

Think back to when you were about 14. Who was a major preoccupation for you then? Did you adore a rock

star, television personality, actor or actress? Were you for
Jason Priestley or Robbie Williams ? Cameron Diaz or
Jennifer Aniston? Who did you dream of meeting and
what did you fantasise would happen to you when you
did? Looking back, what did this mean then and what
does it mean now?

Understanding how you felt at a similar age is a very effective
way of appreciating what your teenagers are experiencing right
now. It follows that activities of theirs that you criticise now
would have seemed much more important to your teenage
self. And while you may be surprised, looking back, at how
strongly you felt about pop or movie stars, few of us would
delete the experience from our background – rather we see it
as part of growing up.

People of all ages define themselves through their interests,
and developing different interests is also part of the way in
which teenagers separate themselves from their parents. If you
think back to your own adolescence, you will probably find
that whatever your parents did not approve of seemed attractive, and pursuits they wanted to encourage you to do, you
resisted. Nothing has changed for your young people.

'My parents would not allow me to read *Jackie*, so I used
to secretly buy it myself and read it in the garden shed,
tearing it into small pieces and putting it in the dustbin
when I had finished. They eventually relented and let
me have *Fabulous 208*, but I can still remember the sad
look they would give me whenever they found me reading
it.' **Mother**

'I liked to collect *Marvel* comics. My parents thought this
a waste of time and money and I ended up piling them
up in my sock drawer to avoid them being tidied up and
thrown away.' **Father**

Having a hobby in common with others, whether it is support for a football team or love for a rock star, is a very empowering thing for a young person. It may provide them with a sense of identity and community, of belonging to a club or group who feel the same. It may, however, become a concern if the enthusiasm spills over into every other aspect of life.

Many hobbies that start in teenage years are about adding order and control, and when everything seems to be changing this can be very comforting to a young person. For example, attempting to spot and list all the numbers for a particular category of aeroplanes or trains, or to compile the complete army of model figures from a series, provides them with something to talk about, and a ready-made circle of friends. It gives them a safe feeling of belonging to something without the need to talk about things that make them sound vulnerable. Many adult men, on meeting together, will tend to talk about travel arrangements (usually motorway routes!) or football, allowing them to communicate at one level without giving away too much; women will talk about the weather or comment on each other's clothes or children. Such things give us all a feeling of security – we can function because we understand the rules.

Some groupings within society allow us to ritualise our lives to an even greater extent, enabling those who take part to feel safe because they understand their place. For example, religious orders, the police and emergency services, the armed forces, or an organisation that requires life-long loyalty (big corporations have always been particularly keen on this) can feed this need; the individual knows precisely what is expected of them at any moment, and this is reassuring. There is no risk of inappropriate behaviour and those obeying the rules won't get teased. This is one of the reasons why so many older people now look back on their time of National Service as a very positive experience.

Those who do not achieve this security within their working

lives may look to get it from clubs and associations after work. Go as a casual observer to any seemingly flexible group of people, from flower arranging to civic societies, and you will see how individuals have adapted what could be a very relaxed structure into a very precisely controlled system in which all who belong feel comfortable and understand the rules.

So, belonging to a rigid interest group is not necessarily a bad thing for a young person to do – but it's a good idea for this not to make up their whole social life! Those individuals who are too dependent on their rituals can find it hard to think 'outside the box', to envisage alternative courses of action when they are not on the prescribed route. And of course they can be completely devastated should disaster strike – sudden redundancy or a move away from the area where they live and the group to which they belong.

## WHEN THE ONLY THING THEY ARE INTERESTED IN IS IN THE MIRROR

Probably most teenagers go through a period of self-obsession – after all, it is a time of great change, and they do not know how they will end up. There is a period of time when most young people obsess about their appearance, their hair, their skin, their height and weight and their secondary sexual characteristics such as muscles and breasts. For most this is a fairly short-lived obsession; they soon get used to their changing appearance and enjoy the benefits it brings, from increased stamina and strength to new-found curves.

However, as we live in a celebrity-obsessed culture, with much of the television, magazine and online content aimed at young people devoted to pictures of the famous and beautiful (with or without surgical assistance), young people can also become overly concerned about their appearance. Traditionally this is something girls may adopt, but increasingly boys are also becoming worried by their physical appearance and body image, with more and more boys developing eating disorders, self-harming or exercising obsessively.

Many parents don't realise that their mirror-obsessed young person is developing a problem until it becomes startlingly apparent – by which time it is difficult to change and professional help might be needed.

All parents can help their child have a realistic view of themselves by being aware of how they (the adults) judge the world around them. Parents who regularly criticise their child's eating habits or the appearance of TV celebrities or strangers in the street are encouraging, albeit unwittingly, their young person to be critical by example. This may then become self-criticism when the common teen feelings of insecurity and inadequacy are added to the mix.

> 'My mother still divides her life into "good" days and "bad" days. These have nothing to do with wars or disasters, nothing to do with feeling up or down – they are entirely decided by what she has eaten. Good days are when she stays within a loose calorie limit, bad days when she eats high calorie foods. She is now 85 years old and has been doing this for as long as I can remember.' **Gill**

Of course we want young people to have healthy eating habits, but obsessing about fat content or calories during the vulnerable adolescent years can feed unhealthy obsessions. And alarming numbers of young women that Gill is in contact with go without meals on a regular basis as a way of keeping down their weight. Many feel guilty or distressed if they eat heartily – even if their hearty meal is a salad! None of these are technically young women with eating disorders, but all have the propensity to become them.

Constantly praising young people's appearance is no more helpful than criticising it – as it still encourages them to see their appearance as overly important, a viewpoint exaggerated by young people's media. Encouraging them to enjoy their bodies from the inside out – by dancing, running, taking part in sport or something they've never done before such as abseiling or kayaking – helps them appreciate a healthy and strong body for how it works and how it feels, rather than just how it looks.

Encouraging young people to take an interest in the world around them rather than just themselves can be difficult during the teen years as they don't particularly wish to share their views with parents. However, regular meals together at home or in a restaurant provide an excellent opportunity to talk about opinions and viewpoints. Try to widen the conversation; talk about what's in the news or what's happening in the local environment – anything other than celebrity gossip, fashion, or how their team is doing.

## SUGGESTIONS FOR HOW YOUR YOUNG PERSON COULD USE THEIR TIME – IN ORDER TO MEET MORE PEOPLE AND ESTABLISH FRIENDSHIPS

- **Societies and groups that create something together.** Working towards a performance with a group of others, for example, can be a very motivating experience; it promotes teamwork, a group dynamic – and can create very strong memories. There are probably a variety of options in your neighbourhood including drama, singing and dance. Be sure to look out for all the options available, not just those you know about already. For example, if your young person is interested in singing, there are probably a wide variety of different styles available, from gospel and rock to *a cappella* and street singing. According to some, choral singing is even beneficial physically as well as psychologically.

- **Organised groups.** The Duke of Edinburgh Award Scheme and organisations such as the Guides and Scouts can offer a very enjoyable experience, often providing young people with the kind of skills that will be invaluable in later life such as conflict resolution and self-reliance. These organisations have undergone great change in the past few years and will probably not be the same ones you remember when you were growing up. They promote teamwork, self-respect and can take young people into new areas of interest as well as an understanding of diversity, global awareness and healthy lifestyles.
- **Discussion groups** may be organised through local libraries, and many political parties have groups catering for the interests of young people.
- **Playing in a band** is as cool as ever, but if your young person is not a gifted musician they may still have other skills to offer – and hence a reason to get involved. Most bands also need additional support – people to manage the obligatory Facebook presence, put together press releases for the media or distribute leaflets.
- **Many gyms offer a youth membership** and there can be classes aimed at younger demographs at which friendships can be formed. Regularly turning up can mean that eye contact is established and other opportunities for discussion arise. Many gyms also have classes included in their membership packages and these will often bring the same people together.
- **Cheerleading** is popular and promotes a strong sense of shared identity as well as an itinerary of events at which performance is required, or possibly competitions to work for.
- **Youth clubs and youth centres** either run by local councils or attached to churches often have extensive programmes of events and impressive facilities, such as band-practice studios and recording studios, cooking

facilities and gyms, while providing a regular meeting point, supervised by trained and qualified staff who try to engage and support young people.

- **Exercise** of all kinds can be a really good way of meeting other people and building a supportive network. Being in a regular team requires stamina and reliability – and in the process mentoring from older team members often results. It can be really helpful to a young person to see how other adults prioritise their lives and value the relationships created in the process.

'Over the years, we have consistently attracted a wide age range in our netball team. In the process we have encouraged many young women to think more ambitiously about their future and take themselves seriously. We are proud that several have now gone on to university who had never thought of it before – and we have watched others make steady progress in their careers.'
**Mother**

- **Charities** may welcome younger members into their organisation – or have a junior section that your young person can join. Organising and taking part in fund-raising events can be a strong group activity – and lead to further involvement in future, as can taking part in special initiatives (e.g. clearing a pond or working on a site that needs rubbish clearance). The charity needs to be their choice rather than that of their parents; if you are suggesting they take part in the junior section of an organisation you support, they may feel a danger of being 'reported on'.
- **Meditation and relaxation classes** may appeal – and there is a variety on offer from yoga to mindfulness.

## QUESTIONS & ANSWERS

Q: My son is spending all his pocket money on an army of 'collectables' and all his spare time with friends playing with them. How can I encourage him to have a wider social life?

A: You don't say whether or not he is happy doing this. For a young man who has found it difficult to make friends, for instance, finding a group of people with whom it is easy to communicate (because you know what to talk about) and the entry point is fairly straightforward (choose which army you want to collect) can be a great relief. It's not unknown for such young people to begin by feigning interest in order to join this ready-made social circle. If, however, you suspect he is becoming institutionalised, you can help him to widen those he mixes with.

Observe how he interacts with other people when he is not with his new friends – with his family and neighbours for example, or on the telephone. Is he able to keep a conversation going or does he avoid eye contact and scuttle back to his collectables whenever possible? Can you extend opportunities to talk to him – for example, from time to time can you make a cup of tea for both of you and ask that you sit down to drink it together? Encourage him to join something else as well, perhaps a sports club, which is an ideal complement to lots of time spent hunched in front of his collection. Is there a local chess club or a pub quiz that you could go to with him? The kind of mind that is attracted to minute detail is often very good at acquiring pub quiz trivia!

Q: My sister's eldest son excels at sport. While his parents are obviously very proud of him, they spent all weekend driving him from event to event with their other two children in tow. How can I encourage them to be fairer to the rest of their family?

**A:** While the arrival of a prodigy can be a source of great pleasure to parents, their siblings can be much less enthusiastic about the experience of growing up with someone very talented.

The response of some parents in this situation is to try to find a different skill or hobby at which others in the family can excel, but this can only serve to make the siblings feel further isolated. It's perfectly possible not to be particularly good at anything, and a lengthy search for a nascent talent other siblings may lack just makes them feel even more inferior.

It's very important for a young person in this situation to have their morale and self-esteem upheld, for parents to assert that what matters is who they are, not what they do: 'The unique mixture that makes you up is what is so special to me.' This may sound a little corny but in my experience I have never found a young person who did not respond well to this kind of sentiment, provided they know it is sincere.

As the children's aunt, could you offer to go and support as well, arranging a separate programme for those not involved in the competition – say a trip to a swimming pool or a picnic? Or what about having the two siblings to stay with you for a weekend? In other words, could you support the family rather than criticise them, as this may be better received!

**Q:** My daughter seems to have no hobbies or interests at all, just a circle of friends she spends time with. The frivolity of this gets me down: they don't do anything, or read anything, they just hang out together.

**A:** Girls often have people as hobbies rather than external interests. They discuss their friends' lives and their problems, they groom each other, they spend a lot of time looking in the mirror and they try on clothes together. They may become their own hobby, becoming preoccupied with particular features of their body or each other's.

Don't worry. This really is just a stage she is going through.

It's part of the process through which women learn to interact with the world around them and is why women generally find it much easier to talk about their emotions than men.

**Q:** My teenage son has no hobbies at all. He just lies on the sofa all day.

**A:** Do you mean all weekend (when he is busy during the week at school) or do you really mean all the time? Youthful indolence can be infuriating to parents, when they see a home full of jobs that the adults have not got time to do.

A starting point could be to ask how content he is. Most of us like an occasional day doing nothing, and may find watching television immensely soothing. But if you suspect the lounging about disguises depression you may need to be a little more cunning.

Telling him to get up and get busy will have the opposite effect; it will show him he has been noticed in his current state and you want him to move. He may be lying there because he wants to be noticed. Look at what he is getting from this behaviour: he is the centre of attention and everyone knows he is there. Change the reward he gets for his indolence, and you may change the behaviour too.

Why not try leaving him on the sofa? Can the television be moved to another room where everyone else can gather? Buy tickets for everyone to attend something and ask if he wants to go. If he chooses not to, get others in the family to tell him what he is missing rather than continue a parental monotone. If you change the payback his behaviour provides, his behaviour may change.

**Q:** We have always gone out to the pub on Friday evenings and taken the children with us – there is a family room we can all be in together and a garden for the summer. Now they are teenagers, my daughter is refusing to come with us, wanting to go to a wine bar instead. I feel hurt that we are no longer good enough for her.

**A:** This is just part of the inevitable process of separation between adult and young person. What one generation adopts, the next will let go, and every generation thinks they have discovered everything for the first time.

It's interesting that she has not changed the activity you prefer on Friday evenings, just the location in which it takes place. It may look like she is being perverse, but the desire to socialise is constant – just much more influenced by her friends than by her parents. Perhaps you should take comfort in that. Young people find it cloying if the happiness of their parents depends on them being there too. Why not continue to go to the pub, but do so with your friends rather than your family?

**Q:** My son is addicted to computer games. He wants to do nothing else. I can't bear the violence of the games he chooses.

**A:** Parents sometimes find the kind of computer games teenagers enjoy very alienating – although they frequently encourage their use with younger children to keep them occupied.

It's helpful to begin by looking at the machine from the teenager's point of view. They really do see things differently – the game you may view as violent may have no relationship to life, and shooting at figures will not necessarily turn teens into serial killers. They look to overcome challenges presented in the game, in the same way that many adults are equally addicted to doing the crossword in the paper or chess. It's possible too that you may have under your roof the source of a multi-million-pound future income – those who design computer games/software, etc. were usually playing games from an early age too! Oscar-winner Nick Park, creator of Wallace and Gromit, thanked his parents in his acceptance speech for letting him, from a very early age, play with the family's video camera.

Read the advice about how to regulate computer use given in Chapter 10. Consider, too, whether you could set up an agreement to limit your young person's use of the computer. For example, two hours a day, no more; one night a week when there is no computer use at all; a regular family night when the TV is turned off and certain family activities are enjoyed, e.g. get a takeaway and play family games together. As a general rule, stick to the censor's boundaries on games and films, and don't let them have over-age games.

## CHAPTER 16

# Writing about the development of children and young people – how this book fits into what else is available

Charles Darwin, most famous for his theory about the origin of species, was one of the first observers of childhood behaviour, keeping a detailed journal of his first son William Erasmus – who was known in the family as Doddy. Doddy was born in December 1839, and Darwin wrote systematic and impressively objective notes on the boy's development:

> 'When little under five weeks old, smiled, but certainly not from pleasure, but merely a chance movement of muscles, without a corresponding sensation.'

His habit of noting Doddy's progress continued until September 1844, when his son was nearly five, and was also taken up by his wife, Emma. But the paper based on his observations, *A biographical sketch of an infant*, was not published until 1877, by which time he and Emma had had a further nine children (five boys and four girls). So in his publication he was able to compare the development of his first child with that of all his subsequent siblings, using the notes he and his wife had made, as well as information gained from the questionnaires he sent out and from the wide range of those with whom he corresponded on a regular basis.

The Victorians are often thought of as the 'inventors' of childhood – and it was during that era that special books, toys and clothing for children started to become more widely available. In part this was made possible through the industrial revolution and the mass-production opportunities that arose, which meant that factory-made toys, including tin and clockwork items, went on sale and were widely available.

It was also during this time that legislation to protect children began. From the 1830s onwards, the Victorians passed a variety of laws aimed at protecting children at work, school and in the home, partly motivated by a growing popular understanding of children as innocent creatures who should be protected from the adult world and allowed to enjoy their childhood. But the legislation was inconsistent, incomplete and not routinely applied – the smallness and dexterity of children was very much valued in the workplace (for example in linen mills where they could nip under machinery to clean it), including up chimneys (where they could access difficult places). Books about children in such circumstances, however, played an important part in bringing their mistreatment to popular attention and awakening consciences. Charles Dickens' *Oliver Twist* was published in 1837–8 and drew attention to the consequences of poverty. Charles Kingsley's *The Water Babies* (1863), a satire against child labour, revealed the other side of the industrial revolution: the poverty and child labour that underpinned the economic comfortableness of others.

The study of child development, through observation and experimentation, got underway in earnest in the 1920s and 1930s in the US with the founding of Institutes of Child Study or Child Welfare in university centres. Child development began as a branch of psychology, influenced by sociology and ecology, and in particular examinations of how family relationships work among animals. This was something that had intrigued

Darwin, and about which he had written in *The Expression of the Emotions in Man and Animals* (1872). The most famous researcher and observer of children, Jean Piaget (1896–1980), began his work in the 1920s and continued throughout a very long life. John Bowlby (1907–90) was working during the same period and his important work on attachment theory also drew heavily on the work of ecologists and those studying animals, such as that of Konrad Lorenz (1903–89).

The study of children was also driven by trends. The first examinations of children (like Darwin's) tended to look at them in their home setting, but in the 1950s and 1960s laboratory conditions were popular for the studies (known as 'clinical studies' or 'clinical psychology'). Today there is a tendency for children rather to be studied within their social context, with as much interest in how children grow up as how they turn out in the longer term.

The study of child development, now generally known as developmental psychology, has now become a specialisation of its own, with a body of associated literature that is growing all the time. There are now increasing numbers of people wanting to study developmental psychology as a field in its own right, and there has been a similar specialisation within the caring professions, where it is now possible to qualify in Nursing Children or Social Work for Children.

A good example of how quickly the subject has grown in recent times is the study of the role of the father in the raising of children. This began in the 1940s and by the 1970s there were many studies, generally based on the role of the father as primarily 'breadwinner' or 'absentee'. Within universities there were attempts to chart and distil the work going on, and relate it to its role within more complex behaviours, but the field was expanding so fast it was often hard to keep up.

'. . . the first two editions of *The role of the father in child development* (Lamb 1976, 1981) contained encyclopaedic

introductory chapters in which Lamb attempted to provide
inclusive reviews of the primary and secondary literature.
Such endeavours were no longer possible by the time of
the third edition (1997) when the reference list for such
a chapter would have occupied more space than any of
the chapters in the book!' Introduction to the 4th edition
(2004), **Michael Lamb** and **Catherine S. Tamis-Lemonda**

There has been a similar explosion of work around the issue
of gender: for example, on whether an understanding of gender
is innate or learnt, and the influence of parents who emphasise
gender when raising their children (e.g. dressing in pink/blue;
providing different toys; having different expectations and
freedoms for children of different genders). Another example
of an area of new speciality is the mental health and well-being
of children and young people. Many centres of excellence,
including several in the UK, have had a strong effect on the
understanding of mental health in children, working across
the age range and considering cognitive and developmental
changes in children as they grow, and what in particular influences them.

Quite naturally the study of children has expanded to the
study of the family as a whole unit, with differing views on
how individuals interact and how such interactions impact on
children. This has led to many studies of siblings and their
impact on each other, parental relationships and break-ups as
influencing factors, as well as considering familial beliefs that
have developed over generations. One of the ways of viewing
families is to see them as systems made of component inter-
connected parts which cannot move or change without affecting
the whole.

Work also often proceeded under a series of specific
perspectives, for example feminist, political (within various
ideologies) and sociological. Disciplinary sub-alliances
were formed and the influences of ecologists, geneticists

and environmentalists ('nature versus nurture') came into play. Some developmental psychologists sought to classify behaviours under types of parenting style (e.g. Baumrind's stages of 'authoritative, authoritarian, indulgent, neglectful'), and the media remained consistently keen on labels that could be discussed by a wider audience. But whereas the media constantly question whether the latest trends in birth (e.g. single mothers, artificial insemination by donor, adoption, fostering, surrogate, lesbian and gay parents) impact negatively on the children created, a general consensus seems to be emerging that:

'The main conclusion . . . is that in considering what aspects of family life matter most for children's psychological well-being, more attention should be paid to the quality of family relationships and the child's relationships with the wider social world than simply to whether the child is being raised in one type of family or another.'
**Susan Golombok**

The starting point for developmental psychologists is often either the work of other psychologists or 'folk' theories about child development – what Slater and Bremner term 'ideas held about development that are not based on scientific investigation'. Theories about parenting, or very strong opinions, are very common in society – because parenting is a common experience, and many people reflect on their own experience when parenting their children (and this too has been studied).

'Folk' theories may ultimately be proven to have a sound basis for acceptance, but need to be tested. Children and parents are required for studies – and all studies have weaknesses. Ideas may be tested through 'cross-sectional design' (people of different ages tested at the same time) or 'longitudinal studies' (more than one observation of the same group of children is made at different points in their development). But studies may be compromised by weakness of design, misunderstanding of the survey or participants' dropping out ('participant attrition'), which may ensure that those who remain ('selective survivorship') are no longer representative of the population as a whole and hence the response and eventual findings are distorted. The popularly is also growing of 'practice as research', where ideas are observed as they are developed – and initial observations and thinking are updated and refined.

## HOW THIS BOOKS FITS INTO WIDER WORK ON DEVELOPMENTAL PSYCHOLOGY

This book is based on regular contact with young people over a 20-year period, through hundreds of workshops in schools with young people, their parents, mentors and teachers, developed and run by educator and trainer Gill Hines. The book also draws on much wider consultation – with parents, teenagers, friends, teachers and many more – who were asked what issues they wanted to consider, what difficulties they faced most often and which they found most tricky to handle. Many of the comments received are included in quotes within the text.

Each chapter begins with an examination of the key issues involved, but then poses a series of questions, which parents often ask. In this way you can see how the advice works in a practical context. Although the observations are thus based on common sense and experience (and so fit the 'folk' category outlined above) they have been trialled through 'practice as research' – and are affirmed by much of the literature relating to parenting and child development. The books have drawn widespread praise from education professionals, the media, parents and children. This book has been widely read by young people, as well as parents, and has been regularly quoted by both parties during discussions and arguments. It consciously offers an analysis and interpretation of parenting seen through the lens of much longer-term developments, through changing educational fashions, stress levels – and online access for sharing thoughts and feelings.

## HOW THIS BOOK CAME TO BE PUBLISHED

The book's route to publication too is similarly significant – it has played its part in the development of the literature on parenting. It grew out of Gill's workshops which Alison, a publisher and parent of four, attended at the schools of her children.

Every seminar was on a different topic, and although the audience changed each time, the experience was similar: ideas were exchanged, difficulties shared and confidence boosted. At the end, many parents would linger to have a chat and one of the most frequently asked questions was: 'Can you recommend a book on the subject?'

As a publisher, Alison was intrigued and she found, on investigating the market, that there was very little published on the effective parenting of teenagers. Spotting a gap in the market she began to approach publishers who had a relevant list of related titles and might consider publication. The responses were entirely negative – for two main reasons. Firstly they cited lack of need; secondly lack of access to the market.

Lack of need seemed unlikely. Publishers swore that parents were interested in buying only books on babies, and that later developmental stages were therefore uncatered for by publishers, who assumed that the market's need for information was being serviced in other ways. There was a strong demand for Gill's courses on parenting issues, and she was being funded by local authorities to deliver them in local schools. She had a variety of course handouts which, she heard, were being stuck up on fridges in the homes of those who had attended. It seemed clear that the main argument convincing publishers that there was no need for such a title was that there were no previous titles. Publishers have a tendency to add to clusters of publishing that are already established – a field without any publications may therefore be seen as a risk rather than an opportunity.

There were also issues of how the market for titles on parenting teenagers would be reached – by the teenage years many parents are back at work and so their shopping habits may have changed. They are perhaps not shopping in town centres so often, so have less access to high street bookshops, and they are also not gathering at the school gate and so less able to hear about what is available that they might find useful. But there were opportunities for selling books through workshops, support groups and online.

Another significant factor was the age and life-stage of the commissioning editors being contacted. They were generally in their early to mid-30s, and so actively involved in planning or becoming pregnant – rather than in the subsequent developmental stages of children. It again became clear that this was having an impact on how the book proposal was being received. Instead a commissioning editor was sought who was slightly older and already had teenagers – a very good match being found in Penny Phillips at Piatkus, who finally commissioned the book. Significantly, Penny had older step-children and spotted the merit of the material immediately:

'I was instantly struck by the plain-speaking obviousness – and yet originality – of Gill and Alison's approach and, yes, by its *importance*. Everything they said not only made irrefutable common sense but also was supported by thoughtful research and corroborated by empirical evidence. And now, a decade later, that remains as true as ever. Relationships between parents and teenagers are all too often categorised as unrelentingly difficult, but Gill and Alison show us that things don't have to be like that, and how by keeping the lines of honest, enlightened communication open we can make life easier – and happier – for everyone.'

As to how to reach the market, this was greatly helped by new ways of accessing customers – direct selling after workshops, the spread of social media and a growing tendency of the market to hunt for material they want rather than necessarily be provided with it (these days, GPs regularly report that patients come to them for a second opinion, having begun with their own information search online). The book has benefitted strongly from word of mouth from existing readers – and been widely appreciated. The format – with explanatory text followed by questions that can be dipped into, was based on Gill's seminars – and both this and the look of the first cover (a pair of old trainers) have since been widely copied. One publisher, who had turned down the original title as having 'insufficient market', even commissioned a lookalike title with a remarkably similar cover and illustration!

Ten years on from its original publication, a new edition of *Whatever!* is proudly presented, especially as it has been hailed as a seminal text and appeared on reading lists for those studying adolescence and preparing to work with young people.

What it offers is very much in the spirit of Darwin, and it is to be hoped that he would have approved. Great and original thinker as he was, he too was often in a state of indecision about what to do for the best for his children – and he too sought to share common situations and seek advice from others. For example, he wrote about the 'awesome state of indecision' (Darwin to W. D. Fox, 10 October 1850) as he and Emma tried to choose suitable schools and careers for their sons. After opting for a conventional education for Doddy, he admitted in a letter sent shortly after the boy had gone to Rugby School in 1852 that 'No one can more truly despise the old stereotyped stupid classical education than I do, but yet I have not had courage to break through the trammels' (Darwin to W. D. Fox, 7 March 1852).

But above all he loved to share his children's company, to talk and laugh with them at home. He encouraged them to develop hobbies and took a keen interest in what they became involved with: collecting stamps, botany, drawing, as well as involving them in his research. He often wrote to his older children about their younger siblings' amusing adventures and in a letter to a Syms Covington, a former servant and later assistant on the *Beagle*, he commented: 'My children, thank God, are all well, and one gets, as one grows older, to care more for them than for anything in this world' (Darwin to Syms Covington, 9 March 1856).

Quite so. I hope you have found this book useful, and if so you will in turn recommend it to others who might benefit.

## Further reading

Baumrind, D., 'Parental disciplinary patterns and social competence in children', *Youth and Society*, 9, 1978, pp. 239–76.

Campbell, A., and Muncer, S. (eds.), *The Social Child*, Studies in Developmental Psychology (Brighton: The Psychology Press, 1998).

Golombok, S., *Parenting, What Really Counts* (London: Routledge, 2000).

Lamb, M. E., *The Role of the Father in Child Development* 4th edn (New Jersey: Wiley, 2004).

Music, G., *Nurturing Natures: Attachment and Children's Emotional, Sociocultural and Brain Development* (Brighton: The Psychology Press, 2010).

Slater, A., and Bremner, G. (eds.), *An Introduction to Developmental Psychology* 2nd edn (Oxford: BPS Blackwell, 2011).

Smith, K., Cowie, H., and Blades, M., *Understanding Children's Development* 4th edn (Oxford: Blackwell Publishing, 2003).

www.darwinproject.ac.uk University of Cambridge research into Darwin's letters. Here you will find complete transcripts, and commentaries, of all the known letters Darwin wrote and received up to the year 1869, with more being added all the time. Particularly recommended is the essay 'Darwin and Fatherhood' by Dr Sian Pooley: https://www.darwinproject.ac.uk/darwin-and-fatherhood.

# Looking to the future: what we want for our young people

The standard of living may be rising ever higher in the Western world, but the number of people looking for happiness is rising just as fast. More and more people seem to be dissatisfied, needing comfort, reconciliation and guidance, and the number of people enrolling on counselling courses, either to deal with their own problems or to help others, is growing exponentially. Most schools now have a counselling service to help young people deal with issues they find difficult, and they are busy. School and college league tables measure performance but do not take into account how pupils cope with attainment – or the opposite. Significantly, whereas many parents choose particular colleges or schools because they feel their young people will achieve the best academic results through them, what they say they want for them relates to much more spiritual values. They want them to:

- Be content
- Be happy
- Be open-minded
- Have good friendships
- Be respected
- Be able to travel
- Enjoy their work
- Have enough money to support the lifestyle they choose

As partway on this path, it's important to help your young people to spot joy, and to encourage them to enjoy experiences; to live in and value the present rather than be always looking forward to the next thing on the schedule.

This is not as easy as it sounds. Lifestyles can be frenetic and parents and young people more concerned with clearing hurdles than taking time to think about how an experience felt. Looking for the positive can be through little steps, such as encouraging them to dwell on how it feels to get positive feedback, or passing on your own experiences. For example, the smell of coffee is often more appealing than the taste of it; opening a new pot of jam and taking the first spoonful when the surface is smooth and the pot not yet sticky feels really good; having a drink of water when you are thirsty tastes better than anything.

Once you get into the habit of making positive statements, it's not hard to move on to those that may have a long-term effect. For example, finally tackling a piece of work that you have been putting off for ages feels good, and the feeling when you finally finish it is even better. Giving blood makes me feel really useful; it leaves me with a feeling that today I have done something that really matters and a good feeling inside, satisfying me at a deep level. Saving up for something you really want is much more satisfying than just buying it outright.

And once you get into the habit of commenting, your young people can often surprise you by pointing out things to you: 'I like mowing the lawn. I feel really proud when I look out of the window and see the results, and think "I did that"'; 'I was really pleased that I managed to discuss this without losing my temper.'

## WHAT HAPPENS NEXT

Having talked throughout this book about how to harmonise and then improve relationships between parents and teenagers, the irony is that the next step is separation.

Separation between teenagers and their parents is vital if they are to achieve what most of us really want for them – to emerge as adults with minds of their own. But the process of separation can be painful. Suddenly what their peers say matters far more than their parents' opinions. They may not want to be with us very much, they are embarrassed by what we say or do, or how we dress. They may continue to want cash handouts and a roof over their head in between flat-sharing arrangements – but little more than this. The intimate relationships of early childhood, when they hid nothing, are replaced by non-communicative teenager ones, when you are told very little.

But the act of separation does not mean they do not care about or love us, just that in order to become independent they have to separate from us. In the long term, they will probably return, but how long this process takes may vary hugely. With some young people it may happen quickly, with children travelling large distances to be with everyone for family meals; others may not recommence full communication with their parents until their own children arrive; others may never achieve an easy intimacy with their parents, and carry on behaving in child-mode whenever they are in their parents' company.

## FEELINGS OF SEPARATION

Admitting how you feel as your children become more independent is as important to your personal development as it is to your child's.

Some people rush ahead and have a new baby to fill the gap, others have been known to start whole new families. It is not uncommon for parents to start encouraging their older children to produce the grandchildren once the younger ones leave home. After investing many years in the care of children and designing lives around their needs, many parents feel life is over as their children move off with barely a backward glance.

It is important for all people of any age to have relationships and friendships outside the family – because these remain constant through all the changes.

It is also important to maintain a personal relationship with your partner through all the parenting years – and not to lose sight of each other. Have shared time and outings together; use the newly increased time to renew interests and travel or visit places you like.

If you are single the world is your oyster! Make friends a priority and get out and about. Since the son of a great friend of mine moved out last year, she has spent all the money she would have spent on him, on travel. She goes on 'adventure' type holidays where singles are welcome. She has renewed old family connections, taken up some new hobbies like gym and tai chi, and stepped up her career a bit too. She stays in touch with her son and has a close and loving relationship with him. She is proud of all he has achieved, and no doubt he feels the same about her.

No one can experience the changes in a relationship with a child without some sadness, but it is important to be aware of your own needs and to meet them honestly. If you feel sad and rejected, look at why and how you can meet these needs rather than cling tighter to your child – which will only drive them away even faster.

Be assured they will not forget you. What they learnt at home will inform the rest of their lives, whether or not they admit it. From you they learn how to get on with people, how to be intimate, how to manage relationships and how to be kind – and of course the negatives that we pass on such as how to deceive, how to avoid compromise, how to get your own way, how to manipulate, how to be unkind and unfair.

And then comes the excitement of getting to know your young person all over again – and the joy that comes from this; spotting parts of the child you knew in the adult that emerges. I will finish therefore by asking you to focus on what you feel you have done well as a parent of teenagers, and encouraging you to spot the signs of success. I have included several examples from my own experience, and that of others I know, and I encourage you to think of more.

'I always wanted to take my children to lots of live theatre. I was thrilled when my youngest child announced, after a performance of *Guys and Dolls*, "That's the best thing I've ever seen." He was responding to what he had seen, but then making a qualitative judgement in the context of all the other experiences.' **Alison**

'When asked to write about something that he would always remember, my teenage son described an occasion when, on the way to school, I stopped the car and we all got out to look at a dead fox at the side of the road. The incident took no more than four minutes, and yet I was so glad I had bothered to make the time.' **Mother**

'I have tried to link my children with adults I respect who will be able to offer them advice when they do not feel able to talk to me. In this I feel I have succeeded – the links are working well and I really do not feel jealous that they tell these people things they do not tell me. I want them to be able to access good advice, even if they do not want to seek it from me.' **Father**

'My son felt strong enough to leave home at 16. He did not take on the kind of job I would have preferred – he went to work for a chain pizza restaurant and rented a bungalow with a friend, but he took on these commitments by himself. Three years on, he has been offered a management place by the chain he went to work for, he is well adjusted, mature and I am proud of him.' **Father**

## A FINAL THOUGHT: HOW DO YOU
## WANT TO BE REMEMBERED?

When being interviewed on *Desert Island Discs* in 2015, cycling legend Sir Bradley Wiggins talked about his mother thinking it more important that he had maintained a relationship for twelve years, and was a good father, than his sporting achievements.

Along similar lines, although John Peel was hailed by one music journalist as more important to the development of popular music than The Beatles, here is how he wanted to be remembered, in an interview given just before he died:[1]

> 'As for how John wanted to be remembered, he knew exactly the answer to that one. "As quite a good Dad," he replied without thinking. "Before you have children you think you know exactly what to do and how they are going to be and how you are going to be with them. But from the moment they emerge from the womb, you can forget all that. They simply aren't going to conform with your notions of what they should be. The fact is that our four children seem to like us and they also seem to like each other immensely, which is really nice."
>
> 'When I asked if that was more important to him than any of the media and broadcasting stuff he does he said simply: "Oh yes. Absolutely."'

---

[1] Sophie Wilcockson, *Sunday Telegraph*, 31 October 2004

# Appendix 1: How to run a family meeting

Giving young people a voice to debate and discuss issues with parents, rather than just telling them what has been decided by the adults, is a great goal to aim at – and a huge challenge.

During workshops on raising teenagers, I often face questions about how to run a family meeting as one way of doing this. But where do you start? Here is a stage-by-stage guide to introducing consultation to your family!

## 1. WHEN?

Ideally, a family meeting should be a regular event, happening at the same time on a regular basis – say every Wednesday evening at two-week intervals. If you are calling one for the first time, your family (and that means everyone who is a regular member of the household) will probably be intrigued – in my family we have never found any difficulty in encouraging everyone to attend. If there are issues to be discussed in a hurry an extra meeting could be called, and children as well as parents should be able to call a meeting.

## 2. HOW LONG SHOULD IT LAST?

The meeting should be for a limited period of time (one-and-a-half hours is plenty; if your children are younger maybe just an hour). If you find you need longer, then perhaps meetings need to be held more often, and vice versa. Imposing a deadline helps keep everyone focused on the job in hand and encourages concise thought!

## 3. WHERE TO HOLD THEM?

The ideal location is somewhere where all can sit down at the same level, which implies equality – around the kitchen table, for example, is ideal. Sitting around a table also gives everyone something to lean on, which can be useful, particularly if the discussion gets heated!

While it's tempting to combine a meeting with a family meal, or with snacks, these can be distracting. It's best to keep the meeting simple and then to eat together afterwards – this can be very bonding.

Before you start, turn off the television (even if it is in another room, the noise can be distracting), switch the telephone on to answerphone (or agree not to answer it should it ring) and ask everyone to turn off their mobile phones. Agree what you will do if there is a ring at the front door. Agree that everyone should be there for the full meeting. Everyone should bring along their diary so that important dates can be noted.

## 4. SHOULD SOMEONE BE IN CHARGE OF THE MEETING?

It's important to have someone to chair the meeting – primarily to ensure that everyone gets a chance to speak. This role is probably best carried out by a parent to start with, to show the family how the system works, but in time it's a great idea to encourage the young people to take over, in rotation. This is excellent practice – both for work experience and for life, encouraging them to be sensitive to the feelings of others and allowing everyone to be heard.

## 5. WHAT SHOULD YOU DISCUSS?

The chair could start by asking everyone to comment on the period since the last meeting. If this is the first meeting, then you could ask everyone to comment on something that has gone well and something that has gone badly/annoyed the speaker in the last 14 days. While everyone has their turn, they should not be interrupted and there should not be any comment at the end – everyone is encouraged to speak and be listened to.

Once everyone has had their initial say, the chair should ask what people want to discuss during the meeting. On a piece of paper write down everyone's suggestions and then agree the order you will discuss them in. Tick off the items discussed as you work through the list – so everyone can see where you have got to and think about how the level of discussion matches the time available. Have a couple of positive/ non-controversial issues ready for discussion to get things started, e.g. what kind of breakfast cereals should be bought. Issues to discuss could include the following:

- Getting up in the mornings. How many calls is it reasonable to expect someone to give?
- Getting to school. In what circumstances can your teenagers expect a lift and under what conditions will they be offered (e.g. being ready on time, being civil in the car)? If lifts are offered to your teenagers' friends, what should they be expected to do (turn up on time, be ready)?
- Where to go on holiday.

It's important that a family meeting does not become a structured telling-off session. Encourage everyone to have their say. If any individual uses the opportunity to talk without being interrupted to accuse another member of the family of something, try to widen the discussion and include everyone.

If there are problems that need resolving, then everyone should be involved in their solution. The person with the problem could describe how this ongoing situation makes them feel and suggest a solution. Others could comment and then a general agreement could be reached on what to do as a result.

If the meeting is running on, you could decide to defer a couple of big issues until the next meeting, and to agree when that will be. Decisions on issues agreed should be put into practice as soon as possible. Information that all agreed was needed could be pinned up in a prominent place.

## 6. HOW TO END THE MEETING

Just before you finish, it's a good idea to bind everyone together again by asking a simple question that everyone has to respond to. For example, you could ask everyone to:

- 'Name one thing that makes me feel part of this family'
- 'Give one reason why I like being a "Brown"'
- 'The best thing about our last holiday was . . .'

While this can sound a little corny, it does give everyone a positive feeling. In my experience, family members (of all ages) tend to say things that matter to everyone present.

# Appendix 2: List of useful websites, services and contacts

While all the sites listed below are helpful, the star rating is a guide to how useful for parents and young people I feel they may be.

## SEX AND RELATIONSHIPS FOR YOUNG PEOPLE

*NHS Choices website*
www.nhs.uk/livewell/sexandyoungpeople/Pages/Sex-and-young-people-hub.aspx

While not the most obviously 'teen-friendly' website available, it is comprehensive and offers all sorts of optional pages on male bodies, female bodies, ten questions to ask yourself to know if you're ready for sex, myths, having safe and safer sex, taking a pregnancy test and lots of Q&A sections.

The website also provides information on local sexual health services throughout the UK via the search option. An excellent website to explore with your teen and bookmark for them to browse at leisure.

Parents ****
Young people ***

*Brook*
www.brook.org.uk

Brook offers a complete service for young people. They have an excellent website with lots of information about all areas of sex and relationships through a youth-friendly and easy-to-navigate website with issues from starting a relationship, cheating and breaking up, to rights and abuse. They also offer a webchat via the website for young people who want to discuss issues.

Brook offers free, confidential sexual health advice and contraception to under 25s at centres across the UK.

Excellent website to bookmark for your young person.

Parents ****

Young people ****

## *FPA*

www.fpa.org.uk

FPA (formerly the Family Planning Association) is a registered charity working to improve the sexual health and reproductive rights of all people throughout the UK. The website contains a guide to contraception and sexual health, information for parents on talking about sex and relationships with their child or children, and links to other relevant websites.

Parents ****

Young people

## SEXUALITY

### *Being Gay is OK*

www.bgiok.org.uk/

Information and support for lesbian, gay or unsure young people under 25. Set up to provide responsible, easy and caring support to the confused or concerned, it covers everything from coming out to homophobic bullying, dating and crushes and safer sex. It has a problem page – not currently taking more questions but reading the existing ones is helpful. A good website for anyone who is either working out their own sexuality or trying to understand difference.

Parents ***

Young people ***

## Childline

www.childline.org.uk/Explore/sexual-identity/Pages/Sexual-Orientation.aspx

Excellent page for young people, with plenty of information and topics to explore, presented in a friendly and usable style. Covers topics such as supporting friends, coming out, homophobic bullying as well as general advice and information.
Parents *
Young people ****

## Stonewall

www.stonewall.org.uk/at_school/education_for_all/parents_and_carers/default.asp

Excellent section for parents covering the issues of gay young people and providing them with support through their teen years. Stonewall also have a Young Stonewall site.
Parents ****
Young people *

# DRUGS INFORMATION AND SERVICES

## FRANK

www.talktofrank.com

FRANK provides free, confidential drugs information and advice 24 hours a day to anyone who needs it, including parents of young people. The key purpose is to ensure that young people understand the risks and dangers of drugs, and know where to go for advice and help. It also aims to provide parents with confidence and knowledge to talk to their children about drugs.

The website is young-people friendly, up to date on all the recent trends and has excellent information on 'legal highs' as well as illegal drugs. Has an information and support helpline for parents and young people.
Parents ****
Young people ****

## DrugScope

www.drugscope.org.uk/

A useful resource for parents wishing to know and understand more about drugs and their use. Also has excellent information on UK-wide drug services, rehab clinics, etc. 'DrugScope is the national membership organisation for the drug sector and the UK's leading independent centre of expertise on drugs and drug use.'

Parents ****

Young people ***

# ALCOHOL

## Drinkaware

www.drinkaware.co.uk

Charity working to reduce alcohol harm and misuse. Website is full of information, with a Q&A section and a good downloadable leaflet for adults about young people and alcohol as well as sexual harassment and alcohol. More geared to adults than young people.

Parents ****

Young people **

## FRANK

www.talktofrank.com

Has a listing for alcohol in the A–Z section that is factual and easy to understand.

Parents *

Young people ***

## How To Drink Properly

http://howtodrinkproperly.com

This is designed to appeal to young people and provides a series of short animated films – but be warned, many adults

may find this upsetting or distasteful as the language used is decidedly colourful. Probably best for 15–16-year-olds up.
Parents
Young people ****

## EATING PROBLEMS

*Young Minds*
www.youngminds.org.uk
   Website providing information about eating problems, a parent helpline (weekdays 9.30–4.00 p.m. 0800 802 5544), a contact Q&A service as well as details of where to get help for your child.
Parents ****
Young people **

*NHS Choices website*
www.nhs.uk/conditions/Eating-disorders/Pages/Introduction. aspx
   Simple, straightforward explanations and checklists to help young people identify when eating issues are problematic for themselves and others, as well as advice on getting support and the different kinds of support available.
Parents ***
Young people ***

## BULLYING (INCLUDING CYBER BULLYING)

*Bullying UK (part of Family Lives)*
www.bullying.co.uk
   The website provides a lot of information about what bullying is, why it happens and how to stop it for both parents and young people. Website slightly confusing about what is for

young people and what is for parents but there is plenty of good information and real-life case histories which young people usually find helpful. The helpline appears to be just for parents but covers all areas of parenting, which is useful.

Parents ****

Young people ***

### Young Minds

www.youngminds.org.uk/for_children_young_people/whats_worrying_you/bullying

Young-people-focused interface, multiracial and modern looking, with Bullying Ambassadors giving their stories. Deals with racism as well as other forms of bullying. Not as much information as Bullying UK but has a more modern feel.

The Young Minds website covers a lot of areas – a really good one to bookmark for your teen.

Parents **

Young people ****

### Childline

www.childline.org.uk/Explore/Bullying/Pages/Bullying.aspx

Excellent webpage for young people, with message boards to read and post messages for peer support. Online counsellors are available to chat with or alternatively there is a phone counselling service. Probably the most well-known service for children and young people experiencing bullying or abuse.

Parents *

Young people ****

## MENTAL HEALTH

### Rethink

www.rethink.org/services-groups/service-types/young-people

This is a comprehensive website for adults and young people experiencing mental health problems. It provides help in recognising different problems, treatment options, support services and groups, advice and help, advocacy, housing and even covers criminal-justice issues.

A useful site for parents or young people experiencing or worried about mental illness including depression or anxiety.
Parents ****
Young people **

### Young Minds

www.youngminds.org.uk

Excellent website for adults and young people, easy to use, easy to understand and covering a wide range of topics. This website is an excellent one to bookmark for your teen – and yourself. Covers OCD, self-harm, phobias, depression and family mental illness as well as many other topics. Has a parent help-line for all queries.
Parents ****
Young people ****

## ONLINE SAFETY

### Childnet

www.childnet.com

This is an effective website designed for parents, young people and teachers. The young people's section is rather dull and wordy although the content and the extensive blog posts are potentially useful. For parents it provides concise help with lots of issues around web safety and young people.
Parents ***
Young people **

### CEOP (Child Exploitation and Online Protection Centre)

www.ceop.police.uk/

For adults and children/young people to report anything illegal or worrying that happens online. Also has a 'one-stop shop' of links to a range of other websites concerned with online safety. Useful to bookmark for quick reference or reporting.

Parents ***

Young people **

## Get safe online

www.getsafeonline.org

Extensive information about everything to do with the online world for parents, including safeguarding tips for social networking, online shopping and gaming sites and how to set up parental controls. Does not offer advice on time limits however. Not particularly useful to young people.

Parents ***

Young people *

# Index

Page numbers in **bold** refer to diagrams.